THE NOMADIC
ALTERNATIVE

THOMAS J. BARFIELD

Boston University

PRENTICE HALL

Englewood Cliffs, New Jersey 07632

LOCATIONS OF NOMADIC PASTORAL PEOPLES
MENTIONED IN THE FOLLOWING CHAPTERS

ICELAND

UNITED KINGDOM

NORWAY

SWEDEN

FINLAND

BALTIC REPS.

RUSSIA

DEN

EIRE

NETH.
BEL.
GER.
POLAND
BELARUS

CZECH.
UKRAINE

FRANCE
SW.
AUST
HUN.
ROM.
21
AZERBAIJAN

KAZAKHSTAN
10
LAKE BALKASH

2

ITALY
ALB.
YUG.
BUL.
GEORGIA
ARMENIA
CASPIAN SEA

ARAL SEA

23

PORTUGAL
SPAIN

TURKEY

UZBEKISTAN
TURKMENISTAN

KYRGYZSTAN
TAJIKISTAN
XINJIANG

GREECE

LEBANON
ISRAEL
SYRIA
IRAQ
IRAN

18

6
AFGHANISTAN

TIBET

NEPAL **8**

MOROCCO

TUNISIA

16
JORDAN

11
15
4
3
PAKISTAN

ALGERIA
LIBYA
EGYPT

SAUDI ARABIA

1

KUWAIT
U.A.E.
OMAN

I N D I A

W. SAHARA

MAURITANIA
MALI
NIGER
CHAD
SUDAN

YEMAN
DJIBOUTI

BANGLADESH

SRI LANKA

SENEGAL
GAMBIA
GUINEA
UPPER VOLTA

NIGERIA
CENTRAL AFRICAN REP

7 **14**

ETHIOPIA

SIERRA LEONE
LIBERIA
IVORY COAST
GHANA
TOGO
BENIN

CAM

EQ. GUINEA
GABON
REP. OF CONGO

9 **17**
UGANDA
KENYA
SOMALIA

RWANDA
12
BURUNDI

ZAIRE

TANZANIA
MALAWI
MOZABIQUE

ANGOLA
ZAMBIA
ZIMBABWE

NAMIBIA
BOTS-WANA

MADAGASCAR

MAURITIUS

INDIAN OCEAN

19 SWAZILAND
LESOTHO

REPUBLIC OF SOUTH AFRICA

Contemporary Nomadic Groups		
Name of Group	**Number**	**Approximate Location**
Al Murrah Bedouin	1	Empty Quarter Arabia
Altai Kazaks	2	junction Russia, Mongolia, China
Baluch	3	junction Iran, Pakistan, Afghanistan
Basseri	4	southern Iran
Buryat	5	region of Lake Baikal
Central Asian Arab	6	northern Afghanistan
Dinka	7	southern Sudan
Drokba	8	central Tibet
Jie	9	northern Uganda
Kazak	10	between Caspian Sea and Lake Balkash
Lur	11	southern Iran
Masai	12	Kenya and Tanzania
Mongol	13	Mongolia
Nuer	14	southern Sudan
Qashqa'i	15	southern Iran
Rwala Bedouin	16	North Arabia (Jordan, Iraq, Syria)
Turkana	17	northern Kenya
Turkmen	18	northeastern Iran, Turkmenistan
Zulu	19	southern Africa

Historic Nomadic Groups		
Hsiung-nu	20	Mongolia/China
Scythian	21	southern Russia/Ukraine
Uighur	22	northwestern Mongolia
Zunghar	23	junction Russia, Mongolia, China

LAKE
BAIKAL

5

-22 – 13

MONGOLIA

20

CHINA

N. KOREA

S. KOREA

JAPAN

BURMA

TAIWAN

THAI

VIETNAM

PHILLIPINE ISLANDS

CAMBODIA

MALAYSIA

SINGAPORE

INDONESIA

PAPUA
NEW GUINEA

SOLOMON
ISLANDS

AUSTRALIA

Library of Congress Cataloging-in-Publication Data

Barfield, Thomas J. (Thomas Jefferson), (date)
  The nomadic alternative / Thomas J. Barfield.
    p.   cm.
  Includes bibliographical references and index.
  ISBN 0-13-624982-5
  1. Nomads—Social conditions. 2. Nomads—Economic conditions.
I. Title.
GN387.B37 1993
305.9'069—dc20   92-15067
                                                          CIP

Production Editor: KERRY REARDON
Acquisitions Editor: NANCY ROBERTS
Copy Editor: HENRY PELS
Cover Designer: RICH DOMBROWSKI
Prepress Buyer: KELLY BEHR
Manufacturing Buyer: MARY ANN GLORIANDE
Page Layout: JOH LISA
Editorial Assistant: PATRICIA NATURALE

© 1993 by Prentice-Hall, Inc.
A Simon & Schuster Company
Englewood Cliffs, New Jersey 07632

Printed in the United States of America

10 9 8 7 6 5 4 3 2 1

ISBN   0-13-624982-5

PRENTICE-HALL INTERNATIONAL (UK) LIMITED, *London*
PRENTICE-HALL OF AUSTRALIA PTY. LIMITED, *Sydney*
PRENTICE-HALL CANADA INC., *Toronto*
PRENTICE-HALL HISPANOAMERICANA, S.A., *Mexico*
PRENTICE-HALL OF INDIA PRIVATE LIMITED, *New Delhi*
PRENTICE-HALL OF JAPAN, INC., *Tokyo*
SIMON & SCHUSTER ASIA PTE. LTD., *Singapore*
EDITORA PRENTICE-HALL DO BRASIL, LTDA., *Rio de Janeiro*

CONTENTS

PREFACE

Nomads have always attracted attention far out of proportion to their numbers. From the earliest writings on clay tablets complaining about the depredations of tent-dwellers living in the badlands of Mesopotamia to the most recent pictorial in the *National Geographic*, the world of the pastoral nomad has impinged upon the sedentary imagination. Historical and anthropological research on them, particularly during the past forty years, has been extensive and continues to grow. Yet in spite of this interest, general works on the topic have been rare and detailed ethnographies, the backbone of anthropology, go out of print in a twinkling of the eye. As in all too many of the social sciences, specialists write mainly for one another in respected but obscure journals where the demand is for highly focused articles. Indeed from reading the academic literature on cattle pastoralism in East Africa or camel pastoralism of the Near East and North Africa, a casual reader might well assume these neighboring regions were islands separated by vast oceans, so rarely do researchers in each area appear to interact with one another. I am myself as guilty as others in this process. My own anthropological fieldwork on pastoral nomads, first in northern Afghanistan and later among the Kazaks in Xinjiang, China, focused on patterns of economic and social change of

particular relevance to the Near East and Central Asia. My historical research examined the process of state formation among the nomads of
Mongolia and their relationship with China over the span of 2000 years.
Of other places and peoples in the pastoral world, I maintained only a
vague knowledge: enough not to seem stupid, too little to appear smart.

I would have, in all likelihood, continued to graze in my own pastures had I not decided to teach a general course on pastoral nomadism. As
any instructor knows, having to explain basic concepts and compare very
different regions forces the specialist to take a broader perspective. It opens
the mind to new and often surprising conclusions. At the same time there
is the difficulty of generalizing from a wealth of a specialist literature without bleaching out the complex shades of opinions on any issue. As a text-
book, *The Nomadic Alternative* seeks to cross this divide by examining a set
of common themes that span the pastoral regions of Africa and Eurasia and
thereby create a more integrated picture of nomadic pastoralists both in the
past and present. Undoubtedly researchers in each area will feel that important issues or peoples have been neglected, while beginning students
may feel there is far more about nomadic pastoralists than they ever
wished to know.

I owe the greatest debt of gratitude to the many scholars whose work
I cite. Without their research such a book would be impossible to produce.
I would also like to thank the students in my *Nomads* classes at Harvard
and Boston University whose direct and well aimed criticisms did much to
improve the quality of the course, and I hope the book. I owe an additional
debt of gratitude to those scholars who took the time and effort to com-
ment on the manuscript during its many stages of preparation, particularly
Professors David Morgan of the University of London, John W. Olsen and
Robert Netting of the University of Arizona, Jill Dubisch of Northern Arizona University, and Walter Sangree of the University of Rochester. At
Prentice Hall, I would like to thank Nancy Roberts, my editor, for first en-
couraging me to write for a larger audience and Kerry Reardon who handled the electronic production with speed and grace.

Thomas J. Barfield
Boston

CHAPTER ONE

INTRODUCTION

It was the season of the nomad migration in northern Afghanistan and our truck ground to a halt, temporarily engulfed by a mass of animals. Dust clouds raised by thousands of sheep filled the sky as strings of camels decorated with beads, tassels, and cowrie shells passed in procession, the clanging of the bells around their necks beating out a rhythm indelibly linked with nomadic movements and caravans. Armed men on horseback preceded and followed the column, while women dressed in bright satins with velvet capes embroidered in rich gold brocade sat atop the camels. The loads themselves were topped with carpets or some other piece of finery. Large mastiffs with clipped tails and ears trotted alongside, capable of eating a jeep for breakfast once the tents went up but surprisingly docile during the march. And then as quickly as they had appeared they were gone, swallowed up by their own dust.

As we resumed our own journey, I asked the driver who these people were, where did they live and where were they going? "God knows, I don't," he replied. "They are *kuchis*, nomads, and they have no home but their tents." His answer was typical, for even in Afghanistan few sedentary people had a clear idea of who nomads were or what they really did for a living. Often what they did claim to know was based on old folk beliefs or strange stories they had heard. If misconceptions were prevalent

Nomads on migration in northeastern Afghanistan crossing a bridge into their mountainous summer pastures.

even in areas where nomads were common, then in other parts of the world the nomadic way of life was only the stuff of legend, a mélange of images that included the haughty Masai warrior of East Africa leaning on his spear, the horsemen of Chinggis Khan overrunning Eurasia, or the simple Bedouin tent pitched at the base of an enormous sand dune.

It was to get behind these images that I later returned to Afghanistan as an anthropologist and found myself stirring up dust in such a nomadic migration. At first I rode a horse, but it died after eating poisonous plants. I was then told of the danger of poisonous plants and learned that the wealth of knowledge it took to be a successful pastoralist did not come cheaply. Through the cycle of winter villages and summer camps, the world of the nomadic pastoralist became less mysterious but more complex with each passing month. They were not isolated in any meaningful sense nor could they be understood except in relation to the sedentary peoples around them. When I later compared my own ethnographic observations with earlier historical accounts I saw that the wide net of relationships nomads established with the outside world were not the products of recent events or acculturation. From their very beginnings nomadic peoples had always been integral parts of larger regional systems.

Anthropological fieldwork in various parts of the world has shown that these conclusions are not limited only to Afghanistan or the Near East. While these studies have called into question the use of "pastoral nomadism" as a unitary phenomenon, they all support the view that the world of the nomad rarely fits the stereotypes normally assigned to it.[1] Nomadic pastoralists developed different patterns of organization depending on their specific cultural, ecological, political, or historical circumstances. Each region has its own pattern of development and interaction. To understand this way of life we must look not only at the tents and animals but at the complex set of relationships nomadic peoples have established with their sedentary neighbors.

MYTHS AND LEGENDS

Perhaps because their way of life appears so different from our own, the world of the nomad has long fascinated sedentary people. Some writers have romantically lauded the nomad as a free spirit untrammeled by the petty restrictions, a theme strongly represented in modern Western literature. But the nomads have also been condemned by their neighbors for these same traits because, in the words of the fourteenth-century Arab social historian Ibn Khaldun,

> The very nature of their existence is the negation of building, which is the basis of civilization.... Furthermore, it is their nature to plunder whatever other people possess. Their sustenance lies wherever the shadow of their lance falls. They recognize no limit in taking the possessions of other people. Whenever their eyes fall upon some property, furnishings or utensils, they take them.[2]

The reality of nomadic pastoral life is, of course, neither idyllic as romantics have imagined it, nor as mindlessly destructive as its critics have complained. Neither view adequately captures the complexity of organizing a society around regular movements nor recognizes the intricate web of economic and political ties that link the nomad to a world beyond the steppe or desert.

In this regard one of the most enduring stereotypes is the myth of the "pure nomad," one who subsists entirely on meat, milk, or blood, abhors farmers, farming, and grain, despises sedentary life in general, and never has contact with villages or cities except when he loots and burns them. Nothing could be farther from the truth.[3] The historical and ethnographic record is full of nomads who also farm, trade, serve as soldiers, smuggle, or drive trucks, just to mention a few occupations. As we will see in later chapters, even those nomads who did appear purely pastoral, such as the Bedouin of the Empty Quarter or horse riders of Mongolia, maintained an ideal of "purity" largely by means of the subsidies they received from neighboring sedentary societies with whom they had important political and economic relationships. While nomadic pastoralists have always viewed animal husbandry as the culturally ideal way of making a living, and the movement of all or part of the society as a normal and natural part of life, they never rejected other opportunities. However, these activities were always viewed as adjuncts to pastoralism which remained the key element of their cultural and social identity.

DEFINITIONS

What is nomadic pastoralism? This basic question is not as simple to answer as it might seem. In general, societies specializing in animal husbandry requiring periodic movements are called pastoral nomads. This excludes such groups as hunter-gatherers, Gypsies, migrant farm workers, or corporate executives who are nomadic but not pastoral. It also excludes Danish dairy farmers and Texas cattle ranchers who specialize in pastoralism but are not nomadic. Thus, although the terms *nomad* and *pastoralist* are generally used interchangeably, at a basic level they are analytically distinct, the former referring to movement and the latter to a type of subsistence.

Nomadic societies built around a pastoral economic specialization are imbued with cultural values far beyond just doing a job. It is as much a way of life as a way of making a living. Organized around mobile households rather than individuals, it involves everyone—men, women, and children—in the various aspects of production. This distinguishes nomadic pastoralists from shepherds in Western Europe or cowboys of the Americas who also make a living herding animals. Shepherds and cowboys are men recruited from the larger sedentary society to which they regularly return. When raising livestock is only an individual occupational specialty firmly embedded in the surrounding sedentary culture, no separate society of pastoralists ever comes into existence. Similarly, alpine villagers, with their heavy fixed investments in land, barns, and houses, are mountain farmers for whom animal husbandry is only a secondary activity. *Heidi* is not the story of a Swiss nomad girl even though she herded cows and goats each summer.

A N I M A L S

The archaeological record indicates that the oldest domesticates were sheep, goats, and cattle. They are first found as components of a sedentary neolithic farming economy that relied on both agriculture and animal husbandry. Only later did nomadic pastoralism emerge as a specialization, associated with the domestication of transport animals such as donkeys, horses, and camels. What set early pastoralists apart from hunters of the same species was their emphasis on exploiting such by-products as milk, blood, wool, or hair which made live animals more valuable than dead ones. Selective breeding for characteristics to meet human requirements was so intensive that domesticated animals eventually became physically distinct from their wild progenitors. For example, the wild sheep has a thick coat of hair with only a thin fleece undercoat, but through selective breeding the hair largely disappeared on domesticated sheep and was replaced by a thick woolly coat. Similarly, milk production in domestic animals is much greater than in wild ones. Domesticated animals became partners in a mutualistic relationship with humans. Taken to seasonal pastures and protected from predators, many breeds could no longer survive or even reproduce successfully on their own. And for pastoralists the health of their herds became the key to their own survival.[4]

For all the cultural variety we see among nomadic pastoralists, the variety of domesticated animal species they raise is surprisingly small, making their comparison a variation on a single theme. The vast majority of nomadic pastoralists raise herds composed of six or fewer species: sheep, goats, cattle, horses, donkeys, and camels. There are, in addition, several species that have restricted distribution: yaks at high altitudes in the Tibetan plateau region, reindeer in the arctic north, and llamas and other cameloid species in highland South America. With the exception of the reindeer, which feed primarily on lichens, all are herbivores that feed on grass or bush species although each has different water and grazing requirements. All these species have in common a gregarious social organization which facilitates control of their movement. Dogs are also kept by many pastoralists for protection. Of course, not all domesticated animals are compatible with nomadic pastoralism. Pigs are a prime example. They do not readily form manageable herds, have omnivorous feeding habits best met in forests or villages, require a moist environment, and have short legs that are not well adapted for walking long distances. Thus history never recorded great migrations of swine-herding nomads with vast numbers of oinking pigs.

There are also analytic divisions within species that are as vital (and obvious) to pastoralists as differences among species. Domesticated herds of animals are controllable because they consist almost exclusively of females and castrated males, for only a few males are reserved for stud. Thus all pastoralists make linguistic distinctions between these varieties and often have large vocabularies to describe animal age classifications, colors, and condition. The pastoral heritage of Indo-European languages provides English with such distinctive classificatory terms as *ewe/wether/ram* for sheep, *cow/steer (ox)/bull* for cattle, *mare/gelding/stallion* for horses, but, since most of us (anthropologists included) are now more familiar with cuts of meat than types of animals, we must learn what pastoralists assume is common sense.

CULTURAL/ECOLOGICAL AREAS

Understanding the comparative ecology of pastoral nomadism is a necessary first start for any analysis. The interactions among the animals, land, and people produce a complex web of ecological relationships. While each species is adapted to a particular set of ecological conditions and the mix of animals in a herd must be appropriate to the environment, our focus cannot be limited to the animals alone. With domestication, animals became intimately dependent on their human keepers for pasture, water, breeding, shelter, salt, and protection from predators. Therefore nomads had to become aware of the environmental relationship of the carrying capacity of the land to the number of animals raised, as well as the human relationship to the number of animals needed to provide a base of subsistence. Pastoralists never became animal ecologists who could quantify this knowledge, but they were always acutely aware that their lives depended on a thorough knowledge of these relationships.

In this book we will focus our attention on the sub-arctic nomadic pastoralists of Africa and Eurasia who occupy an enormous belt of arid and semi-arid territory running southwest to northeast from East Africa to Mongolia. This pastoral area is bounded by the tropical forests of Africa and by agricultural civilizations in Eurasia (Europe and the Mediterranean littoral in the West, China and India in the East). Pastoralists here base their economies on the exploitation of similar sets of animals (that is, even if they specialize in raising only a few species, they usually have had knowledge of and access to the others) and have historically interacted with one another.

It may be argued that this choice of area arbitrarily excludes the pastoral peoples of highland South America and arctic Eurasia. However, both these regions are peripheral to the focus of this study because they depend on the exploitation of a single regionally unique species and are the products of an evolution that was very different from the vast majority of pastoral nomadic societies. For example, the nomadic herders of the northern latitudes raise reindeer, an animal that cannot survive outside of the tundra, while other domesticated grazing animals cannot survive there. Societies engaged in reindeer herding, though undoubtedly nomadic pastoralists, are part of a very different tradition which is best analyzed as the most sophisticated variation in a wide continuum of arctic reindeer exploitation that ranges from simple hunting, to raising the animals for meat harvest alone, to their use for milking and traction. Similarly, llama-raising communities in the Andes are better understood as variations within an alpine farming or ranching tradition, since no distinct society of pastoralists ever emerged there.

Although they share access to a common set of domestic animals, sub-arctic Old World pastoral societies are divided into five distinct nomadic pastoral zones, each with its own style of animal husbandry and social organization.

1. The pastoral zone of cattle raising lies south of the Sahara, in the Sahel running across the entire continent, and in the savanna grasslands of East Africa following the line of the Great Rift Valley. While cattle are viewed as the most important livestock, many pastoralists also maintain flocks of sheep and goats for subsistence and donkeys for transport. Camels are included in herds bordering the northern deserts. With the exception of donkeys, these animals all provide blood, milk, and meat for subsistence. Although many grassland areas also contain herds of wild grazing animals, pastoral tribes rarely hunt them for meat. Horticulture, where it exists, is exclusively in the hands of women. Pastoralists here construct huts, often linking them together to create a cattle pen. This use of a fixed base means that grazing is restricted to areas around the cattle pens, which must be abandoned when the herds are moved to a new area. What is perhaps most striking to an observer familiar with nomads elsewhere is the minimal use of transport animals and the complete lack of tents.

2. The desert zone of camel pastoralism is contiguous with the Saharan and Arabian Deserts. Unlike their neighbors, these pastoralists commonly specialize in raising a single animal, the dromedary camel, on which they rely for food and transport. The camel's fabled ability to go without water and walk long distances allows these nomads to exploit distant desert pastures inaccessible to other stock. (On the desert margin some camel nomads also maintain flocks of sheep and goats, but they must be herded separately from camels.) While for other nomads, let alone sedentary people, the desert is a barrier to communication, for camel nomads the desert facilitates travel. The camel as "the ship of the desert" is no idle analogy. However, even these desert nomads never really supported

themselves simply on camels' milk and meat. They commonly extorted a percentage of the date crop from the oasis farmers of Arabia, sold their male camels to the caravan trade to acquire manufactured goods, and even the classic Bedouin black tent is constructed of a goat-hair cloth not produced by deep-desert nomads.

3. The zone of sheep and goat pastoralism lies north of the arid deserts that support only camel raising and south of the Central Eurasian steppe, running along the Mediterranean littoral through the Anatolian and Iranian Plateaus into mountainous central Asia. Nomads here take advantage of changes in elevations, moving their livestock from lowland winter pasture to highland summer pasture, making camp in their extremely mobile black goat hair tents. The composition of their herds is quite diverse: sheep, goats, horses, camels, and donkeys. Only cattle are missing. Because they require better pasture, more water, and do poorly in negotiating mountain trails than sheep and goats, nomads here associate cattle raising with farming villages. Pastoral nomads in this region are economic specialists and have a symbiotic relationship with their sedentary neighbors with whom they are in constant contact, trading meat animals, wool, milk products, and hides for grain (which constitutes the bulk of their diet) and manufactured goods.

4. The Eurasian steppe pastoral zone is the home of the horse-riding nomads. Running from the Black Sea to Mongolia, it is largely flat grassland punctuated by mountain chains that divide it into eastern and western parts. The forests of Europe, Siberia, and Manchuria mark its northern limits, while the predominantly agricultural regions of the Anatolian and Iranian Plateaus, the deserts and oases of Central Asia and China create its southern frontier. Although today much of this area is devoted to farming, until a few hundred years ago it was controlled exclusively by nomadic peoples. Their pastoral complex consisted of horses, sheep, goats, cattle, and Bactrian camels. They differed from nomads in other regions in their emphasis on horse riding and archery, the use of carts for transport, and the development of the felt-covered yurt for housing. Historically, they had the greatest political impact on their neighbors, founding many great empires and dynasties, including the world's largest empire created by the Mongols in the thirteenth century.

5. The high-altitude pastures of the Tibetan Plateau and neighboring mountain regions impose an extremely harsh climatic regime for humans and animals. The air is thin, ultraviolet radiation strong, and daily temperatures often swing wildly. Winters are severe and strong winds sweep the plains. Yet the vast plateau grasslands offer rich grazing and, because they lie above the growth line for barley, there is no competition from the farmers who inhabit the valleys. To take advantage of this resource, pastoralists on the Tibetan Plateau herd yaks, sheep, goats, horses, and yak/cattle hybrids (dzo). Cattle are restricted to farming villages at lower altitudes and

Kazak women in the Altai Mountains applying a traditional design to a felt mat made of pressed wool. The wool is softened with boiling water and then rolled back and forth until the fibers lock to create a strong bond.

camels are found only along the borders of Mongolia. The yak can survive only at high altitudes and provides milk, meat, and hair, as well as transport. *Dzos* produce more milk than yaks and have a wider tolerance for altitude changes than either of their parent species. Tibetan nomads employ a pitched tent that consists of panels woven from black yak hair. Wool and milk products are traded to valley villagers for barley which is a mainstay of the Tibetan diet.

K E Y   A N I M A L S

In each of the areas described above there is one key animal that appears to define pastoralism culturally. Central Eurasian nomads give priority to the horse. The high altitude nomads of the Tibetan Plateau praise the yak and yak hybrids. In sub-Saharan Africa, cattle are supremely valued, while in the deserts of the Sahara and Arabia it is the camel. The more prosaic sheep and goat take pride of place in the Near East, Iranian Plateau, and Central Asia. The only species apparently not raised to cultural primacy among nomadic pastoralists anywhere is the hard-working donkey.

It is, however, the rare nomadic group that specializes in raising a single animal because in most of Africa and Eurasia pastoralism is only viable when it incorporates a variety of species. The only significant exceptions are the desert camel nomads like the Bedouin of Arabia. On what basis then do anthropologists and nomads alike give such prominence to any single species as a key animal, particularly when their neighbors in an adjacent zone may herd the same animals? We might naturally assume that it is the economically most important species that defines an area, like sheep and goats on the Iranian Plateau, but this is not always the case. Mongolian horse raisers and Tibetan yak breeders also base their subsistence primarily on sheep. What is really at work is an expression of a hierarchy of cultural value, for in each pastoral zone there is one species that excites the imagination and is viewed as the ideal source of wealth and satisfaction. In some societies the productive stock takes pride of place while others give the nod to transport animals. This cultural preference may be so strong that pastoral success is measured only by ownership of a single species, even when other species are more important for subsistence.

The emergence of any key animal as a marker of regional pastoral identity is the product of remarkable synthesis of ecological possibilities and cultural ideals.

Key animals must meet four criteria:

1. The animal must be well adapted to the regional ecological conditions so that large numbers can be supported. There is a high correlation between the original zone of domestication for a species and its emergence as a key animal among historic pastoralists in the same zone. Sheep and goats, horses, camels, and yaks all fit this pattern. Only the cattle of sub-Saharan Africa appear to have been domesticated elsewhere (although some archaeologists dispute this), but in the past the adoption of cattle as key animals was more widespread. The Indo-European pastoralists of the second millennium B.C. were cattle herders, and an echo of the importance they put on these animals remains in the roots of many Indo-European words for wealth, which are ultimately related to cattle and in the veneration of the sacred cow in India.

2. The key animal must be a necessary component of everyone's herd. An animal cannot become the cultural focus of a pastoral society if its ownership is restricted to only a minority of households. The horse is a good example because, while it has great prestige value among nomads in many parts of the world, only Central Eurasian pastoralists can maintain enough horses on the steppe to provide every household with them. Among the camel-raising Bedouin, the horse is a luxury animal (whose Arabian breeds are admired worldwide) maintained by wealthy households only at great cost, since the animal could not normally survive in the desert. Similarly, although horses are used widely on the Iranian Plateau, they cannot be supported entirely on available range land and require regular supplements of grain.

3. The key animal's pastoral requirements take precedence over other stock. The choice of migration pattern and herd composition is limited by which species is considered most important. When there is a mix of ani-

mals, the requirements of the key animal often determine the composition of the herd as a whole. The yak's requirement of a high altitude habitat means that Tibetan pastoralists can only raise specialized breeds of sheep and goats which are also adapted to the rigors of highland living. Similarly, the reason deep-desert nomads specialize exclusively in raising camels is not because they have aversion to other animals, but because only the camel can survive with so little available water. These nomads cannot add sheep to their herds if they wish to exploit the best camel pasture. It is the high-demand animals that limit the mobility of the herd as a whole. While it is possible to overcome such limits by keeping different species in separate herds, this requires more labor and, if the separation is permanent, it quickly becomes impractical. The choice of species herded by nomads is the product of a complex mix of ecological factors and economic opportunities, but it is culture that sets their hierarchical order of importance.

4. The key animal must in some way define a nomad's social, political, or economic relation to the world. What really sets a key animal species apart from the other animals that nomads raise is the way it structures their relations with the larger world. Among East African pastoralists, cattle are the glue for all social relationships. Marriages, friendships, ceremonies, and conflicts all require cattle exchanges: A man without cattle cannot participate in society. Cattle are, to paraphrase Levi-Strauss, not just good to eat but good to think. The camel is the focus of Bedouin life not just because it is well adapted to the desert, but because the camel allowed the Bedouin to maintain the freedom they value so highly. Until recent times, the Bedouin were invulnerable to outside attack because their sedentary enemies could not pursue them, or even find them, in the desert. Among Central Eurasian nomads, the horse was revered because of the military and political advantages it gave the nomads there. Using swift cavalry, even a relatively small number of steppe nomads struck terror into their neighbors and dominated overland trade routes. Literally and figuratively, people looked up to the man on horseback. The emphasis on sheep and goats in the Near East exemplified the more economically integrated nomadic societies there—for their way of life depended on the sale of pastoral products to neighboring towns and villages.

ECOLOGY OF MOVEMENT

Why would people want to become or remain nomadic pastoralists? Sedentary observers often assume it is just a form of homelessness and that nomads would settle if only given the opportunity. Others see it as a primitive relic—a form of simple production, a step above hunting and gathering that has no place in the modern world. Neither view is a fair generalization. Nomadic pastoralism is a specialization that fills an important ecological and economic niche which often provides a standard of living superior to subsistence farming.

Nomads take advantage of the seasonal appearance of vegetation by shifting animals from one set of pastures to another as part of a regular cycle of migration. For example, in mountainous areas nomads may spend the winter in the lowlands, move to the foothills in the spring, to the high mountain pastures in the summer, and return in the fall. If they attempted to stay in any one place the whole year-round, they would soon find themselves both short of pasture and subject to climatic extremes that their animals could not easily survive: in the winter the mountains are covered with snow, while the lowlands in summer are extremely hot. The mix of animals in a herd is also an adaptation to varying conditions, for each species has its own specific grazing requirements. It is the nomads' willingness to migrate with their animals that permits them to raise a far greater number of animals than they could possibly support on the limited natural pasture in any one place.

While the migration from one pasture to another is the most easily recognizable facet of nomadic life, the number of moves pastoralists make is dependent on the types of animals in their herds, the quality of pasture available, the severity of climate, and the availability of water. When pasture is dependable and relatively abundant, nomads may make only a few moves and stay for long periods in a single pasture. Where pasture is more unpredictable or of poorer quality, nomads may make frequent moves and stay for only short periods in each pasture. In other cases, particularly where water is in seasonally short supply, migrations may be related more closely to the patterns of rainfall, with nomads migrating to pastures with temporary sources of water and then returning to areas with permanent ones. In no case, however, do nomads "wander." They know where they are going and why. Similarly, their tent or hut is their home, the fact that they move it periodically does not make them "homeless."

P A S T O R A L
E C O N O M I C   O R G A N I Z A T I O N

Pastoralism is an efficient way to exploit natural grassland areas that are otherwise unproductive. Grass cannot be digested by human beings, so raising animals that can use this resource is a way for people to tap a rich energy source indirectly and open huge areas of semi-arid range land to productive use. Pastoralism that employs such natural range land must be distinguished from commercial animal raising in which livestock are fed grain to produce meat or milk. Such agriculturally based forms of animal husbandry are often accused of being wasteful, particularly when practiced in poor countries, because many more people could be supported by consuming the grain directly. But where animal husbandry relies solely on grassland, milk and meat production does not compete directly with humans for the same resources. Indeed, in many parts of the world pastoral and agricultural production cycles are complementary. In northern Afghanistan, for example, pastoralists grazed their animals on the stubble of harvested fields in the fall and winter, but then left the agricultural valleys during the spring and summer growing season for the natural pastures of the steppe and in the mountains. Nomadic pastoralists can therefore make efficient use of large parts of the planet that are unsuitable for agriculture. In regions where drought is common, reserving land for pasture rather than using it for unirrigated agriculture is often highly adaptive, protecting the soil from erosion while producing needed milk, meat, and hides.

The economics of pastoralism are based on the type of animal raised and what is done with the products. In general, pastoralists make distinctions between productive animals that yield meat, milk, wool, or hides for consumption or trade, transport animals that provide mobility, and protective animals that guard the other animals from predators. Sheep, goats, and cattle are obvious examples of the first category, horses, donkeys, yaks, and camels of the second, and dogs of the last. The distinction between productive and transport animals is sharper in some areas than others. For example, while horses and camels are considered primarily transport animals on the Iranian Plateau and rarely used for food, Central Eurasian nomads consider horseflesh a delicacy, and they milk mares to make a mildly alcoholic drink. Bedouins who specialize in camel raising consider the camel a productive as well as a transport animal, but keep horses as luxury riding animals that they would never consider milking or eating. All pastoral nomads must, by definition, have productive livestock, but acquisition of animals reserved completely for transport developed to meet the needs of nomads who moved frequently and had to move such heavy baggage as tents or yurts, or where animals such as horses or camels gave the nomads a military advantage because they could move more rapidly over longer distances.

Nomadic pastoralism differs in a number of ways from sedentary agriculture in its allocation of resources and labor requirements, but it is the dynamic of herd growth that most starkly sets it apart from farming. While a farmer can increase his output only additively by bringing more land into production or increasing the amount of labor devoted to the same acreage, pastoralists have the potential to see their herds grow exponentially. If all goes well, a flock of twenty breeding ewes can become forty over the course of a few years, forty can become a hundred, hundreds become thousands. The actual rate of expansion is determined by the number of breeding females in a herd and their rate of reproduction. This is particularly apparent in the differential reproduction of large versus small stock. Large stock like cattle, horses, camels, and yaks take longer to mature and breed than small

Kazak woman in the Altai Mountains milking a mare to make *kumiss*, a fermented drink that is a favorite of the horse raising pastoralists of Central Eurasia.

stock like sheep and goats. Large stock therefore represent a greater invest-ment per unit than small stock, and herd size grows at a much slower rate. Whether large or small, the number of livestock needed to support a family is a critical variable. Since animals are both items of consumption and produc-tion, eating or selling too many animals in a single year may lead to future insolvency. For this reason nomadic pastoralists must always balance pres-ent needs with the ability of the herds to maintain future production.

Of course, the pastoral dream of exponential herd growth is largely theoretical. Indeed, exponential herd growth is most commonly seen after a pastoral disaster—when it allows the recovery of a depleted herd—than in good times when too many animals begin to strain both available pas-ture and labor. Although every pastoral group has its story of a man who started with a few animals in his youth and who is now master of many flocks, they have many more stories of wealthy herd owners reduced to poverty in a single season. For the reality is that disease, drought, storms, or theft can easily decimate a herd. Unlike the farmer who can safely store his harvested crop in a storeroom for future use, a pastoralist's surplus animals are continually at risk. They must be cared for constantly, dispersed widely to find enough pasture, and will eventually die. For this reason pastoralists have a strong incentive to exchange surplus animals for other goods or engage in regular patterns of slaughter to prevent waste. In areas where marketing of livestock is not well developed, the high risks of animal raising also encourage the use of animals for social transactions to make marriages, create friendships, provide hospitality, or buy political support. Such investment in social relations is particularly widespread in areas where sedentarization is not a viable alternative and networks of friends and relatives provide an economic safety net in times of disaster.

what are life expectancies?

PASTORAL SOCIAL AND POLITICAL ORGANIZATION

The social organization of nomadic pastoral societies is of particular interest to anthropologists. After all, we have already defined nomadic pastoralism as a societal rather than occupational phenomenon. While nomadic pastoralists display a variety of social organizations, they are generally tribal in nature, that is, they are dominated by kinship relations.

The patterns of movement inherent in nomadism make the household much more autonomous than among sedentary people. Decisions about where and with whom to camp, how to allocate pastoral labor, and the need to create lasting social ties within a potentially changing physical environment force individuals to cultivate their agnatic and affinal ties to other households. Strikingly, almost all pastoral nomads (excluding the Tuareg of North Africa) are exclusively patrilineal in kinship organization: descent, residence, and inheritance rules are always through the male line. Marriages invariably required the payment of a brideprice, sometimes quite substantial, which transferred wealth from the family of the groom to the family of the bride. However, the status of women in most pastoral societies was generally higher than their sedentary sisters. In East Africa, for example, the inheritance of cattle was by means of allocations through the mother; in southwest Asia where village women were secluded and veiled, nomadic women travelled freely and unveiled; in Mongolia, women acted as political brokers for their sons and were even appointed as regents after the death of a khan in the Mongol Empire.

Patterns of local cooperation and hostility were measured by distance of relation. In the Near East this ideal, though often more honored in the

Afghan nomad women are mistresses of their own tents and move about freely in a country where sedentary women are normally veiled and secluded.

breach, gave rise to the ethnographic cliché regularly recited by anthropologists and tribesmen alike: "Me against my brothers; my brothers and me against our cousins; my brothers, cousins, and me against the world." In the absence of an outside power, a pastoralist's political strength was defined by the power of his kinship group. The strongest tribes and clans laid claim to the best pastures at the best time of year, weaker groups could use them only after they had moved on. The tribe was the largest group of effective kinship and marked the outer limits of ordinary identification.

While understanding social organization is necessary for explaining internal organization of pastoral nomadic tribes, it is insufficient to explain the organization of their external relations. Kinship played its most important role at the level of the family, lineage, and clan, but units of organization at the tribal or supratribal level were more political in nature. For example, Central Eurasian nomads formed empires that incorporated hundreds of thousands, even millions of nomads, well beyond the capacity of kinship rules to regulate. Such tribal confederations formed through alliance or conquest always contained unrelated tribes. Similarly, Near Eastern tribes had extremely complex economic relations with sedentary towns and villages that had nothing to do with kinship. It was this relationship with the outside world that was the most important factor in determining the size and complexity of nomadic political organization. As we shall see, regular patterns emerged in which nomads tended to create political organizations that mirrored in sophistication the organization of the neighboring sedentary peoples with whom they interacted. The most complex and centralized emerged facing powerful states such as China, while pastoralists in East Africa, who faced only other stateless rivals, had very decentralized political organizations. In gross terms there was an arc of growing centralization running from East Africa to the steppes of Mongolia with four increasingly complex types of tribal organization:

1. age sets and acephalous segmentary lineages in sub-Saharan Africa where tribal societies encountered few state societies until the colonial era;

2. lineages with permanent leaders but no regular supratribal organization in North Africa and Arabia where tribal societies faced regional states with which they had symbiotic relations;

3. supratribal confederations with powerful leaders who were part of a regional political network within large empires distributed throughout the Iranian and/or Anatolian Plateaus linking tribes to states as conquerors or subjects;

4. centralized tribal states ruling over vast distances on the steppes of Central Eurasia, north of China and Iran, supported by predatory relationships with neighboring sedentary civilizations.

A P P R O A C H E S   A N D   T H E M E S

The complexity of pastoral nomadism is best analyzed by breaking each region into the related pieces described above: ecological base, social and economic organization, and political relations with the outside world. This approach builds a framework in which regional pastoral systems as a whole, rather than their individual elements, can be compared. (However, just as each nomadic pastoral zone has its key animal, each also has its key research issues about which everyone seems to write. Issues researched intensively in one area are, unfortunately, often neglected by scholars working elsewhere.) By building from this framework we can understand the complexity of nomadic pastoral life not only internally, but externally in the relations they established with nonpastoral people through time.

As part of this analysis, however, we must always keep in mind that we are not dealing with an unchanging way of life. Nomadic pastoral societies cannot be understood without reference to their historical development and their contemporary role in the modern world. Nomadic societies, like sedentary societies, have never existed in a vacuum. They have responded continuously to changes in their relationships to other nomads and to neighboring sedentary societies. To appreciate both their organizational strengths and weaknesses, we cannot restrict ourselves to an idealized "ethnographic present." Nomadic peoples exist in a specific time and space like other people. While current ethnographies can tell us much about pastoralism, we must turn to history and archaeology to determine how stable any form of pastoralism was and if it changed through time. This is even more true of nomads in the modern world, for over the past two centuries pastoralists have been adapting themselves to the dominance of centralized sedentary states. With vast deserts or open steppe no longer a refuge from outside authorities, the nomads have lost most of their political and military autonomy. However, unlike hunter-gatherers, pastoralists have adapted their traditional knowledge of animal husbandry to new economic conditions and have found a niche in the modern world. Their degree of success has been determined to some extent by their ability to export their still-valuable pastoral products to new markets. As no one else is as well prepared to exploit the planet's large arid zones, they have a chance to survive as intact cultures far into the future.

N O T E S

1. Rada Dyson-Hudson and Neville Dyson-Hudson, "Nomadic Pastoralism," *Annual Review of Anthropology*, 9 (1981), 15–61.

2. Ibn Khaldun, *The Muqaddimah*, trans. Frans Rosenthal, ed. N. Dawood (Princeton: Princeton University Press, 1967), p. 118.

3. Anatoly M. Khazanov, *Nomads and the Outside World* (Cambridge: Cambridge University Press, 1984).

4. Juliet Clutton-Brock, ed., *The Walking Larder: Patterns of Domestication, Pastoralism and Predation* (London: Unwin Hyman, 1989).

F U R T H E R   R E A D I N G S

GENERAL ISSUES IN THE STUDY OF NOMADIC PASTORALISM

Carmichael, Peter, ed., *Nomads*. London: Collier and Brown, 1991.

Irons, William G., and Neville Dyson-Hudson, eds., *Perspectives on Nomadism*. Leiden: Brill, 1972.

Johnson, Douglas, *The Nature of Nomadism: A Comparative Study of Pastoral Migrations in Southwestern Asia and Northern Africa*. Chicago: The University of Chicago Department of Geography Research Paper No. 118, 1969.

Nelson, Cynthia, ed., *The Desert and the Sown: Nomads in the Wider Society*. Berkeley: Institute of International Studies, University of California Press, 1973.

Spooner, Brian, *The Cultural Ecology of Pastoral Nomads*. Reading, MA: Addison-Wesley, 1973.

Weissleder, Wolfgang, ed., *The Nomadic Alternative: Modes and Models of Interaction in the African-Asian Deserts and Steppe*. The Hague: Mouton, 1978.

CHAPTER TWO

THE CATTLE KEEPERS: EAST AFRICAN PASTORALISM

Nomadic pastoralism in East Africa is most notable for its emphasis on cattle raising. Ownership of cattle is the key determinant of a man's wealth and status. Marriages, friendships, and ritual events all demand cattle exchanges or sacrifices. Migrating seasonally from one fixed cattle compound to another, these cattle-raising pastoralists lack the tents and large baggage animals so intimately associated with nomadic life elsewhere. Instead, they erect permanent huts within fenced compounds from which they take their animals out to graze daily. Although pastoralists often exchange animals with their neighbors for grain or manufactured goods, regular markets for livestock are rare and the land around their camps is usually sown with millet, sorghum, or beans when there is sufficient rainfall. Social distinctions are based on gender, age, animal wealth, and kinship ties. Pastoralists here are unique among nomads in their use of age-set systems to determine the generational status, privileges, and responsibilities of individuals through the life cycle. Political organizations are egalitarian and generally lack permanent leaders. Many of these features are adaptations to the demands of savanna pastoralism but others are the result of the absence of strong state political structures in surrounding societies until the colonial period.

T H E   C A T T L E   C O M P L E X : D E F I N I T I O N / D I S T R I B U T I O N / P R O B L E M S

Both early travelers and modern observers were struck by the cultural importance of cattle in sub-Saharan Africa. This emphasis was most pronounced in East Africa, although cattle pastoralism is also common to West Africa and the Sahel. In this area the prestige associated with cattle ownership appeared to overshadow their economic value to the point of irrationality. In one of the first comparative studies of the pastoral societies anywhere, Herskovits labeled this preoccupation a "cattle complex." He located it in a belt of societies running from southern Sudan, through Kenya, Uganda, Rwanda, Burundi, Tanzania, Zimbabwe, Mozambique, and into parts of South Africa.[1]

Herskovits argued that keeping cattle was essentially nonutilitarian. He supported this claim by citing case after case in which native peoples displayed three seemingly irrational attitudes about cattle. First, they valued cattle as wealth for social rather than economic purposes. Cattle accumulation was an end in itself, for the animals were only "esteemed for the prestige and social status their possession brings."[2] They were apparently exchanged only in the context of social relations such as marriage, where the groom's relatives transferred a brideprice in cattle to the bride's relatives. Second, these cattle keepers appeared to make only limited use of their animals as a source of food. Live cattle were a visible form of wealth so entangled in a web of social relationships that herders claimed they were too important to be used as food or traded for grain. Cattle should be eaten only after they died of natural causes, they said, or when slaughtered for special ceremonial occasions. Finally, there was the strong personal, even emotional, attachment that men held for their cattle, particularly their prized steers, which were associated with every important ritual in the life cycle. Men named their steers, decorated them, and sang songs in praise of their virtues. In Herskovits's view the cattle complex was to be understood as a set of cultural values that bore little relationship to environmental conditions or economic concerns.

The term *cattle complex* is still current and certainly reflects persistent cultural beliefs, but more recent research has shown that Herskovits's well-documented descriptions presented an idealized view of pastoralism in East Africa. For example, most ethnographers agree that women, half the population, do not share the strong emotional attachments to cattle so pervasive among the men. And cattle may indeed be "too valuable" to be butchered except on ceremonial occasions, but their ritual slaughter is often so regular that it constitutes a significant food source. While in terms of cultural categories there may be a sharp distinction between eating meat to satisfy hunger and eating meat in a ritual context, the stomach cannot distinguish between them. So today the debate has shifted from the "cattle complex" to the "complexity of cattle," for in all of these pastoral systems people are engaged in multiple relationships which are simultaneously economic, religious, social, and political in nature. And few of their practices are truly irrational when examined in context. In East Africa, mobile pastoralism provides the economic infrastructure for a cultural belief system centered on cattle, not the reverse.

CULTURAL ECOLOGY OF EAST AFRICAN PASTORALISM

Cattle take pride of place among East African pastoralists but they also raise large numbers of other animals. Sheep and goats are particularly important for both subsistence and trade, often surpassing cattle in numbers. Camel herds are also common among peoples bordering the northern desert areas of Somalia and the Sahara. However, the cultural emphasis on cattle is so dominant that the role of sheep and goats in the dynamics of pastoral production has been largely neglected in most ethnographic descriptions. Even an animal as unique as the camel is treated as if it were an extra-large drought-resistant cow for, unlike their camel-raising neighbors in the Sahara or Arabia, East African pastoralists do not ride camels or use them to carry baggage, which is packed on donkeys.

Raising a variety of species provides a pastoralist with many benefits, including the ability to efficiently exploit a wider range of available vegetation, expand the variety of animal products derived from his herd, and offset losses in one species by gains in another. Of course, it also increases the complexity of herding because each species has different grazing, water, and labor requirements. Cattle and sheep, for example, are grazers that favor grasses, while camels are browsers which eat large quantities of leafy vegetation. Donkeys prefer grasses but will readily munch on thorn bushes, while goats both graze and browse. Establishing an efficient grazing rotation cycle is also complicated because sheep and goats crop the vegetation too low for cattle to use afterward, a fact well-known to fans of American cowboy movies where angry cattlemen are always accusing sheepmen of "ruining" pasture.

The daily cycle of pastoral movement in East Africa is based on taking animals out to graze from fixed compounds to which they return each evening. How often a species requires watering, and how far the animals can travel to find it, sets a limit on how large an area of pasture can be used. The more time the animals spend travelling to reach water, the less time they have to graze and their mortality rate rises accordingly. For example, in a multi-year ecological study of the South Turkana region of Kenya, an area of highly irregular rainfall averaging less than 200 millimeters with a mean temperature of 30° C (90° F), Rada Dyson-Hudson and Terrence McCabe found that cattle were pastured within 6 to 7 kilometers from the wells where they were watered daily. The smaller sheep and goats could not move as quickly as cattle, so they were herded within 4 kilometers of the wells, but needed watering only every other day. By contrast, Turkana camels needed watering only once a week when used for milking and only once every three weeks if not lactating. Camels preferred drinking at springs which averaged 7 kilometers from their grazing areas, although they could also use water sources as much as 35 kilometers distant.[3]

Herding is generally considered men's work, while women are in charge of the milking. For this reason milking animals are often kept close to camp while other livestock are taken to more distant pastures. In addition to lactating cows and young calves, other less mobile livestock may also be left to graze around camp so that the mobility of the stronger stock will not be impaired. The exact labor requirements depend on the species of animal herded, their number, and the seasonal variation in available pasture and water. Camels require the most experienced herders because they are always wandering off, so a man may spend much of his time tracking down lost camels. The straying camels, not realizing they are "lost," often travel considerable distances. Cattle, usually under the supervision of young men, are easier to manage because they stay together, while sheep and goats can be herded by adolescents. Donkeys take care of themselves. In the dry season labor demand rises because water for the animals must be drawn up by hand from wells as deep as 12 meters using chains of people passing buckets from hand to hand, a backbreaking and time-consuming process.

The use of fenced compounds as a fixed bases, known as cattle kraals, is characteristic of East African pastoralism, but is rare among Eurasian nomads because they limit mobility and require a good deal of work to erect. But Eurasian nomads do not face the same degree of risk from predation by wild animals. Surrounded by lions, leopards, hyenas, and wild dogs, the herds must be returned to a fenced compound every night or risk attack. When the animals must be moved to a new pasture the old compound can either be temporarily abandoned while the whole group moves to a new one, or the herds can move off on their own, supervised by groups of young men who take the animals to new pastures with temporary camps beyond the range of the permanent camp. To those familiar with nomads who use black tents in the Near East, or yurts on the steppes of Eurasia, the idea of mobile pastoralists without portable shelters and large baggage animals at first appears strange. Yet from the African perspective, tents are useless if you cannot protect your animals, and without tents there is no need to maintain a herd of baggage animals beyond a few donkeys.

The seasonal migration calculus is a complex product that balances availability of pasture and water to determine when camps must be changed. In arid areas the basic pattern is to scatter the animals when pasture and water are plentiful and concentrate them around wells when they

Fenced cattle kraals act as fixed bases from which pastoralists exploit nearby pasture. (*Source*: Alice Schalek from *Three Lions*.)

become scarce. Since grazing animals will die sooner from thirst than hunger, the availability of water in the dry season is often the critical variable setting the upper limit on herd size. Pasture use is therefore generally unrestricted, while wells are the property of local-descent groups.

How well adapted is East African pastoralism to the regional ecology? The sight of dead cattle, clouds of dust, and impoverished pastoralists that accompanied the severe African droughts of the late 1970s appeared to bear out "tragedy of the commons" prophecy (a prophecy that any property open to all users equally would ultimately be destroyed through over use). Yet nomads had recovered from severe droughts in the past and from epidemics that had killed even larger numbers of their animals. Therefore the controversy over whether traditional pastoralism is destroying the resource base on which it depends has become one of the most critical, yet least well researched, problems concerning nomads.

One problem with laying the blame on a "tragedy of the commons" is that the description of pasture as a commonly held resource is a gloss for a much more complex situation. While from the perspective of the local group pasture is a communal resource, they define who is a member of the community and can restrict access to it or some other vital resource like water.

Similarly, the idea of maximizing the production of animals within a single pasture assumes that their ownership is clearly defined. However, the reciprocal exchange of animals among East African herders and their network of cattle debts often means that the ownership of animals within a grazing herd is so mixed that both risks and benefits are widely distributed.

This said, we must also critically examine the conflicts between the organization of "traditional pastoralism" and the pressures of the modern state. National governments in East Africa have made it difficult for pastoralists to follow strategies of movement that previously prevented overgrazing in the past. (For example, pastoralists often discovered they could not move between traditional grazing areas because they were now in "other countries.") Pastoralists had always used their mobility as a way to adapt to periodic changes: moving into the desert margins during periods of plentiful rain, retreating from them in times of drought. The establishment of international boundaries and the spread of farmers into semi-arid grazing areas restricted this mobility and forced many nomads to stay put in areas which became overgrazed. This was often not immediately apparent because a decade of good rains could make it appear that the nomads had more than enough land for their animals. When drought struck, as it always did in this region, the loss of normal dry-season pasture and the even more critical drought reserve forced pastoralists to overgraze what they had out of necessity. While the nomads received the blame for these conditions, it is apparent that communal ownership of pasture was but a minor element in a much more complicated relationship.

Even where movements were not restricted, ill-conceived attempts to increase pastoral production could often produce unintended disasters. For example, in the Sahel where water rather than pasture was the key variable, severe overgrazing resulted after the introduction of bore wells. Lack of water had previously kept the number of animals below the carrying capacity of the land, but the new wells allowed a substantial increase. Because cattle deprived of food could survive for months on accumulated fat, but for only a few days without water, pastoralists naturally stayed close to the new wells even after the grass disappeared. Here indeed a tragedy of the commons developed: in a period of drought the nomads stayed at the wells instead of moving off to find new pasture and their animals died of starvation.[4]

HAVING LARGE HERDS: SYMBOLS, SUBSISTENCE, AND SURVIVAL

In East Africa the number of animals in a herd has always been more important than their quality. Large herds of scrawny cattle are considered superior to smaller herds of fatter ones. One explanation for this is the symbolic value placed on cattle ownership as an end in itself. If wealth is measured only by the absolute number of cattle owned, then a herder would be naturally suspicious of the proposition that one fat cow was better than two skinny ones. (You would be too if someone said a single new $10 bill was more valuable than two old and dirty ones.) But the question of raising fat versus skinny cattle is often moot because the resources needed to support more productive cattle breeds are absent. Among the Dodos of northeastern Uganda the average weight of a 300-kilogram steer drops 30 to 45 kilograms in the dry season and 15 percent of the animals die from malnutrition.[5] Local varieties of cattle, while they will never win any prizes for productivity, survive under open-range conditions of frequent drought and lack of grazing that would quickly kill most other breeds.

There are also sound herd-management reasons for keeping large numbers of animals. Pastoralism is a risky enterprise with regular cycles of boom and bust. Herds multiply geometrically but periodically suffer catastrophic losses from drought, disease, or raiding. These cycles of growth and collapse have different rhythms depending on the percentage of large stock in the herd and the number of breeding females. In theory the minimum time for a herd to double is 9 years for camels, 6.5 years for cattle, and 3 years for sheep and goats.[6] This means that recovery from a catastrophic reduction is much slower for large stock than for small stock. A pastoralist concerned with the possibility of losing half his cattle in some disaster will attempt to maximize their number as a form of insurance. The larger the number of animals, more specifically breeding females, that survive a disaster the quicker the recovery. Since pastoralists all have similar access to resources, a herder who enters bad times with 20 cattle will be in a much better position in the end than a neighbor who starts with only 10. Thus what to an outsider appears to be a "surplus" of cattle may in fact be the "margin of error" needed by a pastoralist to survive periodic downturns.

The adequacy of herds is judged in terms of meeting subsistence needs rather than market demand. The key pastoral products are milk, blood, meat, and hides. The animals also provide dung which can be used as fuel, an important consideration where wood is in short supply. Cows and camels are the most important milk and blood producers because of their long lactation periods and large size. Milk is by far the most important pastoral product. It is drunk fresh, soured, or made into various forms of cheese. A large number of cows is necessary to maintain an adequate supply of these pastoral products because they are not very productive. A Dodos cow provides between 135 and 180 kilograms of milk annually compared with 3,500 to 5,500 kilograms from an American dairy cow.[7] Blood is less important but highly valued as a delicacy and is often consumed in considerable quantities when milk is unavailable. It is extracted by piercing a vein in the neck of an ox or camel and collecting the blood in a gourd. An animal will not be bled again until this wound has healed, which prevents overuse. Blood is drunk mixed with milk in some areas, while in others it is roasted and eaten or added as favoring to porridge.

Meat production, though not the primary goal of East African pastoralists, makes a vital contribution to the diet and is used as an item of trade. Sheep and goats are regularly slaughtered for food, but cows are kept for milk and steers are surrounded by a system of beliefs that in principle restricts their consumption to ritual occasions. However, a close look at this situation shows that: (1) nonritualistic consumption of animals that die, particularly cows, is pervasive; and (2) ritual slaughter of steers occurs frequently enough to provide a regular supply of beef. Indeed, less meat may go to waste than among Muslim nomads to the north who consider any animal not slaughtered according to Islamic law to be unfit for human consumption.

How can cattle play this dual role in both ritual and subsistence? In a study of the Pokot of west central Kenya, Harold Schneider argued that in spite of claims to the contrary, the recorded ratio of cows to steers could only have been brought about by the selective slaughter or sale of male animals. He observed that, as among other East African pastoralists, the Pokot slaughter of valued steers is limited to ritual occasions, most precipitated by random events like funeral feasts or settlements of disputes. The most common "ritual occasion" is, however, a feast "given by a member of the neighborhood who requests the prayers and goodwill of his neighbors," often at the request of these same neighbors. A large number of people are invited because the meat, if not consumed immediately, will spoil. Those who attend a feast reciprocate in turn (and each man is expected to give at least one meat feast annually) so that they occur locally about forty times a year. The regular spacing of these events, while not entirely linked with a need for food, nevertheless creates a situation in which ritual feasts play an important, if unacknowledged, role in meeting subsistence needs.[8]

THE ROLE
OF AGRICULTURE AND TRADE

Some pastoral groups such as the Masai apparently restrict their diet to animal products alone and do no agriculture, but most pastoral nomads in East Africa are dependent on some farming or localized trade to provide grain which is an essential part of their diet. The amount of agriculture pastoralists do is inversely related to the size of their livestock holdings: the higher the ratio of cattle to people the less intensively they pursue agriculture with the break point for abandoning farming falling at about 6:1 (see Table 2.1).[9] We do need to distinguish carefully, however, between mobile pastoralists like the Nuer, Masai, or Turkana, for whom cattle are

TABLE 2.1

RATIOS OF CATTLE TO PEOPLE IN A SAMPLE OF EAST AFRICAN PASTORAL PEOPLE

	18:1	Barabaig of Tanzania
	17.5:1	Samburu of Kenya
Agriculture lacking	15:1	Masai of Tanzania
or insignificant	9:1	Rendille of northern Kenya
	8:1	Dorobo of Kenya; Uganda Pokot
	6.5:1	Borana Galla of northern Kenya
	6:1	Kenya Masai
	4:1	Karamajong of Uganda
	3.7:1	Jie of Uganda
	3.6:1	Dodoth of Uganda
	3:1	Kenya Pokot
Agriculture important	2:1	Kipsigis of Kenya
in varying degrees	1.7:21	Meru of Kenya
	1.4:1	Teso of Uganda
	1.3:1	Giriama; Kitui Kamba
	1.2:1	Taita
	1.1:1	Turu of Tanzania
	1.1:1	Machakos Kamba

Source: Harold Schneider, *Livestock and equality in East Africa: The economic basis for social structure.* Bloomington: Indiana University Press, 1979:87.

both culturally and economically important, and neighboring sedentary farmers like the Kikuyu who also esteem cattle but keep relatively few of them. In general, pastoral societies in East Africa are those with ratios of cattle to people greater than 1:1.

The primacy of livestock production over farming is particularly apparent in regions where rainfall is undependable. In a geographical study comparing the relationship of rainfall, altitude, and crop patterns with the distribution of pastoralism, Philip Porter concluded that pastoralism predominated in areas where agriculture was undependable or not practicable. The greater the frequency of crop failure the higher the ratio of livestock to people, and conversely, the more dependable the agriculture the less important animal husbandry became. The major exceptions were in areas where tsetse flies or fever ticks (which carry fatal cattle diseases) made cattle production impossible.[10] In marginal areas, however, agriculture and pastoralism play complementary roles. Keeping large numbers of animals acts as a food reserve for those years when crops fail as a result of unpredictable, but regular, disasters such as drought, predation by insects or birds, or even earth-flattening incursions of wild animals like elephants.

Without capital improvements such as irrigation, a mixed pastoral-agricultural strategy may be the most secure way to ensure long-term survival.

As we noted earlier, the definition of a pastoral nomadic society need not be restricted to peoples who raise livestock exclusively. In his classic study of the Nuer, a pastoral society in southern Sudan, E.E. Evans-Pritchard noted that while in the dry season they exploited the flat grassy plains using cattle camps, in the wet season they retreated to villages located on sandy ridges because the surrounding plains were flooded. Here the Nuer planted the gardens of sorghum and maize that were a staple in their diet. If they engaged in such regular agriculture could they really be pastoral nomads? Evans-Pritchard said yes, noting that the structure of their production cycle clearly gave precedence to pastoralism because:

> (1) the Nuer cultivate only enough grain for it to be one element in their food-supply and not enough to live on it alone; (2) that with their present climate and technology considerable increase in horticulture would be unprofitable; and (3) that the dominance of pastoral values over horticultural interests is in accord with ecological relations that favor cattle husbandry at the expense of horticulture.[11]

Agriculture is easier to integrate with pastoralism in East Africa than in other parts of the world because people spend a considerable part of the year in permanent camps, use hoes to turn the soil rather than plows, and have available land for shifting cultivation. More important, the labor demands of hoe agriculture do not conflict with pastoralism because women do most of the work, leaving the men free to tend to their herds.

The widespread prevalence of agriculture among East African pastoral peoples has led many observers to assert that they are therefore self-sufficient and do without trade. It is certainly true that compared with other pastoral regions of the world, trade relationships were underdeveloped. There were few or no regular markets where livestock could be sold, so nomads never became pastoral specialists, exchanging animals for grain and manufactured goods as part of their regular production cycle, as did the camel-raising Bedouin or Iranian shepherds. But did such markets fail to emerge because pastoralists were self-sufficient and lacked interest, or was developing agriculture a response to the lack of exchange opportunities? When Arab caravan traders penetrated East Africa in search of ivory and slaves, they found little difficulty in purchasing large numbers of livestock as well. With no regional political structures to maintain peace in the area, however, nomads themselves were unable to transport their animals through the hostile territory of their neighbors to reach potential regional markets. And within the region most peoples produced the same goods, varying only in quantity. The high value of cattle and small stock relative to grain did create regular patterns of exchange between pastoralists and neighboring farming communities using networks of personal relationships. But lacking markets with cities as their focal points, most nomadic

Although cattle pastoralists in sub-Saharan Africa give primacy to animal husbandry, grains such as millet provide an imortant part of their food supply. They are usually boiled to create a thick gruel. (*Source*: Eugene Gordon.)

pastoralists remained within a closed system of exchange until the advent of colonialism. Cattle themselves remained the basic unit of value.

SOCIAL ORGANIZATION

Nowhere in the world does pastoralism permeate so many aspects of social structure as in East Africa. Cattle exchanges are intimately connected to the formation and dissolution of households, the determination of descent, the rights and responsibilities of agnates, maternal kin, and affines, the establishment of friendships, and the roles of men and women throughout the life cycle. More than one observer has noted, and not facetiously, that without cattle there could be no social life in these societies. Animals are also the only real form of inherited wealth, since access to shifting agricultural land or pasture is obtained by lineage affiliation and is not personally owned.

The family cycle begins with a marriage that creates a new household. A brideprice in cattle must be paid by the groom and his relatives to the father of the bride in order to make the marriage legitimate. While the number of cattle required varies, only by paying a brideprice can a man lay legal claim to his own children. If there is no payment, or the payment is incomplete, a woman's children may be assigned to her father's lineage, not her husband's. This leads to situations that seem bizarre to outsiders. Among the Nuer a man continues to father children as a "ghost husband" long after his death, for having paid the cattle brideprice, he maintains permanent rights to his widow's offspring regardless of their biological parentage. Although formally patrilineal, such societies are perhaps better described as "cattle-lineal."

The allocation of animals to wives is an example of the complexity of cattle transactions. Individual animals are not simple commodities that may be bought and sold at will: they are encumbered with overlapping rights of ownership that give each exchange multiple social consequences. At marriage, a woman is allocated livestock by her husband to support a new household. Formal ownership of animals is restricted to men, so these animals remain part of the husband's herd and he retains the right to dispose of them as he sees fit. However, because a man's animal wealth is transmitted to his sons from the allocations he makes to their mothers (rather than from a pool of common property), women become the focal points of a "house-property" complex in which descent from the same mother is of more immediate importance than descent from the same father.[12] And just as a marriage creates a new human family, so too does a marriage allocation also create a new "cow family" whose lineage of offspring is kept in as much (or more) detail as human ones. In a study of the complex inheritance distribution of a rich Sebei pastoralist, Walter Goldschmidt collected cattle genealogies running back fifty years to the very beginning of the herd's formation. The disposition of each animal was accounted for because when a man exchanged cattle allocated to his wife, or the offspring of such cattle, the return on the investment was owed to the wife's house-property group.[13] A rich cattle keeper is like the manager of a business who decides on how to use the firm's assets, but whose profits and losses must be distributed among various classes of stockholders.

Success in animal husbandry is translated into additional marriages. Polygyny, the marriage of a man to multiple wives, is the norm for older males and a man who does not achieve this goal is considered a failure. If polygynous households are characteristic of African pastoralists (around 30 percent, but often higher), they are relatively rare among pastoralists elsewhere although most permit it. The reason for this difference lies in the ease of accumulating cattle to make multiple marriages, rules of inheritance, age restrictions that keep young men from marrying, and the high value of women's labor in a mixed agricultural-pastoral economy.

In nomadic pastoral societies of North Africa and Eurasia it is nuclear families that are responsible for paying brideprice, so by the time a man has accumulated the necessary animal wealth to finance an additional marriage for himself, his own sons are demanding brideprices for themselves, as well as their share of the herd. In addition, since children divide a common patrimony, each new marriage potentially reduces the share of a future inheritance so that existing heirs will oppose multiple marriages. By contrast, in the East African system, cattle for brideprice are accumulated by borrowing from a wide range of relatives and friends who will be repaid in the future, so that the immediate burden on an individual family is far less. Since sons inherit their share of the herd based on the number of animals descended from those allocated to their mothers at marriage, future marriages have a less direct impact on the patrimony of existing households. Young men in African pastoral societies are often not in a position to demand cattle for brideprice until their thirties because marriage (but not sexual activity) is often restricted to senior-male age sets, temporarily removing younger men from the marriage market. Polygyny has an additional economic value for those African pastoralists who depend on women to provide the labor for hoe agriculture because each marriage increases an extended household's grain production.[14] In pastoral societies in North Africa and Eurasia, women have little role in agriculture, if it is even practiced, so increasing the number of wives does not provide a direct economic benefit unless women have some other specialized economic role, as among some carpet-weaving Turkmen of Central Asia. Pastoralists elsewhere also have greater opportunities to trade animals or invest in goods or land, and so must weigh the costs of additional marriages against other opportunities.

The house-property complex is found throughout the region but the patterns of marriage and inheritance vary depending on the degree of mobility and amount of agriculture. In general, the higher the ratio of cattle to people the more atomistic the family structure because people are more mobile. How the system works in practice is best understood by examining the practices of specific groups. Here we will contrast the Jie and the Turkana pastoralists of northern Uganda and Kenya who claim a common origin and employ similar principles of household formation but, as Philip Gulliver demonstrated in a comparative ethnography of the two groups, evolved in quite different directions (Table 2.2).[15]

The Jie inhabit a semi-arid plain around 1,200 meters in elevation with an annual rainfall of about 635 millimeters. In the dry season (September to February) they are concentrated around a series of wells in the western part of their territory, moving east during the wet season (March to August) to take advantage of new grass and open pools of water. Near their wells is an area suitable for agriculture. With the coming of British colonial rule, permanent villages were established here,

TABLE 2.2

	TURKANA	*JIE*
Population	80,000	18,000
Density	1.3 per square kilometer	5.4 per square kilometer
Cattle	200,000	60,000–65,000
Camels	80,000	---------
Sheep/goats	800,000	70,000
Per capita	3 to 4 large stock	3 to 4 large stock
	10 small stock	4 small stock

Source: Phillip Gulliver, *The Family Herds.* London: Routledge and Kegan Paul, 1955, p. 38.

although the livestock migrated as before. By contrast, the Turkana have their home camps on a hotter and more arid plain around 1,000 meters in elevation with an average rainfall of only 300 to 400 millimeters and only half that amount in the central desert. This semi-desert plain is dotted with scattered mountains 1,500 to 2,500 meters in elevation where the cattle are grazed daily in the dry season between September and July. If it rains during the "wet" season between April and August, the cattle are pastured on the plains. Regardless of where they are pastured, the animals must be returned each day to wells on the plains for water. Because their environment is the more arid one, the Turkana exploit a much larger territory than the Jie on a per capita basis, are more mobile, and maintain a greater variety of livestock. Lacking the possibility for agriculture, the Turkana have also increased the subsistence role of their herds by adding camels (an arid-zone equivalent of a big cow), raising many more sheep and goats, and keeping more donkeys for transportation.

By mixing agriculture with pastoralism, the Jie are able to maintain larger family groups than the Turkana. Overall control of the livestock is vested in the senior male of a set of full brothers. He controls a residual herd of unallocated animals and can requisition allocated animals when needed. In a form of lateral succession, each brother inherits authority over the livestock in turn until the last brother dies. At this point, new house-lines spring up, each consisting of a set of brothers, sons of a single mother, who begin the cycle anew.

The internal dynamics of such corporate groups generate conflict among component households over exchanging cattle for marriages and over cattle ownership as sons mature. Although the order in which younger brothers and sons marry is strictly regulated, married men resent the demands of their unmarried younger brothers or sons who demand cattle for their own marriages, while the younger men consider their elders stingy, too attached to their cattle to part with them. Cattle disputes also arise over conflicting notions of ownership. In the Jie system each wife receives an allocation at marriage which becomes the core of her sons' herd, but legal title and the right to dispose of the cattle resides with the eldest male. As a woman's sons reach adulthood and form their own households, cooperation that involves requisitioning cattle becomes increasingly more difficult as young sets of full brothers attempt to protect their inheritance by slowing the pace of exchanges that benefit their uncles, cousins, or half brothers. Similar tensions arise over the division of the residual herd of unallocated animals when the group breaks up. This process of fission is subsequently offset by a process of genealogical amalgamation later in the family cycle. After the new brother collectivities have established their autonomy and built up their own herds, they begin to ally themselves more closely with other groups by declaring themselves to be descendants of a common grandfather, even though this is only possible by manipulating genealogies and reducing the number of actual ancestors. This justifies cooperation but gives no rights over cattle.

The Turkana system is similar to the Jie in its principles but is much more atomistic. In Turkanaland, larger kinship groups, "children of a common grandfather," exist only for ritual occasions and it is not possible to maintain brother collectivities for any length of time. As with the Jie, a woman is allocated cattle that become her sons' inheritance, and when the husband dies her sons take control of the animals. The residual herd is small and, because the allocations are known beforehand, there is little rivalry between sets of half brothers: each takes his animals and goes.

In the Turkana system, rivalry is more focused on disputes between fathers and sons or among full brothers. Young adult sons are responsible for grazing a separate herd of animals apart from the home camp. They begin to think of this herd as their own and resent a father who exchanges "their" cattle for additional wives, particularly after the sons marry and establish their own homesteads. However, such conflicts are rarely sustained because a man wants to have at least his first son married to ensure the maintenance of his line and he is unlikely to make too many demands on the new household. With an average of thirty years or more age difference between fathers and sons, only a few of the sons are able to marry before the death of their father. Authority over unmarried sons then falls to the eldest brother who often attempts to maintain Jie-like control over his siblings by delaying their marriages and the division of the herd. Younger brothers resent such attempts by the eldest brother to manage the herd as if he were their father and refuse to obey him. Since the Turkana ideal is a man with his own independent camp, once the father dies each married son demands his independence, takes his share of the inherited animals, and strikes out on his own.

The importance of cattle as the social glue uniting kin groups takes concrete form in the reciprocal exchange of animals. These exchanges are used to acquire animals for sacrifice, to make marriages, pay blood money fines, or just establish friendly relationships. Gulliver has labeled members of such exchange networks "stock associates," and they include agnates, maternal kin, affines, and personal friends. All kinship relations, even between brothers or uncles, are only potential until activated by the borrowing and lending of animals which creates future obligations. Even where an obligation is founded on a close agnatic tie, it is perceived as a reciprocal arrangement: "my brother gave cattle to me when I asked, so I must do the same for him later." Over time these stock associate relationships can transform or transcend bounded kinship relationships, particularly with the addition of "bond friends" who may be from other kinship groups or even other tribes. Such a personal friendship is established easily by lending or borrowing cattle and continues as long as there is reciprocity. As products of personal choice, they reflect a man's evolving social network: the more exchanges the closer the relationship. Among the Turkana the total number of exchange relationships ranges from 7 to 50 with a median of about 30, rich men tending to have more stock associates than poor ones.

Starting such a network may begin with young boys but it comes into full flower with marriage negotiations over brideprice. Marriage rules are exogamous, that is, a man cannot marry a woman who is a patrilineal relative, or marry a woman from his mother's lineage, or even from the same lineage as the wife of his brother or half brother. When listed, these rules may seem arbitrary, but they are based on a fairly simple premise: those that contribute cattle for a brideprice should not also receive cattle as part of the same marriage transaction. And this is a sizeable group of people, for making a marriage requires the cooperation of a wide network of kin and friends who are responsible for contributing the cattle that make up the brideprice, as illustrated in Table 2.3 documenting two Turkana marriages.

The first list enumerates the source of fifty-two cattle and camels assembled by a Turkana man making a second marriage. He provided the bulk of the animals from his own stock holdings and those of his agnates (brothers, half brothers, and uncles) who were under an obligation to contribute. If this had been a first marriage, his father would have provided the largest number. He then received some animals from his mother's brother who, though not required to contribute, customarily does so in a spirit of goodwill. (Indeed, in a classic article, Radcliffe-Brown described such a mother's brother/sister's son relationship in southern Africa as particularly close, permitting the casual borrowing of property and joking behavior that would not be tolerated in other contexts.[16]) After a man's first marriage his affines (father and brothers-in-law) become intimate allies and volunteer aid when needed. Bond friends who have become close through cattle exchanges also contributed.

TABLE 2.3

THE COMPOSITION OF A TURKANA BRIDEWEALTH

Groom	22	cattle		
	4	camels		
Full brother	3	cattle		
	1	camel		
Half brother	1	cow		
	1	camel		
Father's full brother	4	cattle	*Analysis*	
	1	camel	Groom's nuclear family	26
Father's half brother	2	cattle	Rest of house	4
Half cousin	1	camel	Rest of family	10
Mother's brother	2	cattle	All others	12
Wife's full brother I	2	cattle		
Wife's full brother II	1	ox		
Sister's husband	1	camel		
6 bond friends (1 each)	6	cattle		
TOTAL	52	large stock		

THE DISTRIBUTION OF A TURKANA BRIDEWEALTH

Father	14	camels		
	5	cattle		
Father's brother I	5	camels		
	5	cattle		
Father's brother II	3	camels		
	4	cattle		
Father's half brother I	2	camels	*Analysis*	
	3	cattle	Father's nuclear family	19
Father's half brother II	1	camel	Rest of father's house	17
	2	cattle	Rest of father's family	14
Father's full cousin I	2	camels	All others	9
	2	cattle		
Son of father's	1	camel		
Full cousin I	1	cow		
Mother's brother	4	camels		
	2	cattle		
Father's sister's son	1	cow		
Father of brother's wife	1	camel		
	1	ox		
TOTAL	59	large stock		

Source: Phillip Gulliver, *The Family Herds*. London: Routledge and Kegan Paul, 1955, pp. 232, 236.

The second list outlines the allocation of fifty-nine cattle and camels received as a brideprice in a different but very similar transaction. The father of the woman keeps as many as half for himself and redistributes the rest to his own stock associates who helped him in the past: agnates, mother's brothers, close affines. As illustrated, the distribution of brideprice is confined to a narrower range of kinsmen. In particular, bond friends tend to reciprocate by giving to each other when requested, and do not expect to receive animals as part of a brideprice distribution. Such influxes of cattle as brideprice for a woman can later finance a marriage for her brother or father soon thereafter. The cattle come, the cattle go, each exchange knitting new knots of kinship and friendship.

It's easy to see why young men short of animals would attempt to maintain networks for borrowing, they need the extra cattle and repayment cannot be enforced. Refusing to reciprocate without good cause simply ends the relationship. With this risk, why are such relationships maintained by everyone, even wealthy men who could as easily draw on their own herds? Isn't this the pastoral equivalent of doing each other's laundry?

In fact, the stock associate relationship has many other facets that make it both popular and profitable. It spreads risk by scattering animals throughout a number of herds so a man's holdings are less subject to catastrophic loss from disease, theft, or drought which can decimate one herd while leaving another intact. Should a man lose his herd in a disaster, he can not only seek the return of the cattle he is owed but request new loans to rebuild. Exchanging animals can also be used to balance herd composition. For example, it is customary to lend a cow to acquire an ox for a ritual sacrifice because it is considered improper to sacrifice one's own oxen. Although not described as an economic investment, such an exchange is profitable to the man who provides the ox. The cow he takes in return will produce milk and offspring over the years well beyond the original value of his ox, and he can always get another ox by returning a cow to the original borrower. In political and social terms, maintaining stock associates creates a personal network of allies or clients who can provide hospitality when travelling, access to water and pasture in their own territories during time of need, and support in disputes. Refusal to participate in exchanges would put even the wealthiest pastoralist at great risk, for accumulating animal wealth is not just an end in itself but a means of facilitating social relations.

The emphasis in many anthropological studies on the utilitarian value of cattle has been a necessary antidote against the too easy labeling of East Africa pastoralism as an irrational economic system. Yet in laying bare its practical aspects we must not lose sight of the fact that in these societies cattle were considerably more than economic commodities in a way that vegetables, or even cash money, were not. The symbolic value of cattle among East African pastoralists was so high and their use in social transactions so critical that they literally defined the cultural order. Their possession alone was the axis for ranking around which the social structure revolved. Why were men superior to women? Because men could possess cattle and women could not. Why did elders outrank juniors? Because elders possessed cattle, while juniors could only aspire to do so. Who was a man of influence? A man with cattle, for a man without cattle was barely human in a social sense. Raiding for cattle, lending them to friends, exchanging them in marriages, sacrificing them in rituals, decorating their bodies and singing their praises was a end in itself: pleasing to the mind and giving life a purpose. A man was traditionally buried beneath the floor of his cattle kraal, so that even in death the pounding hooves of succeeding generations of cattle could comfort him through eternity.

One could never really have enough cattle, just as we find it inconceivable that we could ever have enough money, because cattle, and only cattle, could be used to denote significant social relationships. Thus the number of animals considered "adequate" was only partially related to subsistence needs, additional animals might be considered necessary to meet social obligations even when their maintenance risked exceeding the carrying capacity of the pasture. This cultural definition of a sufficient herd had a direct impact on its management, particularly in the proportion of nonreproducing steers in a herd. It is also, as we will see, still the foremost barrier to transforming East African pastoralism into a form of cash ranching.

P O L I T I C A L   O R G A N I Z A T I O N

INTERNAL

The networks of cognatic kin, affines, and personal friends are the social universe of everyday life, but political relations involve a much larger number of people. Yet what was most striking to outside observers was the relative lack of political integration of pastoral societies in East Africa when compared to neighboring pastoral societies in the Near East, Central Eurasia, or even other parts of Africa. Where permanent leaders did exist, each chief ruled over a specific territory and localized community with little connection to other neighboring chiefs. Where chiefs were absent, supracommunity politics relied on age-set organizations or segmentary lineages, but in each society only one of these principles took precedence.

Chiefly Lineages: Localized Descent Hierarchies

One of the most common forms of political organization among pastoralists in East Africa vested authority in local petty chiefs who were members of dominant local lineages. Such was the case among the Dinka people of the southern Sudan described by Godfrey Lienhardt. At the time of his research they numbered over 900,000 people, spread over a very wide area, divided into about 25 named tribal groups which varied greatly in size from only 3,000 people in the smallest to 150,000 in the largest. This apparent numerical variation in group size was offset by the tendency of larger groups to subdivide into many smaller tribes that acted as autonomous units. The 150,000-strong Rek Dinka, for example, had 27 tribes, while the smaller Malwal with 38,000 members was divided into 6 tribes. Few chiefs of tribes therefore had direct authority over more than a few thousand people with the largest local aggregation being the wet-season camping group known as a *wut*.[17]

Each camp group had its own leadership. The chiefs of these local residential groups were recognized as superior because they represented lineages which claimed to be the original occupiers of the land. There were two types of lineage leaders in each camp: "masters of the fishing spear," who were drawn from lineages in charge of ritual affairs, and warrior lineage leaders who organized raids and defended the camps. Ideally, both leaders and their kin groups had matrilineal ties with one another so that each was in a mother's-brother relation to the other. The autonomy of a camp group was defined by whether it created and initiated its own age sets.

The powers of a Dinka chief were weak, however, because rather than submit to his authority, dissident groups could move to a new territory if they were dissatisfied. This often occurred when a local camping group got too large. Dissident groups were led by younger brothers of the chief (who bridled at the thought of obeying their elders) or by latecomers who felt they had been relegated to marginal camping areas. Each such cattle-camp community was autonomous and, as long as land was available, expansion made it difficult for any local chief to maintain control over a large number of people.

It was this ease of movement and tendency to fission that both facilitated Dinka expansion into an unoccupied territory (at least unoccupied by cattle pastoralists) and, according to Lienhardt, produced the proliferation of local-level chiefs. The history of such fission was reflected in genealogies which traced the relationship of one local group to another, but such genealogical links did not establish any political obligations between them. Nor did it empower the creation of tribal-level chiefs: instead, the leadership of one among the multiplicity of local camp groups would be deemed preeminent at the subtribal level. Similarly, among all the recognized leaders at the subtribal level, one would be deemed preeminent at the tribal level. Nevertheless, no matter how prestigious it was to be recognized as a tribal chief, such a man still ruled directly only over his own camp group. Leaders of other subtribes might look to him for initiative but he could not command them. Indeed, such higher-level leadership was used mostly in organizing the common defense against encroachments on dry-season pasture by other tribes. Structurally, this situation can be compared to an association of state governors in the United States. Some, by virtue of their state's importance or their own charisma, may be recognized as "national leaders," but their legal authority is restricted to their own states.

Age Sets: Organizations Without Structure

Comprehensive age-set systems lay out a series of ranks through which all men pass successively as members of distinct corporate groups. Every rank has its prescribed areas of competence, rights, duties, and obligations with each set filling a distinctive social role.

A classic example is found among the Pastoral Masai who had a population of about a quarter of a million people in the 1960s distributed between Kenya and Tanzania. They did not form a single integrated tribe, but were divided into territorial groups varying in size from a few thousand to over fifty thousand people. In a study of the Masai, Alan Jacobs found that the very definition of such tribal boundaries centered on participation in a common age set, for "[e]ach tribe organized its age-set system separately, and individual heads of compound polygynous families secured rights to communal grazing and water within the tribal boundaries by initiation into a specific tribal age-set."[18] There were seven age sets: uninitiated youths, junior and senior warriors, junior, senior, and retired elders, and ancient elders. Senior elders were heads of established households, who were presumed to have acquired the dignity and experience to set policy, while less established but more energetic junior elders were expected to implement decisions. There were no formal leaders, instead, groups of about fifteen to twenty camps came together to form a local "council of elders." Warriors (*moran*), prohibited from marrying, were stereotyped as carefree and irresponsible, focusing their attention on herding, raiding, warfare, and impressing women. (Masai women did not form age sets, acquiring their social rights and obligations individually through marriage and motherhood.)

While membership in an age set defined the parameters of social life, rules often had to be bent or broken to accommodate the anomalies that arose from age variations within a set or discrepancies between ascribed status and individual performance. A warrior might marry to meet a family obligation before his age set formally advanced in rank, or a cattle-poor elder might find he was rarely asked his opinion on important decisions. Nevertheless, no individual, however talented, could advance in age-set rank except as part of his whole group, and no individual, however ill-suited to his new status, could be left behind.[19]

In the absence of more formal organization, age sets provided a transferable set of relationships that, as among the highly mobile Turkana,

Herding tasks among the Masai are the main responsibility of boys and unmarried men who are members of junior age sets. Members of each age set advance together through the life cycle. (*Source*: Eugene Gordon.)

created a ready-made structure for interaction for "[w]herever a man goes in the course of nomadic movement or in travelling, he finds men who are his age-mates, comrades, and supporters. He also finds his seniors and juniors to whom he can easily adjust his attitude and behavior. He can never be socially isolated."[20] On a larger scale, warriors could be mobilized as a military force or a council of elders could be assembled to designate a spokesman to negotiate on behalf of the group.

Of all forms of political organization found among nomadic pastoralists, the use of comprehensive age sets was the weakest structurally. Age sets created categories of responsibilities, but provided no clear means by which to mobilize people. They served as a framework for political action only where kinship groups were poorly developed, local residence groups unstable, and there was no institutionalized leadership.[21] For this reason, in pastoral societies with well developed kinship groups such as the Jie or Nuer, the use of age sets was relegated to ritual organization. It is completely absent among the nomadic pastoralists of Eurasia and North Africa. In a modified form, however, an age-set organization restricted to unmarried warriors could serve as the basis for a permanent military machine with age-set regiments led by chiefs. Among the Zulu of southern Africa, this resulted in the rapid rise of a highly centralized and very powerful kingdom.

Acephalous Segmentary Lineages: Organization Without Permanent Leaders

A classic form of leaderless, or acephalous, political organization among East African pastoralists employed segmentary opposition as a means of defense against outsiders or as an organization for predatory expansion. If an age-set system created a fraternity of equals across society, segmentary lineages produced ever-changing circles of reciprocity and hostility within a society. Based on the premise that more closely related kinship groups would ally in opposition to less closely related groups, and that everyone would unite against outsiders, relationships were relativistic with no absolute values: a cousin might simultaneously be my opponent in an ongoing family feud, but remain my trusted ally in disputes with neighboring groups. (Divorced from kinship, this is actually a very familiar process: party members who oppose one another in a primary are expected to support one another in the general election on the theory that the most unqualified candidate of their own party is naturally superior to the best qualified candidate of the other party.)

This acephalous segmentary lineage structure was first recognized and described by E.E. Evans-Pritchard among the pastoral Nuer of southern Sudan who numbered around 200,000 in the 1940s.[22] The Nuer segmentary lineage system organized political groups only through opposition. In such a system there was no class of permanent leaders, for there were no permanent groups. When a man was chosen to lead warriors in battle his authority was only accepted in that context, once the war or raid concluded he had no more power than anyone else. A Nuer lineage was composed of living agnates descended from a single known founder. The size and inclusiveness of a lineage varied, depending on whether the common ancestor in question was a father, grandfather, or more distant ancestor. At a higher level, Nuer lineages coalesced into about twenty named clans whose members all claimed descent from common ancestors, although the exact links between the lineage founders and the clan founder was often unknown. While the number of lineages and their sizes constantly fluctuated as new lines came into existence and old ones died away or were forgotten, the number of clans remained fairly stable. The clans composing the Nuer tribes created the largest group for which some binding agnatic kinship relation was presumed to exist, the outer limits of a social "us." Lifting their cattle was stealing, not raiding, and killing them was homicide for which blood-money compensation could be demanded.

This network of relationships created a treelike structure with the twigs and narrow branches representing the local-level lineages, the limbs representing clans, all converging on a tribal trunk. Unlike a tree, however, the genealogical trunk and limbs were purely theoretical, for only the lineage twigs and branches existed as living social units. While named clans were associated with particular home territories, these were not exclusive and did not create strong corporate groups. The Nuer clans and tribes existed only as a mental construct, a genealogical road map explaining how local lineages were related to one another and therefore how (ideally) they should treat one another in times of conflict. It is also important to recall once again that such descent was as much social as biological: the necessity of making cattle payments to obtain rights to children, "ghost husbands," and the incorporation of captured Dinka into Nuer genealogies created lines of descent in which the biological father and the social father might well be two different people.

EXTERNAL AFFAIRS

None of the political organizations described above displayed any tendency toward political centralization because of internal pressures. When there was a dispute, or the number of people and cattle became too great in a single territory, groups would seek to emigrate. In the process they often displaced their neighbors who would in turn seek out a new frontier of their own. Under such conditions, neither political authority nor territorial boundaries were easy to maintain. Even when a leader did unite a number of tribes, especially during periods of conflict, his authority was severely restricted because allegiance to him was strictly voluntary. A great man of war could not command his neighbors beyond the field of battle. Nor did the configuration of the pastoral economy allow leaders to dominate their followers economically. A large herd owner might be rich in cattle, sons, and wives (which gave him great prestige), but pasture, water, and agricultural land were available equally to all members of a descent group. And in a mobile pastoral society, unhappy followers had the option of deserting their leader and taking his cattle with them. With these difficulties it is not surprising that in a survey of African pastoral societies Philip Burnham concluded that their low population density and easy mobility made the internal development of any institutionalized hierarchy improbable.[23]

Yet in other parts of the continent, pastoral nomads who seemed very similar to those in East Africa did evolve much more complex and centralized political organizations. During the late eighteenth and early nineteenth century a large number of Fulani cattle-keeping nomads in West Africa adopted horse riding and united under the banner of Islamic leaders to conquer the settled Hausa and Yoruba kingdoms in Nigeria. At the same time in southern Africa, Nguni cattle pastoralists such as the Zulu also created a mighty empire of their own, although they began with a political organization not much more sophisticated than those found in East Africa. Why did East African nomadic pastoralists display so little development in this direction? To answer this question we need to examine how East African nomads dealt with the outside world.

SEGMENTARY OPPOSITION: THE NUER EXPANSION

East African pastoralists lived in a political world where external relations played a very small role. They did not have trade relations with great urban centers like the Bedouin, or face a great empire in China as did the nomads in Mongolia, or even act as intermediaries in a system of long-distance trade. Their enemies were their neighbors who, like themselves, were cattle pastoralists or simple farmers. Specifically, they faced no state-organized societies on a regular basis. In such an environment segmentary opposition, even without chiefs, was the most effective model of political organization because it provided the maximum external unity with the minimum internal cost.

It may at first be surprising that a society which employed the principles of segmentary opposition without fixed leaders or a master plan could effectively expand against its neighbors and displace them. Yet in the space of about sixty years between 1820 to 1880 the Nuer did just that, enlarging their territory fourfold to 93,000 square kilometers and doubling their population, devouring Dinka cattle, land, and people in the process. In analyzing their success, Marshall Sahlins noted that the logic of segmentary opposition was relentlessly outward: you should attack strangers and steal their cattle and land before competing with related tribes. Nuer conquests often began as raids for cattle which later resulted in the occupation of Dinka land and the incorporation of captured people. Once begun, the process of expansion at the frontier margins could only be stopped by a well-organized defense or when the territory became unsuitable for Nuer pastoralism. Unfortunately for the Dinka, they proved incapable of sustaining a coordinated defense against Nuer incursions and occupation of prime cattle-raising territory.[24] The Dinka were vulnerable in part because while each genealogical segment had a recognized chief, these segments could not coalesce into larger kinship groups. The Nuer, by contrast, had no chiefs but could combine their genealogical segments readily, producing units three times as large as comparable Dinka tribes.

What impelled the Nuer to act so aggressively? In a provocative and richly detailed study, Raymond Kelly has argued that segmentary opposition alone cannot explain their expansion, particularly since the Nuer had a lower population density than the Dinka and were not short of livestock to meet basic subsistence needs. Instead, he argues that the motivating factor behind such aggressive Nuer expansion was their need to acquire large numbers of cattle and maintain them through the dry season in order to meet the demands of a brideprice system that required much higher payments than among the Dinka. As a shortcut to pastoral prosperity, theft of strangers' cattle has much to recommend it. Such a strategy was particularly attractive to young men who could thereby break their dependency on their fathers and other agnates to supply them with cattle.[25]

While segmentary opposition proved to be a highly effective structure for Nuer expansion against the less well-organized Dinka, it proved ineffective when the Nuer confronted state-organized societies. Until around 1900, the Nuer were protected by their isolation. Egyptian military expeditions and Arab traders had found it difficult even to approach Nuer territory. After the incorporation of southern Sudan into the British empire, the Nuer encountered a state-organized society that could put troops in the field on a permanent basis. Used to organizing raids with temporary leaders, the Nuer were unable to cope effectively with this new type of opposition. They could and did organize periodic attacks against the outsiders, but the British were always able to overcome a local defeat and return with another army. Without permanent leaders and an integrated tribal structure, the Nuer proved unable to maintain their independence, though it must be noted that the level of British control over them was quite limited.

TRIBES AND STATES

European Colonial Expansionism

Left to themselves, nomadic pastoralists had little reason to develop hierarchical political structures that united large groups of people under permanent leaders. Segmentary opposition, age sets, and petty chiefs were adequate for dealing with internal disputes and handling relationships with neighboring tribes. This changed when pastoralists had to confront state-organized societies on a regular basis. In such a competition, nomadic pastoralists were forced to develop wholly new forms of organization or lose their autonomy. In fact, drawing on cases from southwestern Asia, William Irons concluded that among pastoral nomadic societies in general, the development of hierarchical political institutions was "generated only by external relations with state societies and never developed purely as a result of internal dynamics in such societies."[26]

In other parts of the world, the nomadic pastoralists had dealt with neighboring state societies for centuries, but in East Africa this was a recent phenomenon dating to only the 1880s in many regions. Of course, state societies had been established on the Indian Ocean coast in medieval times, but these had little contact with the interior until the late eighteenth and early nineteenth centuries when coastal Arab traders seeking ivory and slaves organized armed caravans to exploit the interior. While these invasions often provoked conflict, Arab traders made no attempt to conquer these regions and the pastoralists there remained completely independent. This situation changed dramatically after 1886 when, anxious to establish colonies during the so-called "scramble for Africa," Great Britain and Germany incorporated all of East Africa into their colonial empires.

There was surprisingly little resistance to this loss of political autonomy, in part because its execution was so rapid, but more importantly because the nomads had never experienced a threat of this magnitude. Although East African pastoralists won occasional battles and often assembled large numbers of warriors under the leadership of ritual leaders who transcended kinship lines, they faced an enemy who had modern firearms and the ability to mass men and resources on a permanent basis. It was a challenge well beyond their immediate political and military capacity. These conquests also closely coincided with a series of "rinderpest" epidemics, the product of new diseases that were fatal specifically to cattle. They first erupted in the 1880s and 1890s and quickly devastated cattle holdings throughout eastern and southern Africa. Losses as high as 80 percent were not unknown. For peoples who held cattle to be the core of social life, the impact of these epidemics was close to catastrophic and, since cattle also acted as a food reserve when crops failed, epidemics were often closely followed by famines. It is hardly surprising that in this context, organizing a resistance against a distant but well-armed central government was extremely difficult.

The establishment of a colonial regime in East Africa had a less direct impact on nomadic pastoral peoples than on their sedentary agricultural neighbors. The British administration (which acquired the region's former German colonies after World War I) had little desire to interfere with local affairs among pastoralists except to preserve order. To this end, they attempted to fix pastoral groups to specific territories and prohibited cattle raiding, pleasing those groups which had been targets of attacks and irritating those groups which traditionally depended on stock theft. Land suitable for agriculture was seized from pastoralists such as the Masai, who found themselves dispossessed of large tracts of their traditional territory by European and then African farmers, but most pastoralists were not affected by colonial land development projects because their semi-arid grasslands were not generally attractive to outsiders. The most important political change at the local level was the recognition, or creation, of permanent chiefs who acted as intermediaries between their people and the new state authorities. This policy of indirect rule greatly increased the power of previously nominal leaders who had little or no executive authority in the traditional political system. Finally, although most European accounts of native peoples invariably stereotyped pastoralists such as the Nuer or Masai as "fierce" and "warlike," in practice they posed little threat to colonial authorities. Anticolonial rebellions against the British by the Gusi in Kenya (1905, 1907), the Bunyoro in Uganda (1890 to 1898), and the Maji Maji rebellion against the Germans in Tanganyika (1905 to 1907) were all initiated and sustained by nonpastoral peoples.

The marginal role of nomadic pastoralists in East Africa's recent history was a product of their weak political organization and the short time they had in dealing with new problems. In southern Africa, where the confrontation with Bantu pastoralists and European settlers occurred over a much longer period of time in the context of frontier trade and military conflict, there was a very different outcome: the reorganization of small chieftainships into powerful states. Although outside of the East African area, it provides an important case study of the transformation of political organization among cattle pastoralists.

Zulu Expansion and Empire

Bantu-speaking Nguni pastoralists, who became the modern Xhosa, Zulu, Batsuto, and Ndebele peoples, began moving into southern Africa from the north in the mid-sixteenth century. They combined cattle raising and agriculture in a fashion similar to East African pastoralists. At the tip of southern Africa in the seventeenth century, Dutch settlers known as the Boers or Afrikaners, also engaged in mixed farming and pastoralism, began moving away from the coast seeking new land and political autonomy. Between the two groups were San foraging peoples and Khoikhoi pastoralists. The San and Khoikhoi were poorly organized and retreated before the more aggressive Boer and Nguni invaders. Although they originally numbered around 200,000, by the nineteenth century the Khoikhoi were reduced to only 20,000 people. Decimated by disease and without their own territory, they were largely assimilated by their neighbors, while the foraging peoples were confined to the remote regions unsuitable for pastoralism. The conflict was now between Europeans and Nguni.

The Nguni peoples in southern Africa closely resembled East African pastoralists in economy, household organization, and importance of cattle in social life. They also had age sets and local chiefs, but maintained a greater social distinction between chiefly lineages and those of commoners. Nguni pastoralists also made other hierarchical distinctions such as between elder and younger brothers, or elder and younger house-lines based on seniority of the mother's status. While this cultural conception of rank set was quite alien to their more egalitarian East African counterparts, it did not initially promote greater political centralization. Like the Dinka chiefs, Nguni leaders rarely controlled more than a couple of thousand people directly and, while "royal lineages" might claim ritual superiority over a set of chiefs, they held little actual power because junior lines could reject their authority simply by moving to a new territory. As the anthropologist Monica Wilson explained, "Independent chiefs acknowledged the *seniority*, and right of precedence in ritual, of related chiefs whose political authority they did not recognize, and it is often very difficult to determine whether a particular chief was subordinate to another or merely acknowledged his seniority."[27]

We noted earlier that it was difficult to maintain a hierarchy of leadership among pastoral nomads when subordinates were free to secede and move off on their own. However, by the early nineteenth century the open frontier in southern Africa was closing. The available pasture land was filled with other Nguni pastoralists or by the expanding Boer settlers. Clients could no longer move away easily, and the Dutch and English settlements on the Cape provided chiefs with new sources of revenue by controlling trade with their people. In this environment, the stage was set for a radical transformation of Nguni society, not through a change in technology or economic organization, but by a transformation of their social and political organization. Leaders from previously small tribes centralized power and built a military structure of a size and discipline previously unknown among African pastoralists.

This political process was set in motion by the northern Nguni tribes at the end of the eighteenth century with their reorganization under the leadership of Dingiswayo. He built a standing army by transforming the young men's age sets into military regiments which were then used to attack neighboring tribes to create the Mthethwa confederacy. Conquered groups retained their indigenous leadership, so it was a confederacy of chiefdoms dominated by Dingiswayo and his army. Many tribes voluntarily joined the Mthethwa rather than fight them. The confederacy collapsed in 1818 after Dingiswayo was murdered by an enemy tribe, and Shaka, a subordinate Zulu chief and military commander under Dingiswayo, moved into this vacuum by establishing his own kingdom.

Shaka was successful because he had introduced a number of innovations that made the Zulus much more powerful than their neighbors. These included the use of short stabbing spears and cowhide shields in hand-to-hand combat, the creation of regiments (known as *impis*) that fought as integrated tactical units to envelop the enemy, and a more comprehensive age-set army that conscripted all men under forty and forbade their marriage. Thus, even though the Zulus originally numbered only around 2,000 people, within a year of Dingiswayo's death Shaka became the paramount chief of the region. His army soon numbered around 40,000 soldiers and the previously autonomous chiefdoms became part of a single Zulu kingdom under his direct control. Warfare under Shaka was both more organized and bloodier: his conquests often resulted in the murder of ruling chiefs and wholesale slaughter of enemy tribes, including women and children. Captured people were incorporated into Zulu regiments and any surviving local chiefs continued only as subjects of Shaka. All cattle became Shaka's personal property, although their use was allocated to his regiments. There was no question of Shaka's dominance. He often executed his own followers for trivial reasons, inciting a fear and respect previously unknown among the Nguni. Shaka's excesses soon bordered on the irrational and he was murdered by his half brother Dingane in 1828. Although Shaka had ruled only ten years, he had so permanently transformed the Nguni society that the Zulu kingdom not only survived his death, it remained the dominant state in Natal for the next half century.

Shaka Zulu (*Source*: Royal Commonwealth Society.)

Dingane and his descendents created a powerful Zulu ruling dynasty that survives to this day.[28]

Shaka's legacy was profound and all of southern Africa was affected by it. Peoples who had not been absorbed into the Zulu kingdom had either fled as refugees or adopted its military organization and centralized administration as a defense against them. The Boers moving out of the Cape therefore encountered a well-organized foe and there were many bloody battles between them. The Boers had the advantage in firearms but, as Shaka himself had once noted, a well-disciplined force willing to take casualties could surmount this obstacle if they closed in for hand-to-hand combat. The Zulu kingdom proved an even match for the Boers and remained independent until the end of the 1870s. At that time the British Empire incorporated all the previously autonomous states in southern Africa, beginning with the Boer Free States (1878) and then the Zulu kingdom (1879). Under the leadership of Cetshwayo, the Zulus put up tremendous resistance against British annexation, at the Battle of Isandhlwana inflicting the worst defeat on them since the Crimean War. However, the Zulus suffered even greater casualties because repeating rifles and light cannons made it much more costly to close in on the enemy than previously. Although eventually defeated, the traditional Zulu ruling lineages retained their influence under British administration.

The rapid formation of the Zulu kingdom and other neighboring states is an indication of how nomadic pastoralists could reorganize themselves in opposition to states. In this respect the Zulu kingdom is more similar to nomadic states found in Eurasia than in other parts of sub-Saharan Africa. However, its use of age-sets as the backbone of an army demonstrates that the structure of a nomadic state was rooted in the local cultural environment.

PROBLEMS AND PROSPECTS FOR PASTORALISTS IN MODERN AFRICA

The colonial period lasted about seventy-five years in East Africa, and when it ended the creation of independent African states presented new political problems for nomadic peoples. The independence movements against the British in Sudan, Kenya, Uganda, and Tanzania were led by men who viewed nomads as a socially backward element and an obstacle to economic development. Despite the establishment of different political systems, each of these countries made an effort to sedentarize pastoralists or at least restrict their movements. In particular they abandoned the British policy of indirect rule, with its emphasis on local tribal autonomy, and imposed central authority in which pastoralists were often confronted with threats to their way of life. This policy has reached its most virulent form in Sudan where the successive national governments dominated by sedentary Muslim northerners have attempted to impose their Islamic cultural values on the southern Nilotic peoples such as the Nuer and Dinka who were animists or Christians as well as pastoralists. Whereas in the colonial period they had been politically quiescent, the Dinka have become the leaders in a civil war for autonomy against the north that has lasted, with various periods of truce, for the past twenty-five years. Political unrest in Ethiopia, Somalia, and Uganda has also led to the emergence of well-armed pastoralists who have reverted to raiding with automatic weapons instead of spears in areas that now effectively lack any governmental control.

Unlike small societies of foragers, states could not afford to ignore pastoralists because there were too many of them, they occupied large tracts of land, and could exploit areas that would otherwise be unproductive for furnishing national economies with badly needed supplies of milk, meat, and hides. Nevertheless, the relationship between governments and resident pastoralists about their role in developing national states has been fraught with difficulties. In general, disputes have arisen over attempts to enforce direct political control over nomadic peoples, the status of their land, and their refusal to become closely integrated into the national economy. This is particularly true in Kenya and Uganda where high rates of population growth have put a premium on developing agricultural land in formerly pastoral areas.

For most pastoralists, however, the imposition of central authority itself has not been as much of a problem as have the attempts by the central governments to restrict their movement, particularly to block migration routes that cross international boundaries. These boundaries were arbitrarily drawn by the colonial powers and never took account of natural ecological zones, the distribution of different tribes, or the economic relationship of one region to another. Even the concept of such boundaries was meaningless to pastoralists who defined their relationship to the land in terms of lineage rights, reciprocal obligations among bond friends, and seasonal occupation. The modern state's concern with preserving sovereign borders, preventing "smuggling," and creating a national identity was alien to them. In this collision of values the nomads have generally ended up losers.

Restrictions on movement have led to overgrazing in some limited seasonal grassland areas. But an even greater threat has been the increasing loss of grazing lands to neighboring farming communities. The best pasture can often support unirrigated agriculture in years when there is sufficient rainfall. Indeed, we have noted that pastoralists themselves plant crops in such regions. There is therefore always a temptation to expand permanent farming communities into such semi-arid zones when the population density rises elsewhere. In the precolonial period, such intrusions were discouraged

by the nomads' military power, and during the colonial period the British administration created "native reserves" which were restricted to the pastoral
peoples who occupied them. Since independence, pastoralists have lost both
forms of protection and have been dispossessed in many areas by a growing
population of farmers, by the establishment of game parks that exclude pastoralists, and by legal restrictions to access of seasonally important resources.
Pasture land was often deemed "undeveloped" by governments so that any
agricultural use was judged to be an improvement. In fact, the use of such
land in regions of regular drought has generally proved disastrous. Newly
settled lands have been abandoned when the rains failed. And pastoralists,
forced to keep their animals within smaller ranges, have been blamed for
abusing the range land and suffered from various "de-stocking" programs,
the forced sale of animals to the government.

Attempts to come to terms with national governments has led to a re-
definition of land rights. Under the traditional system, such rights were
never vested in individuals, and even group rights were rarely exclusive.
By registering land to individual owners, or by creating "group ranches,"
governments expected to reduce pastoral pressure on limited resources, assuming that with private ownership: (1) pastoralists would be more in-
clined to limit access to others, (2) they would be willing to make capital
improvements such as wells, and (3) they would become more market oriented. The Masai ranching schemes in Kenya were organized along these
lines, but instead of creating the bounded units the planners expected, the
Masai made sure relatives and bond friends were distributed throughout a
number of ranches so that when drought hit in the early 1970s they moved
their animals elsewhere. While control of land became a new element in
the relationship between groups, it did not transform them. The risks of
breaking social ties to maximize private gain were too great, and the results
so socially unacceptable, that imposing sedentary concepts of land ownership could not transform the pastoral economy.

Part of the underlying failure of these group ranches and other de-
velopment-oriented schemes is due to a fundamental disagreement over
the nature of pastoralism itself. Governments see a future for pastoralism
only if it can be turned into a form of cash ranching. In ranching the ob-
ject is to produce for a market by culling the maximum number of cattle
for slaughter. They argue that the traditional values of pastoralists, in
which cattle themselves are the basic unit of value, creates too much
waste. That is, unproductive cattle are being maintained long after it
would be profitable to sell them. This "wastage" is not apparent to traditional pastoralists because extra cattle simultaneously serve so may different needs: providing subsistence, meeting social obligations, and as
insurance against disaster. Indeed, the social advantages of lending cattle
to bond friends alone can easily outweigh the economic value of selling
them. This is particularly true when the national economies cannot

The sustained development of native grasslands to support livestock has involved local pasto-ralists, national governments and international agencies in a host of projects designed to in-crease productivity. Here a UN official discusses pasture conditions with a herder. (*Source*: United Nations.)

guarantèe that in times of scarcity the money derived from cash sales will be redeemable for needed goods.

Nevertheless, it has been assumed that while the process may well be slow, pastoralists will eventually come to see their cattle raising strictly as a way to make money when they become more integrated into the cash econ-omy. However, recent research has thrown doubt on this premise. In a study of Lesotho pastoralists whose major source of income was cash wages from migrant labor in South African mines, James Ferguson found that in-stead of ruminating about how they could maximize their money, these labor migrants instead attempted to convert their surplus cash into cattle rather than vice versa. Indeed, he found that they invested so much of their money in cattle that Lesotho, supposedly a "cattle producing" region, was actually a net importer of livestock. Nor were these investments simply a bank account on the hoof, for these pastoralists refused to sell their animals during periods of drought even when it was clear that part of the herd would surely perish. Money, they claimed, would burn a hole in your pocket: only owning cattle could make a man both rich and respectable. Investing in cattle was the chief way in which men who were away from home for long periods could main-tain their social networks and prove that no matter how long their absence they would eventually return.[29]

TABLE 2.4 Estimated East African Livestock Production, 1985 (in millions)

	PEOPLE	ARABLE LAND (HECTARES)	PASTURES (HECTARES)	CATTLE	SHEEP	GOATS
Sudan	21.5	12.5	56.0	20	1.5	2.6
Kenya	20.6	2.3	3.8	12	7.0	8.2
Uganda	15.5	6.5	5.0	5.2	1.2	2.6
Tanzania	22.5	5.2	35.0	14	4.1	6.5

Source: FAO Production Yearbook. Vol. 39, (1985).

The role of East African nomads in the modern world is of more than historical or anthropological interest. As Table 2.4 illustrates, livestock production is still a very significant part of the region's economy. The total number of pastoralists in Africa in 1985 was estimated at least 17 million, or 8 percent of the total population. In East Africa, Sudan has the largest number of any country, around 4 million, and there are about 1.5 million pastoralists in Kenya who comprise about 12 percent of the country's population. In Tanzania, pastoralists comprise only 1 to 2 percent of the population but raise more cattle than in Kenya. Because they exploit non-arable land, pastoralists occupy large parts of East Africa: about two-thirds of Kenya and most of southern Sudan are dominated by pastoral groups. They provide an indigenous source of meat, hides, and milk products that are critical for economic development. Yet so many questions remain to be answered. Can nomadic pastoralists who depended on finding new frontiers for expansion when their populations grew maintain themselves within fixed areas? Can the combination of agriculture and pastoralism, so characteristic of many African pastoral societies, be developed to a greater extent? Is the economic future of pastoralism in cattle or will faster-reproducing small stock eventually become the dominant form? The answers will not only determine the future of pastoral societies but of national economies as well.

NOTES

1. M.J. Herskovits, "The Cattle Complex in East Africa," *American Anthropologist*, 28 (1926), 230–72, 361–88, 494–528.

2. M.J. Herskovits, *Economic Anthropology* (New York: Knopf, 1952), p. 269.

3. Rada Dyson-Hudson and Terrence McCabe 1985:89–90.

4. Andre Bourgeot, "Pasture in the Malian Gourma: Habitation by Humans and Animals," in *The Future of Pastoral Peoples*, eds. John Galaty and others. (Ottawa: International Development Research Centre), pp. 165–82; A.C. Picardi and W.W. Seifert, "A Tragedy of the Commons in the Sahel," *Technology Review*, 42 (1976).

5. W.W. Deshler, "Native Cattle Keeping in Eastern Africa," in *Man, Culture and Animals*, eds. Anthony Leeds and A.P. Vayda (Washington, D.C.: American Association for the Advancement of Science, 1965), pp. 153–68.

6. Gudrun Dahl, and Anders Hjort, *Having Herds: Pastoral Herd Growth and Household Economy* (Stockholm: University of Stockholm, Department of Social Anthropology, 1976).

7. Deshler, "Native Cattle Keeping," pp. 153–68.

8. Harold Schneider, "The Subsistence Role of Cattle Among the Pokot and in East Africa," *American Anthropologist*, 59 (1957), pp. 278–300.

9. Harold Schneider, *Livestock and Equality in East Africa: The Economic Basis for Social Structure* (Bloomington: Indiana University Press, 1979), pp. 85–88.

10. Philip W. Porter, "Environmental Potentials and Economic Opportunities—A Background for Cultural Adaptation," *American Anthropologist*, 67 (1965), 409–20.

11. E.E. Evans-Pritchard, *The Nuer, A Description of the Modes of Livelihood of a Nilotic People* (Oxford: Oxford University Press, 1940), p. 81.

12. Max Gluckman, "Marriage Payments and Social Structure among the Lozi and Zulu," in *Kinship*, ed. Jack Goody (Baltimore: Penguin, 1971), p. 242.

13. Walter Goldschmidt, *Kambuya's Cattle: The Legacy of an African Herdsman* (Berkeley: University of California Press, 1969).

14. Jack Goody, *Production and Reproduction* (Cambridge: Cambridge University Press, 1976).

15. Phillip Gulliver, *The Family Herds: A Study of Two Pastoral Tribes in East Africa, the Jie and the Turkana* (London: Routledge and Kegan Paul, 1955).

16. A.R. Radcliffe-Brown, "The Mother's Brother in South Africa," in *Structure and Function in Primitive Society* (New York: Free Press, 1965), pp. 15–31.

17. Godfrey Lienhardt, "The Western Dinka," in *Tribes Without Rulers, Studies in African Segmentary Systems*, eds. John Middleton and D. Tait (London: Routledge and Kegan Paul, 1958), pp. 97–135.

18. Alan Jacobs, "Masai Pastoralism in Historical Perspective," in *Pastoralism in Tropical Africa*, ed. Theodore Monod (Oxford: Oxford University Press, 1975), p. 414.

19. Phillip H. Gulliver, "Age Differentiation," *Encyclopedia of Social Science* (1968), 1, 157–62.

20. Phillip Gulliver, "The Turkana Age Organization," *American Anthropologist*, 60 (1958), 900–922.

21. cf. P.T.W. Baxter, and Uri Almagor, eds., "Introduction," in *Age, Generation and Time: Some features of East African Age Organisations* (New York: St. Martins Press, 1978), pp. 1–35.

22. Evans-Pritchard, *The Nuer*, p. 110.

23. Philip Burnham, "Spacial Mobility and Political Centralization in Pastoral Societies," in *Pastoral Production and Society*, ed. L'Équipe écologie et anthropologie des sociétés pastorales (Cambridge: Cambridge University Press, 1979), pp. 349–60.

24. Marshall Sahlins, "The Segmentary Lineage: An Organization for Predatory Expansion." *American Anthropologist*, 63 (1960), 332–45.

25. Raymond Kelly, *The Nuer Conquest: The Structure and Development of an Expansionist System* (Ann Arbor: University of Michigan Press, 1985); Michael Meeker, *The Pastoral Son and the Spirit of Patriarchy: Religion, Society and Person among East African Stock Keepers* (Madison: University of Wisconsin Press, 1989).

26. William G. Irons, "Political Stratification among Pastoral Nomads," in *Pastoral Production and Society*, ed. L'Équipe écologie et anthropologie des sociétés pastorales (Cambridge: Cambridge University Press, 1979), p. 361.

27. Monica Wilson, "The Nguni People" in *The Oxford History of South Africa*, eds. Monica Wilson and Leonard Thompson (Oxford: Oxford University Press, 1969), p. 118.

28. Leonard Thompson, "Conflict and Cooperation: The Zulu Kingdom and Natal" in *The Oxford History of South Africa*, eds. Monica Wilson and Leonard Thompson (Oxford: Oxford University Press, 1969), pp. 336–63.

29. James Ferguson, "The Bovine Mystique: Power, Property and Livestock in Rural Lesotho," *Man*, 20 (1985), 647–74.

FURTHER READINGS

Cunnison, Ian, *Baggara Arabs: Power and the lineage in a Sudanese Nomad Tribe*. Oxford: Clarendon Press, 1966.

Dyson-Hudson, Neville, *Karimojong Politics*. Oxford: Clarendon Press, 1966.

Evangelou, Phylo, *Livestock Development in Kenya Masailand*. Boulder: Westview Press, 1984.

Evans-Pritchard, E. E., *Kinship and Marriage among the Nuer*. Oxford: Clarendon Press, 1951.

Evans-Pritchard, E. E., *Nuer Religion*. Oxford: Clarendon Press, 1956.

Goldschmidt, Walter, *The Culture and Behavior of the Sebei*. Berkeley: University of California Press, 1976.

Gulliver, Phillip H., *Social Control in an African Society: A Study of the Arusha, Agricultural Masai of Northern Tanganyika*. London, Routledge and Kegan Paul, 1963.

Konczacki, Z.A., *The Economics of Pastoralism: A Case Study of sub-Saharan Africa*. London: Frank Cass & Co., 1978.

Lewis, I. M., *A Pastoral Democracy: A Study of Pastoralism and Politics Among the Northern Somali of the Horn of Africa*. Oxford: Clarendon Press, 1961.

Monod, Theodore, ed., *Pastoralism in Tropical Africa*. London: Oxford University Press for International African Institute, 1975.

Pratt, D.J., and M.D. Gwynne, eds., *Rangeland Management and Ecology in East Africa*. London: Hodder and Stoughton, 1977.

Rigby, Peter, *Cattle and Kinship among the Gogo*. Ithica, NY: Cornell University Press, 1969.

Rigby, Peter, *Persistent Pastoralists: Nomadic Societies in Transition.* London: Zed, 1985.

Schlee, Gunther, *Identities on the Move: Clanship and Pastoralism in northern Kenya.* New York: St. Martin's Press, 1989.

Spencer, Paul, *The Samburu: A Study of Gerontocracy in a Nomadic Tribe.* London: Routledge & Kegan Paul, 1965.

Spencer, Paul, *Nomads in Alliance: Symbiosis and Growth Among the Rendille and Samburu of Kenya.* London: Oxford University Press, 1973.

Spencer, Paul, *The Maasai of Matapato.* Bloomington: University of Indiana Press, 1988.

Stenning, Derrick, *Savannah Nomads: A Study of the WoDaaBe Pastoral Fulani of western Bornu Province, Northern Region, Nigeria.* Oxford: Clarendon Press, 1959.

CHAPTER THREE

*T*HE CAMEL NOMADS: THE DESERT BEDOUINS

Of all the images of the nomad none has been more indelible than that of the Bedouin riding his camel across a harsh desert landscape. Much to the dismay of sedentary residents of the Near East and North Africa, who have traditionally held Bedouins in low esteem, foreigners have stereotyped their whole region as the land of camel raisers. But the nomads have always formed only a small proportion of the region's population and the average city dweller is about as familiar with a camel as the average American is with a Texas longhorn steer.

Yet it is undeniable that the Bedouin and their camels have had an impact on the region's political history far out of proportion to their number. Indeed, the very name *Arab* used to be applied only to those who lived in a black tent, never to sedentary people, and the nomads themselves still retain this usage. It is a mark of the esteem in which these tribes are held in the region's historical imagination that over the past century nationalist movements have successfully transformed *Arab* into an ethnic label for all the Arabic-speaking peoples of the Near East and North Africa. *Bedouin*, a name which we apply to the region's nomads, is derived from *badawi* (singular) or *bedu* (plural), a term used by sedentary peoples meaning "desert dweller."

We cannot understand the importance the nomads have held in the cultural and political life of the region if we restrict our analysis only to their life in the desert. If they and their camels had remained isolated and cut off from their sedentary neighbors, the Bedouin would be but an historical curiosity, marginal groups making a living in an area too poor for anyone else. But this was not the case. In the past, Bedouins produced many ruling dynasties that conquered sedentary kingdoms, formed the core of the armies that spread Islam, and were a vital link in an international and regional trade network that transformed the desert from an impenetrable barrier into an overland highway. Today, the nomadic tribes still play an influential role in many Arabian states, where ruling dynasties (and their armies) are of Bedouin origin. They are a people whose presence could never be ignored.

A   FEW   WORDS   ABOUT   CAMELS

All wild camels became extinct long ago except possibly for a small number located in remote parts of Mongolia and Xinjiang, China. Today, only two distinct domesticated species remain: one-humped camels, dromedaries, that probably originated in southern Arabia between 3000 and 2500 B.C., and Bactrian, or two-humped camels, that were first domesticated in Central Asia between 2500 and 2000 B.C. It is believed that both species originally evolved from wild ancestors with two humps but, since the hump has no boney structure, this is hard to prove one way or the other. However, the fetus of the one-humped camel passes through a two-hump stage during gestation and the evolution of two smaller humps into a single larger one is easier to explain than the reverse. Bactrian and dromedary camels were crossbred as early as the second century B.C. to produce a very strong one-humped hybrid which was used extensively on the overland caravan Silk Route from China. Unlike the better-known mule, which is sterile and obtained by crossbreeding horses with donkeys, such a camel cross was fertile, but in succeeding generations their initial qualities of strength degenerated significantly. Therefore it was necessary to maintain pure stocks of both species to produce quality hybrids. For this reason, the practice ceased sometime during the Middle Ages when breeding experiments finally produced a self-reproducing race of single-hump camels that was both strong and cold resistant. It now dominates the Iranian Plateau and northern Afghanistan.[1]

Dromedaries are by far the most numerous type of camel today and form the basis of desert pastoralism in the Near East and North Africa. They have short hair and are very heat resistant, but do not thrive in cold or wet regions, so their distribution is restricted to the hot, dry lands bordering the Sahara and Arabian Deserts. By specializing in raising dromedaries, the nomads of these regions are able to exploit vast arid zones that would otherwise be inaccessible. Bactrian camels, by contrast, have relatively long coats (the source of most camel's hair for coats and sweaters), are cold resistant, and are found in steppe and desert regions running from central Asia through the Mongolian Plateau and northwest China. No pastoral society in these regions, even in the Gobi Desert, specializes in raising Bactrian camels exclusively, although they do constitute a larger percentage of mixed herds in more arid localities.

Camels are truly remarkable-looking animals and the first question almost everyone asks is about their distinctive hump(s). Contrary to popular belief, a camel's hump does not store water, but rather fat which it draws upon in time of need. Firm fat humps indicate a camel in peak condition, while shrinking humps indicate deprivation. Camels are, however, justly renowned for their ability to go for long periods without drinking. The camel's need for water depends on its breed, type of pasture available, and the heat of the season. At the height of summer in the Arabian Desert when there is little grazing, milking camels must drink about once every four days, while in the winter on moist pasture they need drink only once every four or six weeks. When camels do drink they can consume as much as 100 to 120 liters at a single watering. Since this water must often be drawn from deep wells, watering a herd of camels may take a couple of hours. Dromedaries also have a rare ability among mammals to cope with peak periods of heat by allowing their body temperatures to rise harmlessly as much as 3° C (6° F) before they begin to perspire. They then cool down to their base level at night. This process, and very efficient kidneys that produce a highly concentrated urine, allows the dromedary to minimize water loss, a highly adaptive trait under desert conditions.[2]

The camel provides both transport and subsistence for the nomads who raise them. They can carry riders or baggage long distances with loads of up to 200 kilograms without tiring. The best riding camels are traditionally female, while most of the baggage camels are male. Bedouins rarely slaughter camels for meat except for special occasions, so the main pastoral product of dromedaries is their milk, therefore herds consist largely of female animals. They claim that camel's milk is superior to that of goats or cows because it is richer and more plentiful. A camel can produce milk continuously for a whole year after giving birth with initial outputs of up to 4 liters a day with lesser amounts thereafter. Unlike the sheep and goat pastoralists, who devote considerable effort to processing milk into cheese or dried yogurt for future use, camel raisers consume their milk fresh daily and make no attempt to preserve it. Male camels were kept for stud and to carry baggage, although in the past the majority were sold to supply the caravan trade or, in more recent times, to satisfy the demands of urban meat markets. Even the camel's dung pellets can provide ready fuel in the desert in the absence of wood or brush. (Indeed, in Central Asia dried camel dung is deemed a markedly superior fuel by nomads because it burns so hot.) Small wonder

Sheep and goat's milk cheese is made by the Bedouin living on the margins of sedentary areas, but the deep desert Bedouin rely entirely on fresh camel's milk since they raise no other animals.

Bedouin poetry traditionally extolled the camel's virtues. Other less romantic observers, noting the animal's many qualities but ungainly form, have described the camel as a horse designed by a committee.

THE EMERGENCE OF BEDOUIN SOCIETIES

We often casually assume that the modern camel-raising Bedouin nomads must be representative of a very ancient way of life that extends well back into the mists of prehistory. Surprisingly, this is not the case, because camels themselves were not domesticated until well after urban life and literate civilizations had first emerged in Egypt, Sumeria, and Central Asia. This was also long after the domestication of sheep, goats, cattle, and donkeys, so that in most regions of the world nomads adopted the camel only as a new transport animal capable of carrying more baggage than a horse or donkey. Only in Arabia and then North Africa did a form of pastoralism evolve in which the nomads abandoned the raising of other animals to specialize exclusively in camel pastoralism. By making themselves at home in an environment where no other nomads could survive, they were able to exploit not only a unique ecological niche, but in time a unique political and economic position that gave them an influence far out of proportion to their numbers.

Unlike East African cattle keepers, the camel pastoralists of Arabia developed in an environment where powerful sedentary states were always part of the regional backdrop. Although they raised camels in the desert, from the beginning the Bedouins and their ancestors were tied directly into complex systems of trade and urban civilization. As a result, the archaeologist Carlton Coon has observed that in the Near East ethnic groups were distributed in a mosaic pattern, each with its own economic specialty.[3] The Bedouins were the regional camel specialists but remained dependent on urban areas as markets for trading surplus animals, buying grain, and obtaining tools, weapons, or other handicrafts. As much as they valued independence, the Bedouins were part of a system that they rarely dominated, for as was noted by an Arab historian:

> while (the Bedouins) need the cities for their necessities of life, the urban population needs (the Bedouins) for conveniences and luxuries…They must be active on the behalf of their interests and obey them whenever (the cities) ask and demand obedience from them.[4]

The first written records of nomads come from a series of ancient Mesopotamian texts from the city of Mari dating from the eighteenth century B.C. They record many incidents involving pastoralists, but none which had camels. Instead, they describe nomads who raised sheep and goats and transported their goods on donkeys, a type of pastoralism that would have been restricted to steppe or mountain regions where water was readily available. The earliest (and most contentious) descriptions of pastoralists raising camels are from the Bible in the histories of the first Jewish patriarchs, such as Abraham, dating to the early second millennium B.C. Some scholars argue that "Abraham's camels" are anachronisms, the invention of scribes centuries later who could not imagine nomads not having camels; but others accept their presence while noting that these Biblical accounts describe a type of pastoralism quite unlike that practiced by the Bedouin in the last 1,500 to 2,000 years.[5] Early Biblical pastoralists depended on sheep and goats for their livelihood, as in neighboring

Mesopotamia, but also kept a relatively small number of camels. These were used for milking and to transport baggage, but never ridden; a form of camel usage that still survives today in Somalia.

If the early descriptions of camels are contentious, there is no doubt of their importance by 1100 to 1000 B.C. when invading nomadic groups like the Midianites are described in the Bible as having thousands of camels. What appears to have brought about this change was the growing importance of camels in the expanding incense trade from southern Arabia. Incense was in great demand by the temples of the ancient world and merchants began to employ camels as baggage animals to transport it and other goods from southern Arabia to markets in the north. Camels soon became indispensable to maintain the overland caravan routes through Arabia and then beyond, and the range of the animal spread along with it. The nomads who raised them, however, remained politically unimportant because they lacked the military power to control the wealth that passed through their territory. If a caravan was armed it had little to fear from the desert dwellers and could easily drive them off.

It was not until between 500 and 100 B.C. that this situation changed when the nomads solved a fundamental riding problem: how to fight from atop a one-humped camel without falling off. Before this time, camel riders had very insecure seats that made it impossible to use a sword or lance effectively, so they were restricted to fighting with bows and arrows. The technological breakthrough created a secure seat by building a frame around the hump. Known as the north Arabian camel saddle, it allowed the mounted warriors to fight foot soldiers from above with great success. It did not make the camel superior to the horse in battle, however, and horse cavalry could usually rout camel riders easily (unless the horses were frightened by the camel's appearance). For example, in Central Eurasia horse-raising nomads never used the two-humped Bactrian camel in battle. Even the Arabian desert nomads preferred to use horses when possible and developed the famous Arabian breeds so prized today. However, since horses could not survive in the deep desert there was no way that caravans could maintain cavalry escorts, so the control of the desert caravan routes increasingly fell under the control of the camel-riding nomadic tribes. Some were content with extracting tolls from passing caravans, while others became merchants themselves and established rich trade cities such as Petra in Jordan and Palmyra in Syria which rose to prominence on the margin of the deserts. The very wealth of these cities attracted the attention of their neighbors and even the desert could not protect them from incorporation into the Roman Empire.[6]

It was not until the seventh century that the camel nomads made a deep mark on the history of their sedentary neighbors. Following the collapse of Roman power in the desert margins of the Near East and a decline in the volume of trade along the old incense trade route, the camel nomads

A major camel caravan city in Jordan in pre-Islamic times, Petra, the "rose-red city half as old as time," grew fabulously wealthy through its control of the incense trade over the Arabian desert.

emerged as a powerful military force under the banner of Islam to conquer the Near East and North Africa. It was at this time that camel pastoralism expanded to include all the desert regions suitable for it. But while the early Islamic armies were heavily dependent on camel nomads, the balance of power soon shifted to the large sedentary areas that were converted to Islam. Cities like Cairo, Baghdad, and Damascus which were close to the desert, but not part of it, became the capitals of empires from which sedentarized Arab dynasties ruled the region. The Arabian Bedouins who had made up the core of the early followers of Islam gradually drifted away from the mainstream of Islamic civilization, even to the point of raiding the annual pilgrim caravans to Mecca, until led back to more orthodox practices by conservative Wahhabi missionaries during the creation of the Saudi state in the 1920s and 1930s.

Although the Bedouin tribes themselves became politically marginal, their style of pure camel pastoralism was much more firmly rooted in the region. One reason for this was that the camel raisers had become even more economically integrated into the regional trade network than in ancient times. During the Islamic period, the transport system, even in non-desert regions, came to rely almost completely on overland camel transport to such a point that camels replaced wheeled vehicles. In a fascinating book describing this process, Richard Bulliet, an historian of the medieval Islamic world, has traced the reasons for the disappearance of the wheel. These include the greater efficiency in transporting large loads by camels as compared with carts pulled by oxen or horses, the independence of camel caravans from paved roads, and the disappearance of the skilled artisans who could build carts and wagons. Although wheeled transport was the mainstay of neighboring Europe and Central Eurasia, the dependence on the camel as the sole means of overland transport in the Near East and North Africa did not end until the introduction of motorized vehicles in the twentieth century.[7] Perhaps surprisingly, the modern Bedouins have been some of the greatest fans of trucks, particularly small pickups, because they have always valued the world's best in transport. As in the past when they prized great horses and invested their camel profits in them, so today they prize great trucks and put their camel money there.

THE BEDOUINS OF ARABIA

Among the Bedouin Arabs in Arabia, nomadic camel raising was traditionally considered the most noble form of pastoralism, even though many tribes (or parts of tribes) in the region also raised sheep and some even engaged in casual agriculture. Yet the camel nomads' claim to superiority was not based on the greater productivity of camel pastoralism (sheep and goats reproduce much faster and give greater profits) or on the possession of more material goods (by sedentary standards they traditionally lived in poverty), but because by reputation they took orders from no one. Only in the deep-desert regions could the ecology of pure camel pastoralism sustain such political autonomy against the threats posed by surrounding sedentary states.

Camel pastoralism is one of the most extreme forms of nomadism found in the world, both because of its reliance on a single species of animal and the distances that are regularly covered as part of the annual migration cycle. To best take advantage of the camel's ability to exploit the desert it must be herded separately from other animals: first, because the camel can utilize pastures too far from any water source to support sheep or goats; and second, because camels can browse on thorny perennial plants with woody fibers and a high salt content that sheep or goats cannot digest. Thus a pastoralist who wished to combine sheep and goats with camels either had to stay out of the deep desert and forgo exploiting the best camel pasture, or keep the sheep or goats under separate management and maintain two distinct herds with very different migration schedules. Such decisions had significant political consequences. The owners of less-mobile mixed herds were confined to specific regions and were therefore more vulnerable to control by regional sedentary states. Pure camel pastoralists, by contrast, could retreat into the desert beyond the range of any state authorities, and they were free to raid their neighbors, knowing that direct retaliation was difficult or impossible.

The Al Murrah Bedouin of Saudi Arabia represent a classic, if somewhat extreme, example of camel pastoralism that still survives in the modern world. As we will see, most of the traditional Bedouin tribes which raised camels exclusively well into the twentieth century have today drifted into sheep pastoralism or have even sedentarized. Many Al Murrah tribes in Saudi Arabia, however, remained pure camel pastoralists, nomadizing the Empty Quarter (*Rub' al-Khali*) of the Arabian Peninsula to take advantage of the sparse vegetation that lies within an area the size of France. Because the Empty Quarter is completely uninhabitable except by pure camel pastoralists, the Al Murrah who use it regularly (about one-third of the tribe) have earned the sobriquet "Nomads of the Nomads," although they are perhaps less well-known than the larger groups of northern Arabian Bedouin such as the Rwala, Howeitat, or Shammar. In the late 1960s, when the anthropologist Donald Cole did research among them, they numbered about 15,000 people, divided into seven clans, each composed of four to six lineages.[8]

While the Al Murrah raise dromedaries exclusively, they breed three distinct types: one variety especially for riding, another for carrying baggage, and a third for milk production. The Al Murrah are particularly famous for their milking camels. The herd size varies from 40 to 75 camels, but averages about 50. This makes them quite wealthy as camel pastoralists go, for it is estimated that a family needs only between 15 to 20 camels to meet its basic subsistence needs.[9] Almost all of these camels are females that provide milk, and their daily herding requires the labor of at least two men. The seasonal migrations are determined by the pattern of rainfall, and there is considerable variation in the timing and location of their

Camels must cover vast distances to take advantage of the desert's sparse vegetation. (*Source*: UPI Bettman Newsphotos.)

movements from year to year. The most wide-ranging of the Al Murrah migrate up to 1900 kilometers annually in an elliptical pattern centered on their summer wells. Despite long periods of drought, some rain is likely to fall somewhere within the region, and a single downpour can support up to four years of plant growth. There is no overall coordination of migration, and each family decides where and when it will move, although in the past when raiding was common, many tribes moved as a single body for protection.

A tribe's summer wells mark the core of its territory, even though its owners may be many hundreds of kilometers away during other times of the year, because water rather than pasture is the key limiting resource at this season. The Al Murrah tribe claims ownership of about twenty major wells, and many more minor wells, in their southern range. Their major wells are as much as 45 meters deep and are scattered across the Empty Quarter between 75 and 150 kilometers apart. They were dug before historical memory and individual lineages which claim their ownership today do so by right of inheritance, confirmed by their use and maintenance. They and their animals congregate around the wells for at least three months a year from early June to mid-September, and it is the one time when a whole lineage is likely to be camped together.

During the height of the intense summer heat (above 40° C or 105° F), the camels must be watered every four days. This means they cannot stray far and soon exhaust the limited grazing around the wells. The camels survive this period of want by drawing on the reserve of fat built up in their humps during the winter. When the heat moderates in mid-September (to around 30° C or 95° F) the Al Murrah are able to journey to fresh pastures deep in the sandy wastes of the Empty Quarter, 320 kilometers to the southwest of their summer camps. Each family operates independently and travels with a minimum of baggage, leaving most of its belongings at the summer wells. Herding camps are moved about 11 kilometers every two days to take advantage of new grazing. Before mechanical wells were opened in the Empty Quarter as a result of oil exploration, the camels had to be returned once a week to the summer wells for water, limiting the area that could be exploited.

The major migration of the year is to the winter pastures 1000 kilometers to the north along the border with Iraq and Kuwait, although the Al Murrah may move well beyond these limits in times of drought. The migration normally occurs in December or January, depending on when the rains fall, and is accomplished quickly in a small number of long moves. The route runs past the summer wells where stored baggage and the heavy tents are picked up for the trip north. The winter camp has the best grazing in the annual cycle and open water is often available in seasonal ponds. The pasture is occupied by an assortment of different tribes and there is considerable visiting and feasting among them. The camels graze here until late March or April when the temperatures begin to rise and the pasture dries out. The Al Murrah then return slowly to their summer camps, arriving in late June, to take advantage of grazing they passed over on their way north.

The use of pasture among the Al Murrah and other Bedouin tribes is unrestricted, that is, people are free to graze their animals on any available pasture. This permits the widest possible latitude of movement which is absolutely essential in a region where pastures are undependable. There were, however, indirect ways to prevent pastures from becoming overgrazed. When raiding was common, the freedom to graze was offset by the possibility of attacks by rival tribes so that migrations often steered clear of hostile territory, or paid rent to the dominant tribes as insurance against raids, both of which restricted use of a common resource. Indeed, if there were a concentration of camels in one place so great as to risk overgrazing, their numbers would invariably attract raiders from areas where camels were in short supply because of drought. Louise Sweet has argued that over time such camel raiding traditionally redistributed camels fairly equally throughout Arabia.[10] In the summer pasture areas it was the private ownership of wells that acted as a break against the abuse of pasture, since at this season pasture was useless unless one has access to water. Since even a major well could supply no more than forty or fifty families and their animals during the summer, the population concentrations that exceeded a well's capacity had to seek grazing elsewhere.

THE ECONOMICS
OF CAMEL PASTORALISM

The Al Murrah take great pride in their camel raising, but a look at their diet reveals that raising camels alone cannot provide for the Bedouins' basic needs: the bulk of their food consists of dates, bread or rice, with coffee and tea as standard beverages. And the animal most commonly slaughtered for meat is the sheep, which must be purchased from other nomads or in urban markets.   Indeed, their insistence on describing themselves as exclusive camel nomads tends to disguise their essential links to the outside world. This tendency is even more pronounced in northern Arabia where large tribes like the Rwala are in regular contact with urban areas.   Ironically, as we will see, the very specialization of Bedouin camel raising which makes it so distinctive, so stereotypically "nomadic," would be impossible without close connections with a sedentary world that provides them with their food, clothing, tools, weapons, luxuries, and even goat hair cloth for their tents. These products were all traditionally acquired by trade, extortion, or as subsidies from rulers in neighboring states.

Trade between nomads and their sedentary neighbors was an important part of the Bedouin economy and their migratory cycle always included a swing through at least one market town.   Pastoralists who raised sheep could find a ready market for wool, cheese, and live animals in any town or village, but the deep-desert Bedouin were dependent on large urban centers to market large numbers of expensive camels. Up until the First World War, for example, the Rwala Bedouin alone sold 30,000 to 35,000 camels annually.[11] Only regionally important cities like Damascus and Baghdad could absorb such quantities. They therefore provided a key link between the city-based caravan operators who needed large numbers of camels for transport and the desert-dwelling nomads who produced them.   This was a symbiotic relationship because, since Bedouin subsistence depended primarily on herds of milking camels, they had a regular surplus of male animals that could be sold for use in the caravan trade without impeding pastoral production. Conversely, merchants not only depended on the Bedouins as a source of camels, but also as a market for grain, manufactured items like cloth, weapons, and metalwork, and luxury goods such as coffee.

Unlike the sheep-raising nomads of Iran and Afghanistan, the desert Bedouins could rarely rely on the annual sale of animals to meet their subsistence needs.   Camels reproduced and matured too slowly to assure a family a regular supply for sale. Male camels reached maturity only after four or five years, while female camels were sexually mature between three and four years of age. Calves were born after a gestation period of twelve months and were dependent on their mother's milk for as long as eighteen months. Beyond these biological factors herds were periodically depleted by long droughts or raids and there were periods when they were in short supply. So to meet their basic annual needs the Bedouins relied on their military strength to extract such necessities as dates and grain from neighboring farming communities. In return for not raiding, and agreeing to defend the farmers and traders against attacks by other tribes, the nomads received protection payments, known as *khuwa*. Since the sellers of this protection were the most likely attackers, these offers were hard to refuse. However, because these oasis towns and villages were generally not incorporated into regional states, the nomad "protection racket" was normally significantly cheaper than paying taxes and did provide security where none was otherwise to be had. Indeed, over time, such arrangements became so imbedded in the lives of both nomads and villagers that their coercive nature often receded and developed into a relationship in which the nomad patrons were expected to use their political influence on behalf of their sedentary clients in disputes with other groups. Nor was the relationship static. Tribal groups could sell their *khuwa* rights to other groups and oasis leaders were quick to transfer *khuwa* payments away from Bedouin leaders who failed to prevent raids to those who could.

In addition to regular trade in livestock and direct extortion, many nomads traditionally received substantial payments from neighboring sedentary rulers. In some cases these payments were made for direct services, but more often they were received in exchange for not causing trouble or for the nomads' willingness to serve as a military auxiliary that could be called upon in time of need. While this practice was more widespread in the Near East before the introduction of modern weapons, motorized ground transportation, and air travel, the political value of Bedouin support has remained important in a number of countries where the tribes are considered the strongest supporters of the remaining local monarchs. It was such payments, for example, that allowed the Al Murrah to boast that they never sold their camels. They did not need to because they received generous salaries from the Saudi Arabian National Guard. Similarly, in 1973 when King Hussein of Jordan was threatened by the Palestine Liberation Organization (PLO), he employed his army, largely of Bedouin origin, to expel them from the country.

HOUSEHOLDS AND TENT GROUPS

The household is the key social institution around which nomadic life is organized. The extreme dispersion required by camel pastoralism demands that each household make decisions for itself and act as an economically autonomous unit. The labor needed to run a household depends largely on the

A Bedouin soldier and his son. Conservative monarchies and sheikdoms in Arabia favor Bedouins for recruitment into their armies and police forces because of their physical toughness and tribal loyalties.

number of camels it possesses and how they are divided for daily grazing. A relatively small herd of 15 to 20 animals requires at least one full-time herder, and larger herds like those of the Al Murrah (40 to 75) require the labor of two full-time herders plus some part-time labor. The herders follow the camels out in the morning and return with them at sundown when they are milked. The men are responsible for herding, milking, and watering the camels. The women are responsible for all food preparation in camp. They are also in charge of the tent, and must pack and unpack it and all other household belongings for each move. While the division of labor is along gender lines, these lines may be crossed in time of need. Men cook for themselves when travelling and women take on herding tasks when the family is short-handed. Similarly, in the absence of men, women can assume men's roles to provide hospitality to visitors.

The livestock is managed in trust for the group by the eldest male, but is disposed of only with the consent of the other members. By Bedouin custom, sons have the right to reclaim camels that were given away without their permission even after many years have gone by. Sons may receive their share of the livestock after marriage and set up a new household, but in practice such fission is generally postponed until the death of the father. At that time, the livestock is divided among his surviving sons. Unlike East African pastoralists, Bedouin women are legally entitled to personal ownership of animals which they inherit from their paternal kin or their husbands under some circumstances. For example, among the Rwala Bedouin, a man without sons can even leave his entire estate to his daughter (although he must appoint a male guardian for her) and "in case this daughter marries, her property is inherited by her son, or if there is no son, by her *ahl* [patrilineal kin]; her husband can claim nothing."[12]

The visible manifestation of a household is its large black tent. It is the portable home to a family averaging about six people and, although Bedouin tent households may be established at the time a man marries, they often house an extended family composed maximally of a father or mother, their sons, wives, and children. The size of the Bedouin black tent is certainly much larger than similar ones in Iran and Afghanistan, where each nuclear family must have its own tent, so this pattern may have been more widespread in the past. One important reason for a larger tent is that Bedouin camel pastoralism requires a high degree of self sufficiency. The extreme dispersion of camps during many parts of the year means that each tent must be capable of running its herd periodically without the aid of neighbors. In such situations an extended household based in a single tent is often the smallest possible social unit in which decision making and herding can be effectively organized. This is because nuclear families with small children lack the necessary labor to act alone and find it more efficient to stay within an extended family group until they can become autonomous. Even if a nuclear family does choose to hire extra herders or servants to help out, a large tent is still needed to house them.

The Bedouin tent is constructed of black, woven goat-hair panels which give the tent its distinctive color and effectively absorb the heat of the sun while providing considerable shade. In the past, Bedouin women often wove this cloth themselves, but today it is more often machine woven and purchased ready-made in market towns. The main body of the tent is created by sewing six to eight cloth panels, each 60 to 80 centimeters wide, into a single piece. The tent is pitched with its main entrance facing south, using stakes that are driven into the ground to secure guy ropes which hold the tent cloth taut against the center poles (2.2 meters high) and side poles (1.5 meters high). The width in most Bedouin tents is the same, so their size varies by length measured in the number of center poles needed. The space between each center pole is 3 to 4 meters, so the total length of a two-poled tent is 9 to 12 meters, while a three-pole tent is 12 to 16 meters long; only very wealthy families or tribal sheikhs have four- and five-poled tents. The long sides of the tent can be pitched so that they are open, allowing the wind to cool the interior, or the roof cloth can be allowed to fall closer to the ground, further closing off the sides to preserve heat in cooler seasons. Each of the tent's walls consists of a flat woven cloth (ru'ag) that is pinned to the roof cloth. The same type of cloth is also used to divide space inside the tent to separate the women's section from the men's section.[13]

A household's autonomy is particularly apparent when tents combine to form a camp group. The decision to camp together is a purely voluntary one and families are free to stay or go as they please. There is little economic advantage in joining with other tent households because they do not herd collectively. Each household remains responsible for its own animals whether camped within a group or on its own. However, there are significant social advantages: both the desire for companionship and the possible need for protection induce tent households to camp together. The Bedouins are not desert hermits, for them the only valuable life is a social life, even if this consists of only a few tents pitched together. Unlike some European travellers who have praised the silent beauty of deserts unsullied by man, the Bedouin view such spaces as potentially dangerous and infested with evil spirits. On the practical side, members of a camp group are also under a special obligation to defend one another from outsiders, even against relatives, a consideration that was particularly important when tribal warfare encouraged camel raiding in the region. Although camp groups are often formed by members of the same lineage, they are under no obligation to do so. Close patrilineal kinsmen mark their relationship by pitching their tents together so that the guy ropes cross. Camping with in-laws is also popular because it gives the women a chance to visit their natal families.

Each tent household within a camp group is responsible for providing hospitality, which is raised to a high obligation among the desert Bedouin. At a minimum, the arrival of a guest demands the serving of coffee, which is prepared as part of an unvarying ritual. The beans are roasted and then pounded using a heavy brass mortar and pestle. The rhythmic ring of the beating sounds an invitation to the residents of any neighboring tents to come and join. Water is boiled and the coffee is then brewed in a traditional long-beaked brass pot and served to the guest along with dates. Tea may then follow. A meal should be at least offered to a guest, the lavishness of which depends on the wealth of the household and the status of the guest. Bedouins have high praise for the households that readily slaughter an animal to meet such an obligation, but the extent to which

A Bedouin black tent pitched beneath the towering cliff walls of Wadi-Rum in southern Jordan.

such hospitality is obligatory varies: among the larger northern Arabian Bedouin only prominent sheikhs are expected to host visitors regularly, while more remote groups like the Al Murrah expect that every household should entertain visitors who happen to turn up.

The importance the Bedouin place on hospitality must be seen in the context of their environment. In the deep desert where tents are few, only the reciprocal obligations of ritual hospitality make individual travel possible. In general, nomads have rigorous codes of generalized hospitality to the extent that they themselves engage in regular travel, expect relatively infrequent visits by outsiders, and lack access to such conveniences such as tea shops or inns. Thus while the steppe nomads of Mongolia and the desert Bedouin take the provision of hospitality for granted, nomads in Iran and Afghanistan who are close to towns and villages do not. They are more likely to point a visitor to the nearest caravanserai or provide only a drink of tea unless the visitor is known to them.

LINEAGE MODELS OF SOCIETY

Bedouin social organization appears relentlessly patrilineal. While almost all pastoral nomadic societies are biased in this direction, none comes as close to reinforcing patrilineal ties in so many aspects of social relations. The preferred form of marriage is ideally a patrilineal cousin, residence rules are patrilocal, and families are organized into defined patrilineages. Bedouin tribal organization employs these patrilineal kinship groups to create a structure in which scattered and autonomous households can be united for cooperative action. Composed of nested groups of egalitarian clans and lineages that are assumed to descend from common ancestors, the tribe is designed primarily for political purposes. At first glance this system would seem to be very similar to that of the Nuer described in the last chapter, but in fact, there are a number of significant differences: among the Bedouin, lineages exist as corporate groups even when not in conflict with one another, they have permanent chiefs, and marriage partners are drawn from within the group rather than outside it.

To the desert Arab, the social universe of the region is ultimately divided into Bedouin and non-Bedouin societies, with all Bedouins being assumed to be distantly related and to share common values. Although a genealogical chart that would relate all the Bedouin tribes to a primordial ancestor could be created, such extensions are largely symbolic and they have never served as a basis for any supratribal political organization. The tribe was thus the outer limit of both ordinary identification and political leadership, and it was by the tribal name that a group was most frequently known to the outside world. Most Bedouin tribes have populations in the tens of thousands, but some, such as the Rwala, have as many as a quarter of a million members. The tribe was the key political structure in regional politics. Raids were made against other tribes and tribal sheikhs organized defensive actions on behalf of the whole tribe. However, because tribes rarely united as a single unit for any large-scale actions, it was the tribal section, or clan, that was the usual group for political and military coalitions. That is, what to outsiders was an attack by the Rwala, Al Murrah, or Shammar, was to insiders the work of particular tribal sections within these named tribes.

Clans or sections all claimed descent from a common tribal founder, but segmented along different lines of descent from which they get their names. These were fixed and well-known. Individual clans were composed of a varying number of lineages which traced a common ancestry back at least five generations. In some cases, the named clan and lineage were identical, in other cases, it was composed of many lineages and even sublineages. Within the tribe, the relationship between each lineage or clan rested in theory on segmentary opposition, that is, they were expected to support or oppose one another based on their degree of relatedness. Disputes within clans and lineages of the same tribe, even those involving homicides, were often resolved through negotiated settlements and the payment of fines; outside the tribe, vengeance was the normal recourse.

Within the tribe, it was the five-generation lineage, *fakhd*, that was the basic structure on which the whole system rested. Descendants of a common grandfather might have closer economic ties and tribes were more important for organizing territorial defense, but the maximal lineage was the unit of greatest consequence because its members had absolute rights and responsibilities to one another that could not be abrogated. Each lineage's strength was based primarily on the number of men it could muster in disputes and, while a dominant hierarchy was recognized in practice, no lineage was deemed permanently superior to another by right of inheritance. It was also within this five-generation lineage that marriage was most common and where kinsmen were collectively responsible for taking revenge if one of their members was killed or injured, and for defending even guilty members against attacks by other groups.

It is important to keep in mind that although the Bedouin conceived of the tribal structure as generated through genealogical connections, genealogies did not in fact determine relationships between groups. Rather the reverse was the case: groups with which one had friendly relations and many marriage connections were assumed to be close in genealogical terms, while groups that were on bad terms with one another always categorized themselves as only distantly related. In a study of Rwala kinship, William Lancaster has argued that this is possible because the seemingly fixed composition of Bedouin kinship groups is more apparent to outside observers (including other Bedouin) than to members of a clan or lineage. The term *fakhd* itself is slippery because the same word is often used to label both clans and lineages, so that the level of organization being described is situational. Looked at from the bottom instead of the top, the Bedouin think of their relationships as parts of ever-larger groups of *ibn amm*, or patrilineal cousins. As in English, the term *cousin* seems well defined but is notoriously ambiguous, ranging from a closely linked three-generation *ibn amm* and the jurally responsible five-generation *ibn amm* to a vague category of other Bedouins with whom one is not fighting. Thus, although the Bedouin often imply that their clans and lineages are naturally generated by lines of descent, the five-generation lineage is more figurative than exact. Lancaster discovered, for example, that the named ancestors of the Rwala five generation lineages collected by Alois Musil in the 1920s were almost identical to those he acquired fifty years later, an impossibility if the Rwala were keeping strict account of actual descent. But this is not too surprising, for as Musil himself commented, "every Bedouin knows his great-grandfather whereas of his great-great-grandfather he is likely to be absolutely ignorant."[14]

The lack of knowledge about the links between the various clans and lineages within a tribe was not a product of forgetfulness. By deliberately losing track of ancestors at this level (while keeping exact account of tribal identity and the relationships within one's own lineage) the whole system accommodated itself to reality. Any lineage that attempted to follow actual descent exclusively would soon find its lineages out of demographic balance as some prolific lines would have many members and others only one or two. Instead, many smaller lines were amalgamated in a single larger one by claiming a common ancestor at the fourth- or fifth-generation level, an assertion that would in time become as good as true in an oral tradition where people knew their own genealogies well but not those of other groups. Only old tribal genealogists and anthropologists would then take any interest in the anomalies, and the former at least always had the good taste to avoid publicly discussing them.

By allowing such flexibility of membership, a seemingly rigid system of descent actually functioned quite well. Since all close relationships were presumed to have a genealogical base, if two men or groups were friendly they "must be" kin of some type. In political terms, the breaks in known descent also prevented any lineage from claiming the right to dominate others because of an imputed genealogical superiority. As we will see, while sheikhly lineages did emerge to lead others, they could not use their descent alone to justify such power, as was commonly done among the steppe pastoralists of Central Eurasia who routinely employed genealogical descent to rank tribal sections.

W O M E N ' S   R O L E S   A N D   M A R R I A G E   P A T T E R N S

Men and women inhabit distinctive social spheres. The tent itself is divided by cloth walls into a women's section, which is reserved for family use, and a men's section, where visitors are received. Men completely dominate the public world, and the business of politics, herding, raiding, and revenge is theirs alone. Women are considered exempt from attack during raids, wars, or feuds although traditional tales often describe them beating off attackers with tent poles when the encampment is overrun. Nevertheless, the men could not actively participate in the public sphere without the direct support of women. It is the women who make the vaunted Bedouin hospitality possible because they prepare the food that is needed. They are the core of the household and a Bedouin does not consider himself sedentarized unless he moves his wife from her tent into a house in town. Women's status as neutrals in disputes allow them to carry information from one side to another. And fear of being labeled cowards by their women has turned the tide in more than one battle when the men have been tempted to flee.

As in most traditional societies, marriages are considered too important to be left to chance. Marriages are formally arranged by negotiations between the kinsmen of the prospective bride and groom, although behind the scenes the women are heavily involved, since they can gather critical information through their own networks. The preferred marriage partner for a man is his father's brother's daughter (FBD), or *bint amm*. By custom, a man has the right of first refusal and can prevent a marriage to an outsider by pressing his rights, even to the point of removing the prospective bride on her wedding day. In fact, the actual rate of first-cousin marriages varies considerably, but by extending the ideal of *bint amm* to second cousins and beyond, lineage endogamy is typically quite high. Brideprice is paid, but between cousins it is only nominal and for others it is not a major expense. Divorce is also common and about 30 percent of marriages break up, particularly during the early stages. Divorce does not stigmatize either party and young women find it easy to remarry. While only men can initiate divorce, women who are dissatisfied with their husbands often simply decamp to live with their kin where they remain in this estranged condition until their problems are resolved or the marriage is dissolved. Polygyny is condoned, Islamic law permitting up to four wives, but is common only among the wealthy because (unlike East Africa) wives are not economically self-supporting.

We saw that many East African pastoral societies have lineage structures, but none puts the same emphasis on biological descent as do the Bedouin for whom it is the primary qualification for participation in social life. In East Africa, cattle payments legitimize descent and the identity of the biological father is of secondary importance, but among the Bedouin only biological patrilineal descent, "blood," grants membership in the group. A tribesman identifies himself by his kinship group and not the territory he inhabits, so without a proper genealogy a person is no better than a peasant farmer, a group that Near Eastern nomads view as the very opposite of themselves. Thus while pastoralism is closely tied to Bedouin life, one's purity of descent is in no way determined by the ownership of camels. However, because the "purest" lineages were always considered to be those which stayed in the deep desert where they did not intermarry with other groups, the camel pastoralists were generally perceived as having the best genealogies.

The focus on purity of descent is most noticeable in the preference for FBD marriages among the Bedouin. Anthropologists have long debated why this marriage practice should be so common among the Bedouin and the Near East in general. It violates the cardinal rules of clan exogamy central to marriage practices elsewhere, where marriages between groups unrelated by descent create alliances that are essential for social and political action. For example, we saw that in East Africa the marriage of cousins was rejected because people who give cattle for a marriage should never receive cattle as part of the same brideprice transaction, thus preventing a man from marrying any woman from his own father's or mother's lineage. Among Mongol and Turkish steppe pastoralists, marriage between members of the same patrilineage extending back five, or even seven, generations is considered incestuous, but they do permit cousin marriage on the mother's side so that two unrelated patrilineal clans can create lasting alliances through a regular exchange of marriages.

While the literature on this subject is vast, the most common theories on why the Bedouins forego the advantages that marriage alliances would produce include the preservation of property within the lineage, the reinforcement of patrilineal ties that would otherwise be stained by marital ties, and the emphasis Bedouins place on preserving purity of descent. For camel nomads, the preservation of property is probably the weakest argument because, unlike land, wealth in livestock is periodically subject to catastrophic loss which makes such long-term planning problematic. The question of divided loyalties in such strongly patrilineal societies is a much more important consideration because Bedouin women retain strong patrilineal ties to their natal kin groups even after marriage. As a permanent outsider, she is a potential threat if a dispute should arise between her lineage and that of her husband, particularly at an early stage of marriage. Marriage of patrilineal cousins solves this problem because the couple share the same patrilineal kin, thus guaranteeing loyalty and providing women with protectors within the group to ensure proper treatment. Still, since patrilineal societies which prohibit FBD marriages manage to overcome these structural problems, they cannot be overwhelming. We must therefore look more closely at the cultural values in Bedouin society, particularly their preoccupation with preserving a lineage's honor, for next to descent, a lineage's most prized possession is not its livestock, but its social reputation.

H O N O R   A N D   R E P U T A T I O N

Reputation is maintained by upholding a standard of behavior that emphasizes autonomy and self-control. These values are believed to be closely connected to genealogical descent, that is, some lineages and tribes assert they have more intrinsic honor (or their neighbors less of it) by virtue of their ancestors' deeds. But these reputations are not static: They can be gained or lost by both an individual and a group, so each family or lineage is acutely sensitive to assaults on its status.

Bedouins praise individuals who display courage and initiative, cultural features prominent everywhere among nomadic pastoralists because keeping livestock and moving them regularly is a risky business in which passivity and fecklessness lead to disaster. They also highly value hospitality and political acumen. Traditionally, men gained honor by acts such as raiding for camels and then distributing the spoils to others. Political reputations could be enhanced by the ability to resist the demands of others, bringing others under one's control as clients and allies, or most importantly, by being sought out by others as mediators in disputes. Men or whole tribes could lose honor by abandoning their autonomy to seek protection because of economic need or political weakness.

One of the most common ways to raise an individual or group's prestige was through the camel raids. Camel raiding was bounded by many rules: herders were to be left alone, women were inviolable, enough camels must be left to transport the victims to their relatives, and any killings would provoke a blood feud. The recounting of such raids, successful and unsuccessful, was a major topic for poets and storytellers. The way the raid was carried out was as important as its outcome. Lifting a few camels quietly under the cover of darkness was more likely to be labeled theft than raiding and brought profit but no honor. Similarly, a large raiding party could ensure success but would require the spoils to be divided many ways. The most admired raiding party therefore was a small group of men who would surprise a much larger opponent and run off with a large number of camels. These captured animals could be redistributed within the raider's tribe to enhance his position and political advantage. The sons of sheikhs were particularly attracted to raiding (and suffered a relatively higher death rate) for this reason as they competed to show their daring and bravery.[15]

The question of preserving honor was most spectacularly present in blood feuds, because here the acts of an individual put a large group of kinsmen at risk. If a homicide occurred, blood must be paid with blood or some settlement negotiated for compensation. If left unresolved, revenge killings would set off a series of mutual retaliations that could take years to resolve. The whole five-generation lineage was held collectively liable for acts committed by any of its members, although in practice close kin were held to a higher standard than more distant cousins. In keeping with this logic, a woman's patrilineal kin, not her husband, were ultimately responsible for her actions because even marriage did not supersede their rights and responsibilities.

Bedouin feuds were highly structured in terms of specifying what types of killings were subject to vengeance and the responsibilities expected from the kin groups of both the victim and the killer. When outsiders accused a lineage of an offense, they quickly found that some members refused to accept responsibility on the grounds that they were in fact members of separate sublineages whose five-generation ancestors were different than those who committed the crime. Unless care was taken to restrict revenge only to the known relatives of the offender, a whole new blood feud could be inadvertently unleashed. Not all killings provoked a feud. In discussing the process among the Rwala, Musil noted that while manslaughter demanded compensation, such accidental deaths were not subject to revenge. Similarly, if a thief was killed in the course of a simple robbery, revenge could not be sought. In keeping with the logic of kinship, murders within the family had no possibility of revenge, since the group would be taking retribution upon itself. For example, a man who killed his father was not subject to revenge because this was viewed as an internal family affair, although such a killer could be permanently exiled.

Few Bedouin killings (except in retaliation) were premeditated, but instead generally arose from arguments that got out of control: insults to honor which led to blows and then a stabbing or shooting. Even in raiding and warfare there was an attempt to avoid unnecessary bloodshed because of its long-term consequences. Whether a homicide was justified or not was a secondary matter, for the killing itself set the respective kinship groups into action. The murderer either fled the territory or sought temporary protection from a neutral party who would attempt to mediate the dispute. Since the concept of collective responsibility put whole groups of kinsmen in peril, mediation was sought quickly to reduce the risk of escalation. Negotiations, when successful, often took many years to complete and would result in the payment of substantial blood-money payment before a killer could safely return home. Among the Rwala, blood compensation for a man from a related tribe consisted of a mare, fifty she-camels, and equipment; twenty-five camels for a woman; while only seven camels for a man from an alien tribe.[16] If no compensation was agreed upon, then a revenge killing was almost inevitable, for failure to take revenge in the absence of a settlement permanently blotted a lineage's honor and might encourage future assaults.

On an individual level, the concept of honor was closely tied to personal behavior, particularly the ability to display self-control. The lack of discipline in any area of life, emotionally or physically, was sharply criticized. Self-control was in turn related to the cultivation of 'agl, or reason, which included a sensitivity to context in social relations. It was presumed to grow with maturity and responsibility, and the greater a man's age, power, or wealth, the higher the standard to which he was held. Thus the lack of self-control in a young man might be attributed to his immaturity, but considered a fatal character flaw in a more senior man. Similarly, while a powerful man gained respect by attracting clients, he could lose it if he abused his power. Possessing wealth was also double-edged: distributed generously for feasting and hospitality to create a network of allies it brought fame and goodwill; but if hoarded or spent on personal luxury it yielded only social contempt. In all these cases the sin was less in the acts themselves than what they displayed about the person.

Women stood in an ambivalent position in respect to honor. Their role as dependents prevented them from displaying the autonomy expected of men and they could not participate in the public domain. On the other hand, while women could not gain honor directly, they were vulnerable to losing it through inappropriate behavior, particularly by sexual misconduct. In sedentary societies of the Near East this led to the practice of strict gender segregation in an attempt to prevent compromising situations from arising. Yet this was not the practice of the Bedouin among whom women's freedom of action was generally much greater. One reason for this, of course, was that women could not function as nomads if their movements were sharply restricted. But more important was that the Bedouins invested women with responsibility for their own acts and reputations. They stressed an ideal of modesty to guide a woman's actions rather than using externally imposed restrictions such as strict veiling and seclusion behind high walls.

In a path-breaking study of recently sedentarized Bedouin women, Lila Abu-Lughod has described their world as one in which respect for rigid formal rules was less important than the interpretation of behavior in context. For example, in using their black head scarfs, "women veil for those who have authority over them or greater responsibility for the system. They do not veil for those lower in the hierarchy—dependents and those without honor."[17] Thus the degree to which a woman covered her face in front of men depended on their seniority, status, and kinship relation. Abu-Lughod remarked that when Bedouin women from Egypt's western desert visited cities like Alexandria or Cairo they went completely unveiled because such city folk had no honor worth respecting, but on the journey they took care to cover themselves when passing through Bedouin settlements because they were inhabited by respectable people.

Abu-Lughod also demonstrates that women, particularly in their poetry, have created a private social domain. Now the importance of poetry among the Bedouin has long been recognized, but the emphasis has always been on the publicly recited poetry that focuses on battles, raids and political struggles. In a study of heroic Rwala poetry, Michael Meeker argued that this genre, by glorifying the honor code and the need for men to respond to dangerous challenges, expressed the core problems of Bedouin society: the uncertain nature of political relationships and the centrality of struggle between armed mounted men which seemed to leave no recourse except violence.[18] Abu-Lughod's research, while not denying that these are key issues in the public sphere, has responded that Bedouin also had another, private, poetic discourse which ran counter to these values. For most people it was impossible to live up to an unrealistically high standard of autonomy in the real world where individuals and lineages were not equal, where compromises had to be made, and where personal tragedies weighed more heavily on the heart than could ever be directly admitted. In their position as dependents, women felt this most keenly and therefore cultivated an emotional poetic genre that was widely appreciated and adopted even by men as a way to deal with their own emotions without admitting any weakness in the public sphere. Metaphorically, it provided a way to communicate feelings that could not be publicly expressed in other ways and yet, because such poetry could always be dismissed as "meaningless," honor was never called into question.

T R I B E S   W I T H   L E A D E R S : T H E   R O L E   O F   S H E I K H S

Bedouin political structure was organized around tribes composed of egalitarian lineages of similar size in segmentary opposition to one another. Unlike the Nuer who also have segmentary lineages, the Bedouin tribes had permanent and formally recognized chiefs, or sheikhs, who could act for the tribe as a whole. Though sheikhs were normally recruited from only a minority of a tribe's lineages, this never resulted in the evolution of a social hierarchy because each Bedouin lineage considered itself to be the equal of any other. In fact, Bedouins rarely displayed much formal respect toward their leaders and felt free to argue with them and dispute their decisions.

The office of sheikh itself had little inherent power because the ability to command without consent was severely limited. Leaders in such egalitarian tribal organizations gained their positions by displaying special skills in mediating problems within the tribe or successfully organizing raids and wars against other tribes. A sheikh also required access to considerable wealth in order to provide hospitality to visitors and to aid destitute members of his own tribe. It was thus an achieved status that was not automatically inherited by a man's heirs, although a sheikh's son had an advantage over other rivals if he could call on his father's network to aid him. Instead, succession to leadership was determined by whom the people would follow. Power rarely remained permanently within a single lineage, for at the tribal level there were at least two or three rival lineages competing to supply the paramount sheikh.

The necessity to prove leadership by building a social consensus was seen most clearly in the mediation efforts of a Bedouin tribal sheikh. His effectiveness was judged by the number of problems he handled and extent of his reputation, for he needed the respect of both disputing parties in order to initiate negotiations. Such mediation efforts required the sheikh to possess both political acumen and keen verbal skills, for these were his only tools for resolving disputes. For example, in mediating a blood feud a sheikh lacked the authority either to impose a punishment on the murderers or to force the murder victim's kin to accept blood money. He could only persuade the disputing parties to settle by putting his own reputation on the line, allowing the rivals to claim that any compromises made were "out of respect for the mediator," and therefore involved no loss of honor. All negotiations demanded intensive work over an extended period of time, but success brought prestige and more followers.

Based on research done among the Libyan Bedouin, Emerys Peters has disputed the extent to which this accepted ideal of structural equality ever really existed, except as mystified folk belief, because ruling lineages there periodically emerged to dominate their neighbors through their control of land.[19] But such attempts at domination had to contend with a very real ideology of egalitarian political relationships which identified such power with oppression (zhulm), undermined its growth, and eventually brought about its collapse. If set against the example of the acephalous segmentary organization of the Nuer, a Near Eastern or North African tribal sheikh and his lineage might appear despotic and permanent, but (as we will see in the following chapters) when compared with a Central Eurasian tribal khan whose political role is much stronger and whose lineage has ruled for centuries, status differences among lineages within Bedouin tribes are minor and of only temporary duration.

This was particularly true in Arabia where, unlike North Africa, the dominant "noble" lineages did not control agricultural land or other resources through which they could enforce the dependency of others. As Michael Meeker has noted, in Arabia "noble" tribes were simply those that raised camels as opposed to those who raised sheep and goats. And within these tribes each lineage was autonomous because it possessed its own military force of armed camel riders. All military and political organization was ultimately voluntary because "no one could unite or lead these little groups unless they wanted to be united or led, and there was no occasion on which they wanted to be led except when they were threatened by other groups of camel-herders."[20] Arabian Bedouins thus did not need supratribal leadership to organize attacks. They could and did arrange raiding parties at the local level. Indeed, their propensity to attack their neighbors independently of any central organization was the bane of tribal sheikhs whose long-term strategies of promoting alliances among different tribes and facilitating intertribal diplomacy were constantly undercut by the aggressive acts of their own people who could rarely be controlled or punished.

TRIBES
AND STATES IN HISTORY

The relationship between the Bedouin tribes and the surrounding sedentary states historically has been extremely close. The best analysis of this relationship is one of the oldest in all of the social sciences, the work of the medieval

⌐ social historian Ibn Khaldun (1332 to 1408). In his classic book, the ιν..ｑaddimah, he argued that there were two fundamentally different environments in which all human cooperation and social organization developed: the desert life of the tribal societies, and the sedentary life of towns and agricultural villages. Among the tribal desert peoples he included subsistence mountain farmers such as the Berbers of North Africa, sheep pastoralists such as the Turkish tribes that did not venture far into the desert, and the camel nomads of the deep desert. Of all these groups, he argued, the camel nomads best displayed the constellation of virtues that allowed them to periodically conquer sedentary states.

Ibn Khaldun claimed that the Bedouins were closer to being good in a moral sense than were sedentary people because (of necessity) they lived a spartan life with few luxuries in food, clothing, or dwellings. It was not that they were innately better people, but that desert life offered fewer opportunities for corruption, and that Bedouin life was grounded upon ideals of honor and hospitality absent in towns or among peasants. Ibn Khaldun also observed that the Bedouin were more courageous than sedentary folk because they had no walls or hired militia to protect them from attack. Finally, the Bedouin displayed more self-reliance and had more freedom than people in cities because they refused to be governed by despotic rulers and because the life of a nomad demanded independent decision making, while city life induced passivity.

But what gave the nomads the most cohesion in dealing with the outside world was their "group feeling," or 'asabiya. 'Asabiya was the product of close kinship ties, or patron-client relationships, that developed most strongly among tribal peoples because:

> [t]heir defense and protection are successful only if they are a closely knit group of common descent. This strengthens their stamina and makes them feared since everybody's affection for his family is more important than anything else...It makes for mutual support and aid and increases the fear felt by the enemy.[21]

In warfare, such bonds better ensured mutual aid and cooperation than did the weaker political or economic interests motivating the mercenary armies employed by states, because a man would rather die than be disgraced before his kinsmen. Since Ibn Khaldun observed that genealogical descent groups lost their cohesion in cities or when farming on fertile land, it was the deep-desert camel nomads who refused to intermarry with other people among whom "group feeling" was most highly developed.

Ibn Khaldun believed that leadership in Bedouin societies had a natural lifespan, as did their conquests of sedentary societies. The prestige and power of each rarely lasted four generations. Since in an egalitarian political structure "nobility" was never viewed as an innate characteristic of any lineage, there was no ideological barrier to prevent the rise of new leaders from previously subordinate groups which then established precedence by their power. Ibn Khaldun described the dynastic founder of such a ruling lineage as "the builder of glory," a man who understood the difficulties inherent in establishing political dominance and after obtaining power retained the personal qualities that had allowed him to succeed.   These included parsimony and the love of a simple life even when surrounded by available luxuries. The son of the founder assumed his leadership role and, having observed his father, learned the basic lessons of leadership from him.   However, as "experience is always superior to learning," leadership in the second generation might be adequate but lack the vitality and originality displayed by the founder.   In the third generation, leaders became content with simple imitation and reliance on tradition.   That is, they displayed no independent judgement and were content to implement policies by rote, even when these had lost their effectiveness.   By the fourth generation the qualities that brought the family to power and preserved its rule were lost.   These fourth-generation leaders assumed that the right to rule was theirs by birth and expected the automatic respect of their subjects without remembering how it originated.   Their arrogance and misrule led to disaffection, and allegiance was transferred to a rival leader who installed his own dynastic house.

In dealing with regional states, sheikhs negotiated on behalf of their tribes and, as men of influence, were expected to mediate disputes that arose between their fellow tribesmen and state authorities.   However, their ability to negotiate was limited by the knowledge that they could impose nothing on their followers.   Even the politically prominent tribal sheikhs of the Rwala Bedouin who today deal regularly with Syrian, Jordanian, Iraqi, and Saudi Arabian government leaders can enforce no agreement that their followers find objectionable.[22]   Bedouin sheikhs rarely achieved what Ibn Khaldun called "royal authority":

> It is more than leadership. Leadership means being a chieftain, and the leader is obeyed, but he has no power to force others to accept his rulings. Royal authority means superiority and the power to rule by force.[23]

Without a strong group of retainers who stood outside the kinship network to do his bidding, leaders of egalitarian tribes were always potentially at the mercy of their followers no matter how great their past achievements.   Thus, even effective leaders were rarely able to organize their own tribes, let alone other tribes, into political units for extending their influence.   Warfare conducted by such tribes in Arabia, for example, was traditionally limited to camel raiding or extorting local oases.   Yet despite these difficulties, the Bedouin camel raisers had an important impact on regional political and economic systems.

The virtue of small, tightly defined tribes lay in their 'asabiya, or "group feeling," yet this very strength made it difficult to organize groups of tribes where group feeling was absent and where leaders refused to subordinate themselves to someone else's command. Like the inverse square rule for diffusion of light, the strength of tribal 'asabiya fell off rapidly as it grew beyond the local lineage. Leaders could only become powerful political players by overcoming these inherent divisions. One way out of this dilemma was to organize tribes around a common nontribal principle. As Ibn Khaldun observed, in the Middle East this principle was traditionally Islam:

> Bedouins can acquire royal authority only by making use of religious coloring, such as prophethood or sainthood, or some great religious event in general. The reason is because of their savagery, the Bedouins are the least willing of all nations to subordinate themselves to each other, as they are rude, proud, ambitious, and eager to be the leaders. Their individual aspirations rarely coincide. But when there is religion (among them) through prophethood or sainthood, then they have some restraining influence upon themselves. The qualities of haughtiness and jealousy leave them. It is, then, easy for them to subordinate themselves and to unite (as a social organization)....This is illustrated by the Arab dynasty in Islam. Religion cemented their leadership with religious law and its ordinances, which, explicitly and implicitly, are concerned with what is good for civilization.[24]

The growth and spread of early Islam was strongly associated with the movement of tribal peoples out of the Arabian Peninsula in the seventh century. Much has been written about why the desert tribes, which had been weak and divided in Roman times, suddenly became powerful enough to create an empire. From a tribal perspective, Islam provided a new style of organization and leadership which, while composed at least in part by tribesmen, was not dependent on tribal principles. The concept of umma, the community of egalitarian believers, was congruent with the traditional rejection of social hierarchy, while jihad, holy war against the unbelievers, provided the ideological base for a new type of segmentary opposition for expansion into vulnerable sedentary territories. On a smaller scale, religious orders such as the Sanusi in Libya or the Wahabi in Arabia provided this framework for uniting the tribes in political dealings with the outside world.[25]

However, unity through pantribal movements, even when cloaked in religious garb, was a temporary phenomena because such cooperation demanded that the Bedouin abandon what they held most dear: their autonomy. Such movements might grow powerful and establish states led by rulers of Bedouin origin, but having reached these heights they inevitably fell into conflict with their own tribal base which was either incorporated into the state and had lost its identity, or had severed its ties and returned to the desert. Thus although the many dynasties, and even modern states, that have "Bedouin" origins are powerful, the sedentary rulers have rarely succeeded in bridging the political divide between the town and the tribe.

THE BEDOUIN
IN THE MODERN WORLD

Bedouin camel raising has been on the decline for at least the last seventy years. This is a product both of the profound economic changes in the region and a changing balance of political power which has given sedentary states much more control over formerly autonomous tribes. Nevertheless, at the end of the twentieth century nomadic pastoralism has not disappeared, nor has Bedouin identity receded into the realm of folklore. Both economically and politically, the Bedouin still play a role disproportionate to their numbers, if not as camel raisers then as sheep pastoralists, smugglers, truck drivers, or mercenaries; occupations that fall within their own ideology of culturally appropriate livelihoods.

The best documented example of change among the camel-raising Bedouin is that of the Rwala because we have what is still rare in anthropology: ethnographies by competent observers fifty years apart that between them trace over a century of Bedouin history in northern Arabia. The fieldwork of Alois Musil in the 1920s and William Lancaster in the 1970s (not to mention the extensive literature produced by travellers and various political agents fascinated by the Bedouins) begins with living memories of a period when camel raiding was in full flower on the borders of the Ottoman Empire and extends through the age of oil wells and Chevrolets. During this era, the camel-raising Bedouin experienced major changes in regional political organization, saw the market for their camels collapse, and transformed their economy by heavy reliance on sheep raising and wage labor. Yet in spite of this, camel pastoralism did not disappear and Bedouin society has not divided along economic lines. That is, Bedouin cultural values and social organization have not been transformed to the same extent as has their economic life.

Until the First World War, camels were still in demand for the caravan trade. Of course, for long-distance transport the use of camels had been in decline for centuries due to competition from ships and then railroads, but they remained important in the regional transport network until the widespread adoption of motorized vehicles finally put camel caravans out of business. While there remained a market for camel meat in major cities, raising them was less profitable than sheep which were also in greater demand. At the same time, farmers who had avoided the desert margins in the nineteenth century out of fear of Bedouin attacks began expanding into land that had previously been used as pasture. Islamic law had always held that anyone who cultivated wasteland became its legal owner, so the Bedouin often lost title to traditional grazing lands, particularly to new dry-land farming techniques made possible by tractors, which were seen as improvements by sedentary governments.

Politically, the Bedouins were also at a disadvantage because the introduction of motorized vehicles meant the desert was no longer a refuge from sedentary political authorities. During the Ottoman Empire, it had proved impossible to permanently subdue the Bedouin. Like the rulers before them, the Turks maintained garrisons to defend important oases, cut deals with tribal leaders, and attempted to retaliate against the most fractious tribes as a lesson to the rest. Nevertheless, while the nomads never threatened Turkish control of the region, they could make frontier life very difficult and expensive, a strategy made visually famous in the film *Lawrence of Arabia*. Following the First World War, this strategy became less tenable. Armies could now drive into the desert and camps could be bombed from the air. Boundaries that had been only lines on a map now took on real meaning as postcolonial states attempted to forge a national identity. Some, like Egypt, looked upon the Bedouin as a backward element that should be sedentarized out of existence for their own good, while in Jordan and Saudi Arabia they were granted a preferred status because they were perceived as the most reliable supporters for the region's ever-shrinking number of kingdoms.

The Rwala Bedouin first adapted to these changes by becoming more subsistence oriented. With no raiders to fear, the Rwala saw their herds reproduce to previously unheard-of levels between 1935 and 1958 when families owning hundreds of camels became commonplace. This provided a large surplus of camels for sale and more than enough milk to meet everyday demands. As it turned out, however, such numbers put too great a stress on the available pasture and when a severe drought struck between 1958 and 1962, the camel population collapsed. Faced with the difficult prospect of rebuilding herds of slow-breeding and expensive camels, many Rwala were forced into other occupations. Of these, sheep raising and wage labor were the most important.

Sheep raising has always thrived on the margins between the true desert and irrigated agricultural areas. Traditionally the province of lower-ranking tribes, or lower-ranking sections within tribes, sheep raising was usually treated as an afterthought in studies of the Bedouin because they gave cultural priority to camels. This was in part because the camel-raising nomads traditionally saw themselves as part of a pastoral elite that dominated others from the safety of the desert. With their fading political influence, however, the social distinction between them and sheep raisers disappeared and increasingly more Bedouin shifted to sheep production which allowed them to continue their pastoral life in a different form. Sheep raising was more profitable than camel raising because small stock reproduced and matured much faster than large stock. Sheep also required less labor to herd, were more readily marketable for meat than camels, and provided wool and milk to meet subsistence needs. While sheep production tied the Bedouin more closely to urban markets and limited their migration routes more than camel raising, the drilling of wells in the desert and trucking water to sheep allowed them to use much greater areas of pasture than in the past. Indeed, in parts of Syria and Jordan this led to overgrazing because too many animals could be moved into a single district. Keeping sheep did not mean a total abandonment of camel raising because extended families could divide their herds into components that migrated separately and reap the best of both pastoral worlds: profits from sheep and the status from camels.

Wage labor constituted the other major adaptation to the changing conditions in the Near East. The discovery of oil in what had been land used only by nomads opened economic opportunities for the Bedouin in positions that did not require a formal education such as guards, mechanics, and drivers. Wages could also be had by serving in the military. In the years following the collapse of the camel economy, any type of steady wage labor seemed good to the Rwala, but by the mid-1970s, young men realized that most such positions would never allow them to accumulate the resources necessary to acquire the proper reputation so important for social advancement in Bedouin society. This was important because, in spite of their nonpastoral employment, they retained strong economic and social links with their pastoral kinsmen by investing their money in livestock which was herded by relatives pending their return. More important, they continued to participate in the Bedouin moral economy in which the giving of wealth to others in order to acquire a reputation was more compelling than the accumulation of private wealth as an end in itself. While camel raiding may have lost its importance, the values it embodied remained. Lancaster found that the occupations such as smuggling and trading were more highly valued than farming or office jobs because, like raiding, they offered the possibility of windfall profits that regular work could never produce and demanded the same set of risk-taking characteristics that the Bedouin poets of old traditionally praised. The economy and political position of the Rwala may have changed, but not their response to life.[26]

Like the East African pastoralist's emphasis on cattle, the Bedouin still gives pride of place to the camel because of its cultural significance as a symbol of true nomadic life, even as the number of true camel herders dwindles to insignificance. Anthropologists and Bedouins alike hold the camel nomad in high esteem and often reinforce each other's visions of a world gone by, even as the contemporary Bedouins themselves adapt to the world around them by replacing their camels with trucks. But, like the image of the American cowboy, the Bedouin ideal lives because at its heart it sets out a cultural standard which people value even when they cannot live up to it. The Bedouin emphasis on personal independence and honor prescribes a way to live your life, a way to relate to others, and a way to value action in a hostile world. From the Bedouin perspective, it is this that ideally distinguishes the nomad from the sedentary, not the ownership of camels or even living in a tent. Unlike the East African pastoralist who is a social nobody without cattle, or the sedentarized Iranian nomad who immediately enters the peasantry

The process of sedentarization often begins when a Bedouin family leaves the desert to pitch its tent on the edge of an oasis seeking work that will eventually lead to its absorption into sedentary society.

and retains no rights by virtue of his tribal origin, the Bedouin is not necessarily dependent on his camels to maintain his cultural identity. But in a sedentary situation, under the thumb of a local governor and economically dependent on non-Bedouins, their honor is enough at risk to make the life of camel raising seem ideal because it is where their most cherished values are least threatened and where they can preserve their most manifest dignity. Besides, in a region with five millennia of recorded history which has experienced the rise and fall of many great empires, known both wealth and poverty, and where even rights to wells are centuries old, the Bedouin nomads have coped with change before. They are not about to abandon their cultural traditions because of a few decades of development. Keeping camels and maintaining their own skill at herding them, even if only as an adjunct to their present economic activities, may still be the best insurance policy against an uncertain future when the oil runs out.

N O T E S

1. Richard W. Bulliet, *The Camel and the Wheel* (Cambridge: Harvard University Press, 1977); Marvin K. Mikesell, "Notes on the Dispersal of the Dromedary," *Southwestern Journal of Anthropology* 11 (1955), 231–45.

2. Hilde Gauthier-Pilters, *The Camel: Its Evolution, Ecology, Behavior, and Relation Ship to Man* (Chicago: University of Chicago Press, 1981), pp. 59–77.

3. Carlton Coon, *Caravan, The Story of the Middle East* (New York: Holt, Rinehart and Winston, 1964).

4. Ibn Khaldun, *The Muqaddimah*, trans. Frans Rosenthal, ed. N. Dawood (Princeton: Princeton University Press, 1967), p. 122.

5. W. F. Albright, *The Archaeology and the Religion of Israel* (Baltimore: Johns Hopkins University Press, 1942), p. 96; Joseph Free, "Abraham's Camels," *Journal of Near Eastern Studies* 3 (1944), 187–93.

6. Bulliet, *Camel*, pp. 57–86.

7. Bulliet, *Camel*, pp. 259–68.

8. Donald Cole, *Nomads of the Nomads, The Al Murrah Bedouin of the Empty Quarter* (Arlington Heights, IL: AHM Publishing Corporation, 1975).

9. William Lancaster, *The Rwala Bedouin Today* (Cambridge: Cambridge University Press, 1981), p. 99.

10. Louise Sweet, "Camel raiding of North Arabian Bedouin: A Mechanism of Ecological Adaptation," *American Anthropologist*, 67 (1965), 1132–50.

11. Max Freiherr von Oppenheim, *Die Beduinen* (Leipzig: Otto Harrassowitz, 1939), I, 102; Anatoly M. Khazanov, *Nomads and the Outside World* (Cambridge: Cambridge University Press, 1984), p. 208.

12. Alois Musil, *The Manners and Customs of the Rwala Bedouins* (New York: American Geographical Society, 1928), pp. 664–65.

13. Shelagh Weir, *The Bedouin, Aspects of the Material Culture of the Bedouin of Jordan* (London: World of Islam Festival Publishing Co. Ltd., 1976), pp. 1–6.

14. Musil, *Manners*, p. 48.

15. Lancaster, *Rwala Bedouin*, pp. 140–141.

16. Musil, *Manners*, pp. 489–503.

17. Lila Abu-Lughod, *Veiled Sentiments: Honor and Poetry in a Bedouin Society* (Berkeley: University of California Press, 1986), p. 163.

18. Michael Meeker, *Literature and Violence in North Arabia* (Cambridge: Cambridge University Press, 1979).

19. Emrys Peters, "Some Structural Aspects of Feud among the Camel Raising Bedouin of Cyrenaica, *Africa*, 32 (1967), 261–82; cf. Talal Asad, "Political Inequality in the Kababish Tribe" in *Studies in Sudan Ethnography*, eds. Ian Cunnison and Wendy James. (New York: Humanities Press, 1972).

20. Meeker, *Literature and Violence*, p. 195.

21. Ibn Khaldun, *Muqaddimah*, pp. 97–98.

22. Lancaster, *Rwala Bedouin*, pp. 73–97.

23. Ibn Khaldun, *Muqaddimah*, p. 108.

24. Ibn Khaldun, *Muqaddimah*, pp. 120–121.

25. E.E. Evans-Pritchard, *The Senusi of Cyrenaica* (Oxford: Oxford University Press, 1949); Henry Rosenfeld, "The Social Composition of the Military in the Process of State Formation in the Arabian Desert," *Journal of the Royal Anthropological Institute*, 95 (1965), 75–86, 174–94.

26. Lancaster, *Rwala Bedouin*, pp. 139–50.

F U R T H E R   R E A D I N G S

Asad, Talal, *The Kababish Arabs: Power, Authority, and Consent in a Nomadic Tribe.* London: Hurst and Company, 1970.

Bailey, Clinton, *Bedouin Poetry from the Sinai and the Negev: Mirror of Culture.* Oxford: Clarendon Press, 1991.

Behnke, Roy H., *The Herders of Cyrenaica: Ecology, Economy and Kinship among the Bedouin of Eastern Libya.* Urbana: University of Illinois Press, 1980.

Briggs, Lloyd Cabot, *Tribes of the Sahara.* Cambridge: Harvard University Press, 1960.

Daumas, Melchior, *The Ways of the Desert.* Austin: University of Texas Press, 1971.

Dickson, Harold R., *The Arab of the Desert: A Glimpse into the Badawin Life in Kuwait and Saudi Arabia.* London: Allen and Unwin, 1949.

Doughty, Charles, *Travels in Arabia Deserta.* London: Johnathan Cape, 1936.

Evans-Pritchard, E. E., *The Sanusi of Cyrenaica.* Oxford: Clarendon Press, 1949.

Grossman, David, *Rural Process-Pattern Relationships: Nomadization, Sedentarization and Settlement Fixation.* New York: Praeger, 1991.

Hobbs, Joseph, *Bedouin Life in the Egyptian Wilderness.* Austin: University of Texas Press, 1989.

Ingham, Bruce, *Bedouin of northern Arabia: The Traditions of the Al-Dhafir.* London: KPI, 1986.

Janzen, Jörg, *Nomads in the Sultanate of Oman: Tradition and Development in Dhofar.* Boulder, CO: Westview, 1986.

Keenan, Jeremy, *The Taureg: People of the Ahaggar.* New York: St. Martin's Press, 1977.

Lavie, Smadar, *The Politics of Military Occupation: Mzeina Allegories of Bedouin Identity under Israeli and Egyptian Rule.* Berkeley: University of California Press, 1990.

Lewis, Norman, *Nomads and Settlers in Syria and Jordan, 1800–1980.* Cambridge: Cambridge University Press, 1987.

Marx, Emmanuel, and Avshalom Shmueli, eds., *The Changing Bedouin.* New Brunswick, NJ: Transaction Books, 1984.

Marx, Emmanuel, *Bedouin of the Negev.* New York: Praeger, 1967.

*T*HE *GOOD SHEPHERDS:*
PASTORAL TRIBES OF
SOUTHWEST ASIA

S H E E P   A N D   G O A T S

Throughout the Anatolian and Iranian Plateaus and into Central Asia lies the heart of the pastoral world which is based on the raising of sheep, sometimes in herds mixed with goats. Moving from lowland to highland pastures on a seasonal basis, these nomads also possess camels, donkeys, and horses which carry baggage and people, as well as vicious dogs that protect the herds from predators. These nomads do not share a common language, social structure, or political organization, but rather a common economy. It is the least romantic and most businesslike of the nomadic regions of the world. Nomads here value their sheep as money or goods on the hoof. They are invested with none of the special cultural attributes that endear cattle to Masai, camels to Bedouins, or horses to Mongols. There are no odes to sheep, no praise poems for goats. Donkeys are more common than horses and camels carry only household baggage or women during migration, not men into battle. Yet their very movement, tribal organization, and the productiveness of the pastoral economy have given them both more autonomy and political influence than their numbers alone would warrant. And of all the world's nomadic pastoralists, the sheep raisers are probably best adapted to cope with the forces of change in the modern world that threaten the very existence of nomadic life elsewhere.

Raising sheep is hardly unique to this region. We have seen that small stock comprise a large percentage of the herds in East Africa, that the Bedouins on the margins of the desert keep large flocks of sheep, and that horse-riding nomads on the steppe lands of the north also depend on sheep raising for their basic subsistence. What makes this zone distinct is that pastoralism here is embedded within a larger sedentary regional agricultural economy. Nomads have close symbiotic relationships with farmers in surrounding villages and merchants in local bazaars. While they may appear to be radically distinct from their sedentary neighbors because of the primacy they give to animal husbandry, their use of tents in seasonal migrations, and their tribal political organization, they are in reality pastoral specialists who trade milk products, meat, wool, and hides for the grain that makes up the bulk of their diet. Like most of their sedentary neighbors, all the nomads of this region now share the Muslim faith, most practicing Sunni Islam with a minority of Shiite believers.

Pastoralists also form an integral part of the regional political system, and must cope with the existence of sedentary states that have traditionally claimed sovereignty to the lands through which they migrate. This has led to cycles of conflict and coexistence: conflict when states have attempted to destroy the nomads' political autonomy by imposing direct rule on them; coexistence when they have either ignored the nomads or attempted to employ indigenous tribal leaders as allies in a form of indirect rule in marginal regions. Nomadic political organization in this region is therefore designed as much (or more) to organize relations with neighboring sedentary states as it is to resolve the internal problems of nomadic society.

PASTORAL ECONOMICS

Sheep and goats are man's oldest domesticated animals (after dogs) dating back to the Neolithic period (circa 8500 B.C.) in the Near East. Originally domesticated as a source of meat, generations of selective breeding have created varieties that could produce substantial amounts of wool and milk. Sheep and goats then became more highly valued for these products than their meat. Since this early animal domestication occurred in tandem with the domestication of wheat and barley, most archaeological evidence from this period points to the emergence of a mixed economy based on sedentary villages. Although the old evolutionary model of hunters becoming pastoralists and then becoming farmers is still strong in the popular mind, in fact, it appears that nomadic pastoralism was an economic specialization that emerged only after sedentary agriculture was well established. Thus from their earliest origins, pastoralists in the region developed close (if not always friendly) relationships with the agricultural villages and cities along their migration routes. They kept herds not only for subsistence, but for exchange.

To be a successful pastoralist requires both productive animals for subsistence (sheep and goats) and transport animals for movement (donkeys, horses, camels). Dogs are also kept to protect the livestock from wild predators and human thieves. The exact composition of a herd depends on local environmental conditions. For example, the percentage of goats is higher in regions with marginal pasture because goats can browse on plants that grazing sheep would not touch. For similar reasons, the number of horses is highest where pastoralists have access either to dependable pastures or to grain or hay purchased from farmers. In arid areas, particularly along the edge of the deserts where raising horses is an expensive luxury, camels and donkeys often completely replace them. Cattle are not included in nomadic herds in this region, because they are believed to fare poorly on long migrations and they require better pastures and more regular watering than is available in most semi-arid environments. According to a Baluch proverb, "If you see a cow you are near a village, if you see a goat you are near a camp, if you see a camel you are lost."

The seasonal nomadic migration of people and animals takes place for a very simple reason. Many more animals can be supported by moving them from one pasture to another than by keeping them in one place. While some nomads, like the Baluch who inhabit the southern transborder areas of Iran, Afghanistan, and Pakistan and make horizontal migrations across long stretches of semi-arid and arid terrain, most nomads in this region rely on vertical migrations that take advantage of changes in altitudes. In the winter they occupy low-lying plains or river valleys, in the spring they migrate to the steppes and foothills, and in summer they move into the high mountains to take advantage of seasonal pastures there. Such a migration schedule also accommodates the annual farming cycle, enabling the nomads to graze harvested fields in the fall and winter, while depending on steppe and mountain pasture in the spring and summer when the crops are growing. In one of the most spectacular silent films ever made, *Grass*, Merian Cooper and Edward Schoedsack (who later went on to make the original *King Kong* in Hollywood) documented the Bakhtiari spring migration through snowbound passes and across swollen rivers into their summer pastures high in the Zagros Mountains.[1] Although the captions are somewhat melodramatic, even today this film holds its audience spellbound as the nomads overcome all obstacles in their quest for grass!

Regular migration requires the use of tents, yurts, or huts that can be easily assembled and disassembled and are light enough to be transported by camels, horses, or donkeys. The black tent of woven goat hair is the most common type. It consists of between two and five panels of tent cloth, each measuring about a meter in width and three to four meters in length which are pinned or tied together to create the top and sides of the

All a nomads' belongings must be easily transportable. The heaviest loads are packed on the camels and small children are often strapped to the top of the load to keep them out of trouble.

tent. It is pitched by driving stakes into the ground to secure the guy ropes that hold the tent cloth taut upon poles or a frame. Women take responsibility both for erecting and packing the tents, a task that they can often complete quite rapidly. Unlike Bedouin black tents described in the last chapter, these generally house only a single nuclear family. On the borders of Central Asia, huts and yurts are more common than black tents. This is in part because the yurt provides more protection against the high winds, rain, snow, and frigid winter temperatures that are found in the higher latitudes. However, because black tents are lighter in weight, easier to erect, and less costly to maintain, nomadic groups that moved out of Central Asia into milder climates eventually abandoned the use of the yurt in favor of black tents.[2]

The organization and timing of seasonal migrations depends on a number of variables: distance to be travelled, difficulties of topography, quality and dependability of pasture, access to water, rights of use or exclusion, and competition from other nomads or sedentary farmers.

The length of an annual migration depends primarily on the location of pastures and how long they remain productive. In some instances, seasonal migrations are very short, a day's move from pastures in a river valley to the surrounding steppe, or from the bottom of a mountain to its peak. But most involve periods of considerable movement that require many weeks, or even months, of travel. Such long migration cycles often demand significant coordination when large numbers of different tribes are involved. In a classic article, Fredrik Barth outlined the concept of *il-rah*, or tribal road, by which

Women take primary responsibility both for packing and unpacking the baggage animals. *Source*: Donna Wilker).

migrations were traditionally synchronized in southern Iran. He found that each group had its own migration route which, like a train schedule, melded time and place. That is, each group claimed exclusive access to a particular pasture at a specific time of year. The start of the migration was determined by the tribal leaders and, in general, the strongest tribes had access to each pasture area at its peak, although they were preceded by some tribes and would be followed by others. Like series of trains using the same track, such nomadic migrations funnelled many thousands of families along the migration route while minimizing conflict.[3]

While the organization of migrations in southern Iran are exceptionally complex, most nomads do follow the same routes and use the same pastures each year. Indeed, when pastures are both dependable and of high quality, nomads not only return to them regularly but attempt to restrict their use by others. The most common way of doing this is to vest ownership of pasture in kinship groups of various sizes (tribes, clans, lineages) which restricts access to outsiders while regulating pasture use among themselves. In many parts of northern Iran and northern Afghanistan, summer pastures are treated as the private property of the individual families who use them. Pastoralists without sufficient pasture are therefore forced to rent it from neighbors who have an excess, or buy (sometimes steal) pasture rights from families who have sedentarized. Unlike private farmland, however, what these nomads "own" is the exclusive right to pasture their animals at that particular season, not title to the land itself.[4] Such a limitation is of little importance, however, since most mountain pastures are covered with snow at other times of the year and can serve no other purpose.

During the spring nomad migration in northeastern Afghanistan the main trails are often so crowded with families that they create lines of traffic waiting to use key passes and bridges.

The rules of land use change with the seasons. During the spring and summer migrations, farmers and pastoralists are often in conflict. The nomads claim the farmers plow grasslands that are rightfully theirs, while the villagers complain that careless pastoralists allow their livestock to trample standing crops and exhaust local grazing lands with their large herds. Yet in the fall and winter these same farmers actually encourage nomads to graze the stubble of their harvested fields because the animal dung left behind fertilizes the soil.

THE CENTRAL ASIAN ARABS OF AFGHANISTAN

Northeastern Afghanistan provides a typical example of the complexity of these cyclic movements and relationships between nomads and settled people. In a study of the Central Asian Arabs conducted during the mid-1970s, Thomas Barfield found that pastoralists fill a specialized economic niche in which animal husbandry is closely integrated into the agricultural cycle. Though pastoral specialists themselves, their diet is based on grain (wheat and rice) and they support a large number of artisans in nearby towns who produce the equipment necessary for nomadic life.[5]

The ecological zones in northeastern Afghanistan are determined by elevation. Low-lying river valleys support irrigated agriculture and many villages which grow wheat, rice, cotton, and barley. The lowlands are also home to the region's cities and transportation links to other regions of the country. The highland areas are dominated by small villages dependent on unirrigated agriculture, (wheat at lower elevations, barley in the high mountains) where markets are few and transportation is difficult. In the fall and winter, the nomads graze their sheep in the sheltered marshes of the Amu River valley (330 to 350 meters in elevation) and on adjacent fields of harvested wheat or cotton. In early March, they move out of the valley and onto the nearby steppe (400 to 500 meters in elevation) to take advantage of a green carpet of grass dotted with red poppies that can temporarily support hundreds of thousands of animals. Although less than a day's journey from their winter villages, these spring pastures provide enough new grass to support large numbers of sheep without interfering with the growing crops in the valleys. By the middle of May the steppe dries, the grass withers, and the nomads begin a three-week migration to the pastures in Badakhshan, a mountainous province in northeastern Afghanistan. These pastures lie at elevations between 2,000 and 3,000 meters and their animals graze there until late July or early August when the threat of cold and snow at high elevations causes the nomads to begin their return trek. As one nomad explained, "We chase the snow up into the mountains, then the snow chases us down." The return migration to the lowland pastures is always more leisurely in the spring because the animals can linger to graze on the stubble of harvested fields.

Sheep raising lies at the heart of the Central Asian Arab economy, both as a source of money through the sale of live animals, wool, or skins, and as a source of milk and meat. Even the animal dung can be used as fuel where wood is lacking. Contrary to popular conception, sheep-raising pastoralists slaughter relatively few animals for their own consumption because they are deemed more valuable for sale and as a source of milk. Consumed immediately or processed into dried yoghurt or butter for later use, milk is the herd's greatest direct contribution to the domestic household economy. Processing milk is also the women's major economic activity during the spring and summer. In addition, sheep provide wool which is spun into thread for the production of cloth, used to make felts, or sold to other groups for carpet weaving. The economic mainstay of the pastoral economy is, however, the cash sale of large fat-tailed sheep to urban markets in the fall and winter, supplemented by the sale of *qarakul* lambskins (the internationally famous "Persian lamb") in the spring.

The sale of animals and animal products is a critical part of the annual production cycle because pastoralists need to purchase grain for bread which makes up the bulk of their diet. It can be bought outright for cash, or taken on credit to be repaid at the end of the pastoral cycle. Since the nomads have baggage animals and move regularly, they take advantage of the cheapest source of supply. In northeastern Afghanistan, migrating nomads are the major buyers of wheat purchased from small farmers in the mountains who would otherwise be unable to transport it to market. Manufactured items, tea, cloth, weapons, and luxury goods are all purchased in the local markets for cash. The close connection between nomads and sedentary peoples can also be seen clearly in their investments, for in this region nomads with substantial profits from animal husbandry often invest them in land and thereby become landlords as well as pastoralists. This process is far advanced among the many Central Asian Arab groups which acquired legal ownership to their winter camps in the 1920s. Once settled, they abandoned their yurts for permanent houses, but most continued to migrate as usual, leaving some family members or hired workers to watch the crops, because sheep raising is considered more profitable than agriculture.

Pastoral labor is divided into two spheres: the maintenance of sheep and the procurement of raw materials on the one hand, and the processing activities on the other. The first are male roles associated with daily herding, seasonal marketing, transportation, and protecting their herds from wild animals and thieves; the second are female roles associated with milk production, weaving and felt making, maintaining and moving the camp, and cooking. This division of labor is not strict, however, for men and women help each other out when work needs to be done. In shepherd camps where women are absent, men even do the cooking, but the quality of the bread makes it clear that this is not something they do well. What is most important about the sexual division of labor is that it allows a family to obtain the maximum return in money and products from their herd. This is critical for subsistence-oriented pastoralism where nothing is left to waste. In a region where sedentary women are often secluded, the nomad woman's freedom of movement and lack of veiling is striking. Nomad women have a reputation for independence and competence that is both respected and even feared by sedentary villagers. As one old grandmother explained, she knew how to shoot a rifle when necessary and had used it more than once to defend the family's tent. Unlike sedentary village women, whom she disparaged as "useless," she took the initiative in making many decisions in the absence of male relations.

FAMILY CYCLE

Like individuals, households have their own cycles of development. Among the sheep-raising nomads in southwestern Asia it is the household, or tent, that is the basic social and economic unit. But what role such individual households play depends on which stage of the family cycle they are in, the rules of property inheritance, and the degree of cooperation required to successfully run a herd.[6]

New households are created by marriage, at which time (or upon the birth of a child) the couple receives its own tent or yurt. With few exceptions,

tents house only a single nuclear family or a stem family consisting of a surviving parent living in the tent of a son. When marriages are polygynous,
each woman expects to have her own tent. However, there are significant
differences between pastoral societies in which the nuclear or stem family is
the maximal level of household organization and those in which the extended or joint household is the ideal. As Richard Tapper explains in a comparative analysis of the nomadic societies on the Iranian Plateau (Table 4.1):

> The size and form of households depends largely on a few variables: whether the ideal
> is patriarchy and the interdependence of close agnates, or the independence of each
> married man; whether a household should be self-sufficient in labour as well as flocks;
> and the ages which men first marry and procreate.[7]

The dynamics in each system are quite different. In both, the majority
of the households are nuclear or stem, but for different reasons. Where independence is the ideal, sons break away from their fathers at marriage by
means of anticipatory inheritance to form autonomous households. Marriage not only creates a new household, it permanently drains the wealth of
the parent household in terms of animals and labor. Under such conditions, men tend to marry late because they first need to acquire a herd large
enough to run independently. Where the joint-family ideal prevails, men
do not expect to become independent at marriage but instead pool their
labor and animals under the direction of their father. Here marriage is an
investment which increases a family's political strength and provides new
labor for the group. Thus men tend to marry younger, both because extended households often command greater wealth and can more easily
raise the necessary brideprice, and because marriages do not threaten to
break up existing relationships. But the extended household can only be
achieved at specific stages of the life cycle: when a man actually has grown
sons to work with him, or when brothers agree to cooperate after their
father's death, and such collective groups never survive into the maturity
of the third generation. Many families also lack the necessary pastoral
wealth, or social harmony, to support an extended household.

The labor demands of each systems are also quite different. The joint
household is normally self-sufficient in labor and migrates as a single camping group, although if there are a large number of animals (or the family has
investments in land or business) they have the option of deploying nuclear
families to different pastures during some seasons. To be most effective,
however, they must control enough livestock to put their available labor to
good use. If this is lacking, they may agree to take other people's sheep on
contract or release sons to serve as hired shepherds for other families.
Among pastoralists where the nuclear households are the ideal, the organization of labor is more problematic because the family cycle of growth is rarely
synchronized with labor needs. New households are generally short of
labor because small children cannot help with the herding, while mature

TABLE 4.1

GROUP	SAMPLE SIZE (HOUSE-HOLDS)	MEAN NUMBER OF PEOPLE	NUCLEAR OR STEM FAMILY	JOINT FAMILY	PERCENT PATER-NAL	PERCENT FRATER-NAL
Shahsevan (northwestern Iran)	114	7.3	63	37	24	13
Basseri (southern Iran)	32	5.7	97	3	3	0
Turkmen (northeastern Iran)	59	7.1	66	34	29	5
Yörük (southeastern Turkey)	171	8.3	64	36	34	2
Lurs (southern Iran)	49	7.7	76	24		

Sources: Jacob Black-Michaud, *Sheep and Land*. Cambridge University Press, 1986, p. 166; and Richard Tapper, *Pasture and Politics*. New York: Academic Press, 1979, p. 242.

households have too many hands for a single herd. Therefore in this situation, efficient herding requires families to camp together and pool their animals into a single herd for management, but unlike the joint household, such herding groups are temporary, formed and broken at will depending on the needs of the partners who need not be related.

The joint-household pattern appears to be most closely associated with regions where pastoralism is highly productive, such as Turkey and the northern parts of Iran and Afghanistan where seasonal pastures are dependable, in many cases privately owned, and pastoralists make relatively few moves. For example, the Central Asian Arabs migrate quickly between specific camp sites where they remain for the whole season. In the arid zones of southern Iran and Baluchistan, pastoralism is more precarious because pastures are less dependable and quickly exhausted. While the migration cycle may be regular, the campsites are not. Among the Basseri, grazing areas change every few days (they break and make camp about 120 times a year versus about 35 times annually for the Central Asian Arabs) and their pastures were periodically redistributed by the Basseri chiefs so that kinship groups did not have permanent access to any particular pasture.

In the family cycle, the marriage of children is a key variable. All pastoral societies in the region employ some sort of brideprice system, that is, the family of the groom is expected to compensate the family of the bride with payments in cash or animals. Accumulating the necessary animals or cash is the key impediment to early marriage for men, and often results in

Turkmen women are world renowned for their skill at carpet weaving which employs traditional geometric designs woven from memory. (*Source*: Donna Wilker).

a ten-year age differential for women in their late teens who marry men in their late twenties or early thirties. To the casual cost-accounting observer it would seem that in such a system it would be better economically to have many more daughters than sons, because by receiving brideprices, families would accumulate animals at the expense of families with many sons which had been periodically depleting their herds. In fact, this is not the case, particularly among pastoralists who operate joint households. In his study of the Yomut Turkmen in the late 1960s, William Irons found that although households with many sons were periodically depleted of wealth to make marriages, that this investment paid off in the long run because they were acquiring more labor. His statistics showed that over the course of a lifetime the brideprices received by households with many daughters rarely did more than maintain stable or declining holdings, while households with many sons saw their herds expand.[8]

Each household is responsible for managing its own resources, and disagreements that cannot be settled by compromise are resolved by camping apart. The ability to move away from people with whom you are not getting along, either by pitching your tent at the opposite end of an encampment or moving to another encampment entirely, is one of the great psychological advantages of being a nomad. It also highlights the common belief that once a household, however defined, establishes its autonomy, its success or failure is individual. Autonomous households are neither expected to share any increases with relatives nor, should disaster strike, can they expect to be saved by the generosity of kinsmen. (Indeed it is the very refusal to cooperatively share risks and gains which initiates the breakup of a joint household.) This puts a very high priority on individual success in an enterprise that celebrates the potential geometric growth rate of sheep as the royal road to wealth, while at all times being aware that the sudden onset of disease, severe weather, drought, or theft can destroy years of growth instantly. And the price of failure is not only economic ruin, but in many cases the loss of tribal identity itself.

MODELS OF SEDENTARIZATION AND THEIR CONSEQUENCES

In *Nomads of South Persia*, a study conducted of the Iranian Basseri in the late 1950s, Fredrik Barth asked an extremely important question: how do nomads stay in long-term balance with their environment, particularly when the animals are privately owned but their pasture is held in common? Since each Basseri family is attempting to maximize its own production, it would appear that they could very easily exceed the carrying capacity of the land and thereby destroy the very grasslands on which they depend. The problem is potentially even more critical, since the Basseri have a high birth rate that bears little direct relation to the size of their herds. Therefore, Barth argued, since they have historically maintained a balance both in terms of the number of animals they graze and the size of their total population, such a "long-term balance between pastures, herds, and people and consequent stable pastoral population can only be maintained if the rate of *sedentarization* is sensitive to the population pressure of *animals* on the pasture." In other words, there must be some pressure for families to leave the pastoral economy before the number of animals degrades the environment.[9]

For many camel- and cattle-raising pastoralists in other regions of the world, sedentarization was often not a viable option and mechanisms of collective insurance existed to keep people within the pastoral economy. For example, the Bedouin chief was responsible for supplying destitute tribesmen with replacement camels, and in East Africa, a network of bond friends could be relied upon to make good the losses. In addition, where pastoralism was perceived as the only possible way of life, people who suffered losses would attempt to recoup not only by seeking the aid of chiefs or kinsmen, but by raiding their neighbors for animals. Indeed, in both East Africa and Arabia, livestock raids were endemic. Ironically, these societies were also able to maintain failing members because they usually had access to alternative resources so that while animal husbandry was the ideal basis of economic life, subsistence was not directly tied to owning a specific minimum number of animals. The Bedouin extorted the dates that made up the basic part of their diet, while many East African pastoralists like the Nuer engaged in subsistence agriculture and fishing. In both of these areas, sedentarization was normally a process that affected groups of people, or whole tribes, not individual families.

On the Iranian and Anatolian Plateaus, it was a different story. As pastoral specialists, nomads here derived almost all of their income from livestock production. They lacked alternative occupations or other resources to fall back on if their herds fell below the minimum needed to support a family. There were no collective groups, such as the bond-friend networks created by cattle exchanges in East Africa, that protected individuals against risk. Even raiding more prosperous neighbors for livestock, a strategy so popular among the camel-raising Bedouin, was difficult because strong tribal chiefs maintained organized police forces that prevented individuals from engaging in wholesale raiding. Although casual theft of livestock was well-known, running off herds of small stock was also both more difficult and less profitable than raiding for large stock. Indeed, among the nomadic pastoralists who did employ systematic raiding as a strategy, their targets seem to have been primarily high-value large stock (horses, camels, or cattle). One never hears of successful donkey or goat raiders.

Since each family is responsible for its own economic fate, and no help can be expected even from close kinsmen, pastoral households are economically isolated. This creates a situation in which "the population becomes fragmented with respect to economic activities, and economic factors can strike differentially, eliminating some members of the population without affecting other members of the same population."[10] Among the Basseri, such economic autonomy and pastoral specialization produces two very different paths to sedentarization: one through the accumulation of pastoral wealth, the other through impoverishment.

In southwest Asia, sheep pastoralists experience faster herd growth than the cattle-raising East Africans or camel-raising Bedouin because their herds of small stock can potentially double in three years, which is more than twice the reproductive rate of cattle and three times that of camels. However, these regular gains are normally offset by large periodic expenses that drain a household's income, particularly when it comes time to arrange for sons to marry. Among the Basseri, brideprice payments often require the sale of animals to raise cash and, more important, anticipatory inheritance draws down even large holdings significantly because it is based on a percentage of the total livestock holdings. While these expenses can be calculated in advance, a large herd is always subject to unexpected and even catastrophic losses from diseases or severe weather. This means that even the largest herd is continually at risk. With no protection against such losses in the pastoral sphere, wealthy herd owners attempt to diversify their holdings by purchasing agricultural land along their migration routes. By converting pastoral surpluses into landholdings they obtain three advantages. First, they gain stability, for nomads are fond of saying "land never dies" and is therefore a more secure investment than sheep over the long run. Second, such land can be farmed by sharecroppers and the grain it produces can be used to meet household needs. The nomad family is thus relieved of the need to purchase grain, a major annual expense. While nomads may have little desire to be farmers themselves, they have a keen respect for the productive value of agricultural land. Finally, especially in Iran, land ownership brings prestige and social advancement in the nontribal world. Barth argues that when the importance of these landholdings begins to exceed the profitability of sheep, which declines dramatically among the Basseri if hired labor must be used, then a wealthy family may decide to leave the nomadic life altogether and settle permanently on their investment properties as landlords.

Sedentarization through the accumulation of wealth, however, is much less common than settlement through impoverishment, because their very integration into the sedentary economy puts pastoralists at risk of bankruptcy if they suffer losses. The Basseri are dependent on purchased grain as their primary source of food which they obtain by means of an annual exchange with "village friends" who advance them grain on credit in exchange for wool, clarified butter, and lambskins. The nomads are expected to make full payment at the end of each pastoral cycle. In a normal year, the natural increase of the herd should easily pay off this debt and provide a standard of living much higher than the average village farmer.

However, a series of bad years can begin a cycle of declin
hard to reverse:

> The first stage is that of carrying large debts to a trading partner ove
> the next. Chances are that, in spite of moderate herding luck, only a p
> ~~~~ will
> be paid off next year, in addition to financing the family's needs during that year. To
> meet such debts, and the running demands of his household, the herder is forced to in-
> vade his productive capital, slaughtering female lambs and selling livestock. Once this
> downward spiral starts, it tends to accelerate in spite of all efforts to cut down on con-
> sumption—the disparity between the minimal rate of consumption and the productivity of
> the declining capital grows geometrically.[11]

Barth found that when families lack enough animals to support themselves
they are forced to seek agricultural work in the neighboring villages unless
they can find a herd to run on tenancy terms. Such agricultural labor makes
nomadic life impossible and rarely provides enough income to purchase
sheep to reenter the pastoral economy in the future. Sedentarized families
soon lose their tribal status and are permanently absorbed into the peasantry.

Barth's elegant model of sedentarization is widely cited and has become perhaps the most influential theory in the study of pastoralists. It has
a dynamic that produces a pastoral society which loses both the wealthy
and the poor, leaving only a homogeneous group of middle-class pastoralists. But it is important to realize that it can only work if certain conditions
are present: (1) that other pastoral work is unavailable to nomads in economic trouble; (2) that there are no nonpastoral subsidies available to support poor families; and (3) that nomads can be socially and economically
absorbed by the neighboring peasant villages. As we will see, in other
parts of this region where pastoralism is geared to the demands of the cash
economy, quite a different dynamic emerges.

TRIBAL KHANS AND NOMADIC CONFEDERATIONS

As among the Bedouin camel pastoralists of Arabia, the political order among
nomadic pastoralists in southwest Asia was based on tribal organization.
However, unlike the Bedouin tribes in the Iranian and Anatolian Plateaus,
these political units were typically composed of hundreds of thousands of people and were led by hereditary leaders who had the power to compel their followers into action and to enforce their decisions by coercion if necessary. While
the Bedouin sheikh could only mediate, the Iranian khan had the power to
command. Additionally, the Iranian tribal confederacy made no pretense that
its component tribes shared a common ancestry; it was recognized by all as a
political organization that combined not only tribes of different origins, but

even of different languages, into a single unit. Since the organization of sheep pastoralism itself did not demand such a high level of centralization, we must turn to the nomads' relationship with the outside world to understand the emergence and continued existence of large and powerful confederations.

TRIBAL POLITICAL ORGANIZATION

Tribal political structures employed, in theory, a model of kinship to build corporate groups that acted in concert to organize economic production, preserve internal political order, and defend the group against outsiders. Relationships among individuals and groups in such systems were mapped through social space rather than geographic territory. That is, political units and the territories they occupied existed primarily as products of social relations: rights to use land and exclude outsiders were based on tribal affiliation, not residence.

Because most tribal systems appear segmentary, composed of successively larger units of incorporation, it is often assumed that each level must be the product of the same principles applied to an ever-expanding number of people. Yet what are perceived as "actual" kinship relations (based on principles of descent and affiliations by marriage or adoption) are empirically evident only within the tribe's smaller units: nuclear families, extended households, and local lineages. At higher levels of incorporation, clans and tribes often maintained relationships of a more political origin: client- or slave-descent groups that had no proper genealogical connections but were nevertheless an accepted part of the tribe; alliances or rivalries between descent groups that appeared to violate their genealogical charters; cooperation among networks of people that crosscut kinship relations; or the blatant rewriting (or re-reciting) of genealogies. For example, in the last chapter we saw that the Bedouin, who insisted that the purity of descent was the only proper basis of tribal organization, tacitly accepted all of these exceptions as necessary for making the system work. In examining nomadic political organization, we therefore need to distinguish analytically between a tribe, which is the largest unit of incorporation based on a genealogical model, and a tribal confederation, which combines unrelated tribes to create a supratribal political entity.

Confederations swallowed up whole tribes and made local leaders subordinate to the central rule of a khan. They were created by the imposition of political order that was the product of reorganization enforced by division from the top down rather than alliances from the bottom up. Some tribes joined voluntarily, others were conquered, and still others developed within the confederation after its formation. Although over time the specific tribes and clans that made up the confederation might change, the confederation itself often had a life span measured in centuries. The creation of such powerful long-lived confederacies by the nomads on the

Iranian Plateau was in striking contrast to the fragmented political system of the Bedouin tribes of Arabia. These differences had both cultural and political roots.

Among tribes in Arabia, success in maintaining large-scale political organizations was limited by narrower cultural definitions of political legitimacy. Where tribes were composed of egalitarian lineages whose leaders ruled by means of consensus or mediation, and could unite rival groups only through the use of segmentary opposition, the maintenance of a large-scale confederation for longer than a single lifetime was extremely difficult. As Ibn Khaldun noted, only a leader who stood outside the tribal system could expect to gain the cooperation of quarrelling tribes in the name of religion. On the other hand, the nomads in the highland plateaus of Iran and Anatolia had a very different concept of political organization. Largely of Central Eurasian origin, they drew on a cultural tradition that had its origins among the horse-riding peoples on the steppes to the north. These Turco-Mongolian tribal systems accepted the legitimacy of hierarchical differences in kinship organization that made social distinctions between senior and junior generations, noble and common clans, and between the rulers and the ruled.[12] There was no honor to be lost in serving as a subordinate and, once acquired, the authority of a ruling dynasty became strictly hereditary and was rarely challenged from below. A leader in this type of system therefore found it much easier to create a confederation using local lineages, clans, and tribes as the building blocks of a political/military organization that could present a united front to the outside world. These tribal confederacies incorporated hundreds of thousands of people from a variety of tribes, whose political unity was often all they held in common.

TRIBES AND STATES

The impetus for forming large confederations was external. Nomads throughout the region were either surrounded by powerful states and empires or lived on their borders. The creation of a tribal confederacy was a means by which nomads confronted the threats posed by sedentary states. In general, the degree of centralization was correlated with the power of the states the nomads faced. For example, those inside Iran itself formed the large confederations with powerful khans, while nomads on the borders maintained a much looser political organization. Historically, the interaction between nomads and states in this area produced three very different political relationships: (1) nomadic confederations which used their organization to conquer sedentary states; (2) nomadic confederations which used their organization to maintain autonomy from state control; and (3) nomadic confederations that were manipulated by sedentary governments to rule mobile populations.

Nomadic Conquerors

Although the age of nomadic conquests ended centuries ago, the historical importance of nomads as rulers of sedentary states should not be overlooked. The invasion of southwestern Asia by tribal peoples from Central Eurasia has a long pre-Islamic history dating back at least to the Bronze Age when, during the middle of the second millennium B.C., cattle-keeping, Indo-European-speaking peoples overran Iran, Anatolia, and India. Later, the most important dynasties of the western Iranian world—Achaemenid (558 to 330 B.C.), Parthian (250 B.C. to A.D. 224), Sassanian (224 to 637)—all had their origins there. Following the Islamic conquest, the list of the region's important empires and dynasties for the next 1,000 years appears to be a roll call of Turco-Mongolian peoples turned imperial conquerors: Ghaznavids, Saljuqs, Mongols, Timurids, Aqquyunlu, Ottomans, Mughals, Uzbek, Qizilbash, Qajars, to name just some of the more prominent. Of course, once they became rulers they dropped their nomadic ways and took up the task of governing, oppressing peasants and tribesmen without distinction when it served their interests. But, since the majority of the region's dynasties had a nomadic heritage, they understood the tribes better than leaders of sedentary governments elsewhere, and accepted tribally organized nomads as a natural part of the political landscape. They had to: It is estimated that the tribal nomads who occupied Iran in the early nineteenth century made up half the country's total population of approximately five million people, a percentage that declined significantly only because of the rapid growth in the sedentary population.[13]

The relationship between tribes and states was always problematic under dynasties of tribal origin. To the extent that they claimed kinship with the ruling dynasty, they posed a threat to its stability by assuming a too-active role in politics. For example, nomadic tribes and clans played key roles in succession struggles and civil wars where members of the sedentary ruling family needed their support in battles for supremacy—the practice of a steppe tradition known as bloody tanistry in which the contender who succeeded in killing all his rivals was accepted as the legitimate ruler of the tribe or state.[14] The periodic struggles of the Aqquyunlu elite (1378 to 1508) always involved rival leaders seeking support among the empire's component tribes.[15] On the other hand, tribes were also an auxiliary source of troops that could be used in frontier wars or to put down rebellions. The Saljuq (1055 to 1194) and Qajar (1779 to 1924) dynasties in Iran depended almost exclusively on tribal levies. But in such situations, tribal leaders often expected to be rewarded with military fiefs or administrative positions in return for their aid. To prevent such tribes from building a strong political base, dynasties such as the Mongol Il-khanids (1256 to 1136), Safavids (1501 to 1722), and Ottomans (1281 to 1924), often uprooted whole confederations and moved them to the edges of the empire, far removed from the court.[16]

Autonomous Confederations

Tribes that formed dynasties were the most easily visible consequence of the immigration of Turco-Mongolian peoples from Central Asia, but even among victorious conquerors, most of the confederation's tribes soon found themselves in opposition to state authority. Because in Iran their territories were inside the boundaries of large empires, they could not adopt an *ad hoc* policy of flight whenever faced with trouble, nor could they rely on help from outside states. They could maintain their autonomy only by forming large-scale confederations in opposition to the state structures that surrounded them. To be successful, these confederations needed permanent rulers who could negotiate and act on behalf of the entire confederation in dealing with state authorities. In Iran, such confederations became characteristic of nomadic political organization. Indeed, the Bakhtiari, Qashqa'i, and Khamseh confederations of Iran have all survived in some form until the present day, although they were much more powerful in the past.

One striking aspect of these confederations was their political resilience and ability to transform themselves in the face of state opposition. The range of strategies they employed was quite diverse. Leaders of some strong tribal confederations served as allies of a ruling dynasty, acting as its governors for their own regions. Since control of marginal places and peoples could be had only at great financial cost, such alliances were seen as beneficial by both sides, particularly when the state was weak. When the state was powerful, the tables were often reversed, with the state administration attempting to destroy the tribal leadership of confederations or co-opt it in a policy of indirect rule by using official appointments and subsidies as tools. Between these extremes, ruling dynasties established a *modus vivendi* with the leaders of tribal confederations in which they simply acted as intermediaries between the state and the nomads. (And just who was manipulating whom in such relationships was often difficult to tell.)[17] Tribal confederations in Iran regularly moved from one relationship to another as state power waxed and waned over the centuries.

What distinguished a confederation leader from other political actors was his role as the accepted legal authority for the tribes he controlled. Inside the confederation, the khan was equivalent to the government, regardless of whether he was perceived as an oppressor acting as an agent for a powerful dynasty or, more favorably, as the protector of local tribal territorial and political integrity against outside demands. Ruling over hundreds of thousands of people, the khan met Ibn Khaldun's definition of *royal authority*: possessing the right to command obedience (by using force if necessary), collect taxes, administer justice, and handle all external political relations.[18]

Observers familiar with Bedouin sheikhs or Mongol khans might naturally assume that the leaders of the great Iranian nomadic confederations would be the most prominent pastoralists in their region. With great herds of sheep and large tents, they would be close to the land and people they loved: organizing migrations from horseback, dealing with culturally alien state officials whom they despised, and proclaiming the virtues of the nomadic way of life. While a few leaders did fill such an ideal role, it came as something of a shock to travellers in the nineteenth century (and to anthropologists in the twentieth) that most members of the nomad ruling elite were based in cities and thoroughly at home in the elite sedentary society where they were active participants in national as well as tribal politics. For example, the leadership of the Khamseh confederacy was vested in the Qavam family who were originally merchants from Shiraz, while the Bakhtiari khans spent most of their time in Teheran. True, they often visited their tribal followers, and the Qashqa'i khans celebrated their tribal heritage, but although they set up chiefly camps to receive their nomad followers when the weather was nice, their way of life could not have been more different from the tent-dwelling pastoralists who made up the vast bulk of their followers. Yet the nomads themselves saw no contradiction in this. The job of paramount khan did not revolve around sheep raising, but politics. And just as they migrated to seasonal pastures, their confederation leaders migrated between centers of power. From palaces in provincial towns and the national capital, or even hotel rooms in foreign countries, they played politics on a grand scale.

The Qashqa'i. One of the classic examples of a powerful confederation is that of the Qashqa'i of southern Iran whose leaders have been key figures in regional, national, and international politics for the past two centuries. Beginning with their appointment as governors of the tribes of Fars province in the late eighteenth century, an unbroken line of the Shahilu rulers, or *il-khans*, created a powerful confederacy out of a diverse set of tribes. They owed their success to: the strategic location of their territory along key trade routes to the Persian Gulf; the fact that their territory possessed substantial resources for agriculture as well as pastoralism; and the fact that both nomads and the Iranian state sought them out as political intermediaries to meet their needs. During the First World War, even foreign powers such as the British and the Germans competed with each other for the support of the Qashqa'i khans. As Lois Beck explains in her detailed study of the Qashqa'i confederation's evolution and development, their paramount leadership both "defined the state and the tribe for each other while simultaneously drawing its vital sources of power from both."[19]

The internal organization of the Qashqa'i tribal confederation provides a clue to its strength and longevity: its residential and productive units conducted their local economic and political affairs independently and left regional government to the *il-khan*. As we can see in Table 4.2, the confederation (*il*) was composed of four basic levels. At the top were

TABLE 4.2 Qashqa'i Sociopolitical Organization (1960)

	TOTAL NUMBER	RANGE	AVERAGE SIZE
Qashqa'i (*il*)			>200,000 people
Tribes (*tayefeh*)	14	1,000 to 50,000 people	15,200 people
Major tribes	5	20,000 to 50,000 people	35,000 people
Minor tribes	9	1,000 to 10,000 people	4,300 people
Other units	ca. 20	50 to 10,000 people	
Subtribes (*tireh*)		4 to 60 per tribe	20 per tribe
Lineages		2 to 9 per subtribe	5 per subtribe
Households (*oba*)		30 to 250 per subtribe	100 per subtribe
		15 to 50 per lineage	30 per lineage
Individuals			5 to 6 per household

Source: Lois Beck, *The Qashqa'i of Iran*. New Haven: Yale University Press, 1986, p. 175.

the *il-khan*s who handled the relationship between the Qashqa'i and the state and maintained regional order within the confederation. Each of the confederation's component tribes had a hereditary leader, *kalantar*, who handled the affairs of his own tribe (*tayefeh*) working through a series of subordinate khans who led large clans. In their turn, such subordinate khans relied on headmen, *kadkhuda*, who were responsible for the affairs of the local lineages and households that formed the basic camping units of nomadic society.

For the average Qashqa'i nomad, the confederation structure had a number of advantages. It protected the right of component tribes to maintain access to seasonal pastures and provided a way to handle disputes between different groups. Since the Qashqa'i had to compete with the rival Bakhtiari and Khamseh confederacies as well as the government, it was important that individual tribes have some sort of protection against outsiders. The migration routes of the Qashqa'i and other nomads also made large-scale coordination imperative. In moving from their winter pastures in the south to their summer pastures in the north there were a number of bottlenecks, particularly near the cities of Shiraz and Isfahan, where nomad families were vulnerable to government controls and needed the protection of their powerful khans to avoid taxation or untimely delays. As people on the move, the nomads expected the khan to act as their agent in legal disputes with sedentary authorities. A powerful member of the local elite, he had a vast network of connections that could be used to benefit his people. The price for such services was relatively small. The Shahilu elite collected some taxes, but traditionally most of its wealth was derived from large landholdings worked by sharecroppers, sheep herded by poor Qashqa'i, urban investments, and trading monopolies. The power of a confederation leader lay not his ability to tax or exploit his own people, but in his ability to mobilize them for political or military action.

The leadership of the Qashqa'i and other Iranian confederations proved remarkably long lasting. While their histories are filled with often bloody disputes within ruling lineages, confederacy leadership remained within these lineages for centuries. This was due in part to a cultural pre-disposition in Turco-Mongolian political culture to limit supreme leader-ship to the descendants of the confederacy's founder. In such a tradition, completely new leadership could come about only with the creation of a new confederacy. For example, the confederacies we see today in Iran all have ruling dynasties that can be traced back to each confederation's founding. Yet few of these have a history more than 200 years old (and many date only to the nineteenth century), before which time we find a whole host of other confederations occupying the same territory. Internal revolts against ruling khans, or their destruction by external forces, brought about new confederations with new names, not the reorganization of existing ones.

Border Tribes and Decentralized Political Systems

The centralization of tribes into large confederations was primarily a product of the relationship between nomads and the state. In border areas where state power was weak the nomads were organized into much smaller groups. Here, nomads maintained their autonomy either by inhab-iting the frontier zones between states (allowing them to play one power off against another) or by fleeing from the territory of one state to another. The strategy of border tribes, of course, depended on the existence of a po-litical no-man's-land between two states and beyond the control of either. Because these frontiers were political rather than ecological, their bound-aries could shift over time as state power expanded or contracted. The freedom of nomads could be destroyed if an expanding empire encapsu-lated such an area by conquering it, or if both states became powerful and turned what had been an ill-defined frontier into a garrisoned border.

The frontier between Central Asia and northeastern Iran in the late nineteenth century provided a classic example of the ability of nomads to exploit the rivalries between weak sedentary states to their own advantage with very little formal organization. At this time, Central Asia was divided among a number of Uzbek khanates, based in such major cities as Bukhara and Khiva, whose rulers were the descendants of the nomadic tribes who had conquered the region in the early sixteenth century. They controlled the major river valleys and surrounding territory, but the nomadic tribes along their margins, such as the Kirghiz in the mountains to the east, the

Kazakhs on the steppe to the north, and the Turkmen in the deserts of the west, were independent of any sedentary political control. Although they generally had close economic ties and peaceful relationships with the Uzbek khanates, they refused to pay taxes or accept any orders from the khans of these states. The Uzbek khanates also had a number of disputes with their sedentary neighbors to the south. They periodically fought with the Afghans for control over disputed territories along the Amu River and, as Sunni Muslim rulers, were hostile to the Shiite rulers of Iran.

Of all the Central Asian tribes, the Turkmen who straddled the borderland between northeastern Iran and the Uzbek khanates of Central Asia were in the best position to manipulate this situation. When either the Iranians or Uzbeks attempted to coerce them, the Turkmen employed movement as a strategy to resist state authority, transferring their camps from one side of the frontier to the other to avoid taxes or to escape military retaliation. In general, it was observed that those Turkmen who lived closest to towns and cities were the most law-abiding, while those who inhabited the more distant deserts were prone to violence. Many of these took up slave raiding as a profession, selling captive Iranians in the bazaars of Central Asia or holding them for ransom. Turkmen who were despised as savage robbers in Iran were welcomed as valued customers in Khiva and Bukhara. Of course, such an infamous commerce could only thrive as long as the states of Iran and Central Asia were simultaneously too weak to police their frontiers and too hostile to cooperate with one another. The Turkmen strategy ultimately failed, however, when the expansion of Czarist Russia into Central Asia first cut off their slave markets and then led to their conquest in 1884 with the capture of the oasis of Merv. With no place to run, the Turkmen lost both their political independence and their military power.[20]

POLITICAL ENCAPSULATION
BY THE MODERN STATE
IN THE TWENTIETH CENTURY

The relationship between nomadic tribes and states in the region began to change dramatically after the First World War. Innovations in transportation, military technology, and political ideology transformed what had been a relationship of equality into one where states held a paramount advantage over nomads.

The revolution in transportation, including the introduction of railroads, trucks, and airplanes, changed the very conception of movement. It shrank the effective distance between urban and rural areas, and people and goods could now be moved rapidly to formerly remote areas. In general, cities expanded at the expense of rural areas, and those parts of the region not tied into this new network became economically stagnant. Although the traditional overland caravan trade had been in decline since the sixteenth century, the new transportation technologies put a nail in its coffin and the nomads lost their market for baggage animals and their old role in regional trade. Some nomadic traders, like the Pashtun in Afghanistan, adapted to this situation by buying trucks themselves, abandoning pastoralism, and using their tribal networks as the basis for a new enterprise. Most, however, continued their pastoral existence as they had in the past. For in their remote mountain, steppe, and desert pastures there was little investment in roads or railroads, so pastoral nomads retained a competitive advantage.

The changes in the technology of transportation were also accompanied by changes in military technology that put the nomads at a severe disadvantage. Traditionally, the nomadic tribes themselves had constituted an important military force. They could easily put an impressive cavalry in the field and often served in military campaigns for ruling dynasties. If attacked, they could use their own mobility to shield their people from retaliation or to mount offensives against an invader. While the introduction of cannons in the sixteenth century had made sedentary armies superior in a pitched battle, and made it practically impossible for nomads to overrun cities as they had done in the past, the availability of rifles in the eighteenth century evened the odds by adding firepower to the mobility the nomads already had. The twentieth century, however, shifted the odds almost completely to sedentary states. With planes, tanks, armored cars, and air power, the nomads were both outgunned and could no longer use retreat as a military strategy. And these new armies were no longer just seasonal levies of peasants led by a few officers, they were now standing armies led by professional soldiers.

These technical innovations were also accompanied by new national ideologies of modernization. Although their political content varied widely, all theories of modernization insisted on imposing direct government rule everywhere, without the use of intermediaries such as tribal khans, and tended to view traditional forms of agriculture and pastoralism as backward and in need of transformation. Nomad khans who traditionally had been viewed as key components in a policy of indirect rule were now labeled obstacles to direct rule. This left no room for the nomad elites who had acted as brokers between tribes and states. Indeed, it left no room for the nomads themselves who were now declared a hindrance to programs of economic development and made targets of sedentarization projects.

Nowhere was this policy of sedentarization and the vilification of nomadism more prominent than in Iran under the rule of Reza Shah in the 1920s and 1930s. In Turkey, nomadism had been on the decline for centuries because all of the Anatolian Plateau was suitable for agriculture so that over time the expansion of farming had significantly reduced the number of pastoralists and their political significance. In Afghanistan, the central government was too weak and the country too fragmented to even consider a policy of sedentarization. As in previous centuries, the nomads were simply accepted as a natural, indeed economically vital, part of the economy and left alone. In Iran, on the other hand, nomads were both economically and politically important. Their tribal confederations dominated the southern part of the country where their khans were often the *de facto* rulers of their regions. As late as 1909, the Bakhtiari tribes were instrumental in deposing a Qajar shah, Mohammad Ali Shah, and replacing him with his son. When the Qajar dynasty fell in 1925, Reza Shah seized power and was determined to break the power of the nomadic confederations, first by eliminating their political elite through exile and execution, and second by destroying the pastoral economy itself. In a thinly disguised novel about the Qashqa'i, *The Last Migration*, Vincent Cronin described the nomads' historic struggle with Reza Shah and their continuing disputes with his son Mohammad Reza Shah, who was toppled from power by Khomeini in 1979:

> The continued presence of nomad tribes Reza Shah considered a blot on his progressive country. Conservative by tradition, they opposed many of the usurper's innovations. They refused for instance to wear the compulsory new dress for men: Western-style suits with peaked hats; and the new gendarmerie found it difficult to enforce this rule on a sturdy people forever on the move in mountainous country. Seeing in the tribes a challenge to his policy and a potential threat to his throne, Reza Shah decided to settle the most powerful among them as the surest means of crushing their spirit and ending their backward ways. The task was entrusted to the Army and carried out in haste. No suitable agricultural land existed, water was lacking, implements were not provided, and the climate on the plains proved fatally severe. Weakened by this strange sedentary life, many tribespeople fell ill and died.[21]

Of course, since movement between seasonal pastures was the key to herd management, impeding it had a devastating impact on the pastoral economy. Only the most powerful families, who often had significant landholdings to fall back on, were able to keep flocks by bribing officials to ignore the prohibition. This policy remained in force until 1941 when Reza Shah was deposed by the British and Russians.

Although nomadic pastoralism suffered a severe blow under Reza Shah, it did not disappear. Migrations resumed and the herds were rebuilt. The attempt to destroy nomadic political organization was also only partially successful. The tribal khans still retained considerable influence and because local affairs had always been handled by local leaders, the rest of the tribal political structure continued to operate in the absence of the paramount khans so that the Qashqa'i or Bakhtiari identities remained intact. Indeed, after the fall of Reza Shah, the Qashqa'i khans attempted to cultivate even closer ties to their tribal followers and represent their interests in national politics. During the reign of Mohammad Reza Shah, they once again found themselves in opposition to Teheran, but upon his fall they attempted to reassert their authority by taking up arms against the Khomeini regime, from 1980 to 1982. Although unsuccessful, their attempt displayed the resilience of nomadic political organization which, as the twentieth century drew to a close, had outlasted most of the governments that had sought to destroy them.

PASTORALISM AND ECONOMIC CHANGE

Just as their political environment was subject to change because of the growing power of national states, pastoral nomads in southwestern Asia also experienced a shift in the structure of economic relations with their sedentary neighbors. Pastoralism has always been an important part of the region's economy. In the late 1950s, animal products constituted one-third of Iran's non-oil domestic production and a similar fraction of its exports, and at least half of this was produced by migratory peoples.[22] Similarly, in Afghanistan, 30 percent of the country's foreign exchange was officially derived from the export of livestock, mostly sheep, and this did not include the trade in animals that were smuggled into Iran and Pakistan.[23] Nevertheless, the price for sheep was relatively low compared with other commodities until after the oil boom in Iran during the 1970s. With new roads, more truck transportation, and a growing demand for meat in the region's cities, pastoralists saw the value of their sheep rise sharply and many became more closely tied to urban markets. Although apparently outwardly unchanged, nomadic pastoralists in fact responded to these conditions by reorganizing their production in a way that had profound consequences. The model of sedentarization that appeared to account for the relative stability of nomadic societies in the past was suddenly found inadequate to explain these new developments.

MODELS OF SEDENTARIZATION REVISITED

Conducting research among the Luri nomads of southern Iran from 1969 to 1970, Jacob Black-Michaud observed a system of economic organization quite different than that described by Barth for the neighboring Basseri.[24] Among the Basseri, both the wealthy and the poverty-stricken sedentarized and left the pastoral economy, while among the Lurs, the rich hired the poor and both remained within the pastoral economy. This meant that Basseri society was composed largely of self-sufficient households that were socially and economically similar to one another. By contrast, Luri society was marked by extreme social stratification, with the majority of pastoralists working for a few affluent families which had formed "agro-pastoral combines" that mixed land ownership with sheep raising on a large scale. Far from abandoning their pastoral assets, wealthy Luri landowners had continued to invest heavily in sheep raising by employing impoverished Lurs as contract herders to oversee their flocks which were grazed on traditional tribal pastures. The Luri data thus appeared to turn Barth's model inside out and raised questions about its general validity.

Black-Michaud traced the development of inequality among the Lurs to their historical experience with forced sedentarization in the 1930s. At that time, the government of Iran under Reza Shah prohibited nomadic migrations. In response to this policy, the most powerful Luri families seized control of the limited tribal land best suited for agriculture and made it their private property. They were also able to use their money and political connections to evade the restrictions on movement and continue running sheep. The majority of ordinary nomads, on the other hand, lost their flocks during this period. Thus, when Reza Shah fell in 1941 and nomads were free to renew their migrations, most families lacked enough sheep to begin again on their own. Wealthy sheep owners in need of labor stepped in and made flocks available on contract to poor families, but these herding contracts rarely provided enough profits for shepherds to become independent. Although the reopening of traditional pastures allowed the flocks to recover from earlier losses, the distribution of ownership was radically transformed.

Since the Lurs lived under similar ecological conditions as the Basseri in a neighboring region and had a similar history, why were their experiences so different? The major structural difference between the two systems appears to hinge on the existence of herding contracts. Because so few contract herds were available to poor families among the Basseri, those pastoralists who lost their sheep had no alternative but to sedentarize. Among the Lurs, where contract herding was the norm, those who lost their own livestock could remain pastoralists by herding other people's sheep.

Barth attributes the relative absence of herding contracts among the Basseri to the falling rate of profitability as the number of sheep rises and the poor care they receive when not herded by their owners. Black-Michaud, on the other hand, claims that his figures demonstrate just the reverse. He argues vigorously that while all owners complain about the problems of supervising the work of shepherds, the return on sheep raising is far too high to be casually abandoned. Indeed, at the time of his research, city-based merchants had begun to invest in sheep as a way to earn high profits. He implies that Barth is guilty of perpetuating an ethnographic illusion, seduced by an egalitarian ideology which paints an idealized picture of nomadic political autonomy while disguising its underlying structure of economic inequality. For example, in spite of the large differences in relative power, the Lurs still insist that, since all herding contracts are entered into on a voluntary basis, rich herd owners and poor shepherds alike are equally free decision makers and therefore autonomous.[25]

Who's right? As in many debates, the available data are insufficient to resolve the issue directly. Barth's model is elegant, but the number of cases he had the opportunity to observe during his short stay among the Basseri (three months) was small. Black-Michaud has much better data for the Lurs, but these are not necessarily applicable to the Basseri. In fact, a closer look at the structure of herding contracts supports the conclusions of each author. For while both societies depend on pastoralism, the profitability of sheep as a cash investment is quite different in each system.

Among the Basseri, sheep run by their owners are very profitable, but sheep run under contract are not. At the time of Barth's research, in the 1950s, a mature ewe valued at 80 *tomans* ($11.50) produced wool, clarified butter, and lambskins that could be sold for 60 *tomans*, leaving the other milk products and lamb's meat to be consumed by the family, for a combined annual return of 100 percent for owner-operators. If these same ewes were run under a Basseri herding contract, this relatively high rate of return declined significantly. Under the terms of a shepherding contract, the owner received only a fixed cash payment of 10 to 15 *tomans* per ewe and the promise that his flock would be returned intact (with the same size and age composition) at the end of the year. In exchange, the shepherd got to keep all the pastoral products, including any increase in the herd. Effectively, this meant that there was a 6:1 or 4:1 split of the cash value of the flock's annual production between the shepherd and the owner, a rate very unfavorable to the owner. More important, the owner could not profit from the anticipated reproductive increase of his animals, which is one of the key advantages in running sheep. Given the potential risks inherent in pastoralism from disease, weather, or herding mishaps, even the promise to return the same number of animals was a perilous proposition because a shepherd with a few ewes of his own could hardly be expected to meet this obligation if he suffered heavy losses. The Basseri contract system therefore appears geared to meeting short-term labor demands because, as a long-term investment, it is only marginally profitable. It is hardly surprising that those wealthy families who invested in land subsequently abandoned sheep raising when they could no longer run their own flocks.[26]

Among the Lurs, the value of contract sheep is much higher. Not only do the owners receive a much larger share of the herd's income, but they also specialize in selling yearlings to urban meat markets, a cash business not shared by the Basseri.[27] Luri herding contracts for ewes call for an exactly even split between the herd owner and the shepherd: "Lambs of both sexes, ewes' and lambs' wool, dairy produce, skins of dead ewes, and the proceeds from the yearly sale of barren animals are all pooled and divided 50:50 between patron owner and herder client."[28] In addition, the shepherd is financially responsible for providing any additional labor needed for herding, paying for veterinary care, and supplying any necessary winter fodder. Shepherds are not responsible for any losses, however,

Afghan shepherds packing wool sheared from qarakul lambs in their mountain pastures for transport to urban bazaars where it is in high demand for carpet weaving and felt making.

although they may find themselves unable to renew their contracts if ewe mortality is excessive. Little or no cash changes hands in such arrangements and contracts between herders and owners often extend over many years. These contracts are popular with herders because they can use their share of the milk, meat, and wool to improve their families' standard of living and, by receiving their income mostly in live animals, they can build the nucleus of their own flocks.

Luri yearling contracts are more market oriented than ewe contracts and are viewed explicitly as cash investments by both shepherds and owners:

> There is nothing traditional whatsoever about attitudes to male lambs and yearlings which, from the moment they are separated from the ewes, cease to be regarded as anything other than money on legs endowed with potential growth. Yearling contracts are distributed to anyone—be he agnate, affine or total stranger—according to the single criterion of herding efficiency.[29]

The profitability of raising yearlings lies in the fact that most Luri households must sell their male lambs at an early age to meet expenses. Rich Lurs are therefore able to buy up large numbers of them cheaply for fattening before selling them to urban meat markets the next year. Flocks of yearlings yield no milk products or lambs, of course, so they are valuable only for the price they will bring at market and sometimes the value of their wool. The profit on the sale of the animals is split 50:50 (or less commonly 60:40) between owner and shepherd, with both being similarly liable for the cost of any lost animals. Yearling contracts are inherently speculative, but can yield great returns to both owners and shepherds if conditions are right. On the other hand, if a substantial number of yearlings die, a shepherd may find his return reduced to little or nothing.

These differences reflect the value of sheep as a cash investment in each system, a situation structurally similar to the economics of peasant households as described by the nineteenth-century economist Chayanov in his classic study of agriculture in Czarist Russia.[30] Chayanov observed that Russian peasants often made an excellent living by farming under conditions which would bankrupt absentee investors. This was because a peasant family never thought of its own labor as a real cost of production, and therefore its "profits" were considered any money left over after paying all other expenses. An absentee investor, on the other hand, had to pay the same expenses plus the cost of labor as well. If his return did not exceed the cost of production, including the cost of labor, he went out of business. So too with pastoralists: where sheep give high cash returns to investors after paying the cost of labor (as among the Lurs), the wealthy remain pastoralists; where sheep are more highly valued for subsistence and provide low cash returns to investors (as among the Basseri), the wealthy leave.

The dynamics of each system depend on the value of sheep and the cost of labor. If either or both of these variables change, then there can be a radical reorganization of the pastoral economy similar in significance to changing from a subsistence crop to a cash crop among farmers. Yet with nomadic pastoralists, such a change may not be easy to see, since the people, the pastures, and the animals appear the same as always. Timeless-appearing nomads on migration can disguise an important change in which subsistence pastoralism becomes a form of cash ranching. The Central-Asian Arabs, whom we discussed earlier, provide an example of how this process works and the consequences for nomadic social organization.

PASTORALISM AS CASH RANCHING

The Basseri, with their local village partners, weak links to urban markets, and limited outside investment in pastoralism, represent a classic form of subsistence pastoralism. And Barth's model of sedentarization and economic opportunities undoubtedly reflects the dynamics of such a system. However, with the construction of new roads and the development of strong national markets for sheep to feed meat-hungry urban residents, the value of livestock rose considerably and previously marginal pastoralists were drawn into the cash economy. The Luri response to such changes was to invest heavily in the sale of yearling wethers (castrated male sheep) run under contract to meet this demand. Unlike traditional ewe-herding contracts, in which little cash changed hands and subsistence products were very important, yearling contracts were cash investments in which owners and shepherds split the profits. The Central Asian Arabs have moved another step beyond the Lurs and transformed their pastoralism into a form of commercial ranching. In northern Afghanistan, all the components of pastoralism (sheep, pasture, and labor) could be purchased and carried a specific monetary value. Nomads there had also already developed strong links to urban markets, raised breeds of sheep to meet the specific demands of those markets, and could explicitly determine profit and loss. When the cash value of their livestock began to rise, running sheep soon became a business handled by shepherd crews who were paid cash wages by absentee sheep owners. Many households which remained dependent on the pastoral economy no longer directly participated in it as family groups. Wealthy families in particular sedentarized and lived off the profits of their contract herds, effectively abandoning milk production which was so central to subsistence pastoralism. Under these conditions, Black-Michaud's model of a pastoralism that attracts wealthy investors who sustain a class of poor wage-earning shepherds applies even more strongly than among the Lurs.

Pastoralism in northern Afghanistan has always been integrated into the market system, and selling live animals or lambskins in urban bazaars is a long-standing tradition. However, because closed borders with the Soviet Union prevented nomads from trading with their traditional customers in Bukhara and other Central Asian cities, the price they received for their animals locally was low. While pastoralism provided a good living, it did not attract outside investors because such a high percentage of a flock's value lay in its milk products, meat, and wool that could be consumed directly by its owners. As with the Basseri, when the number of animals rose to a point where hired shepherds were required, wealthy pastoralists found that their rate of profits declined significantly.[31]

The traditional Arab herding contract called upon the owner to pay his head shepherd (*chopan*) approximately one ewe for each hundred animals herded for each six-month contract period. Each additional assistant shepherd (*chakar*) received slightly more than half this rate. The employer was expected to provide food, some equipment, and pay the cost of salt in the mountain pastures during the spring/summer contract. Because shepherds milked ewes only to meet their own daily needs, most of their subsistence value, so important in a family operation, was lost. An independent herd numbering 600 animals that required a shepherd and two or three assistants would therefore cost an owner approximately thirty ewes annually, that is, between 10 and 15 percent of his reproductive stock, depending on his herd's composition. The insistence on wage payments in ewes, instead of lambs, was unusual among pastoralists. It reflected the fact that: (1) each shepherd contract was for six months and only in the spring/summer period were there new lambs; (2) the contract herds of wealthy Arab pastoralists traditionally contained a high proportion of wethers so that shepherds might find themselves herding lots of nonreproductive stock while the owner kept as many ewes as possible in his own flock for milking. In any event, paying in mature ewes cut into the owner's most important asset: his reproductive capital. The more animals herded by shepherds, the slower their growth rate. But such payments also allowed the shepherds themselves to accumulate the nucleus of their own flocks and made it possible for families who were poor in stock to rebuild their holdings.

This situation changed radically in response to a sudden rise in the price of sheep in northern Afghanistan. Until the 1960s, the region produced large agricultural and pastoral surpluses. But because there were few local markets and no opportunities for export, commodity prices remained low. When the Salang Pass through the Hindu Kush Mountains opened in 1964, demand surged and prices rose. Sheep prices doubled a year after the pass was opened and doubled again over the next ten years. These advances were well above the average inflation rate. Sheep, which had been valued mainly for subsistence, now became valued as investments. In response to the price increase, the owners of livestock changed the herding contracts to a system of cash payments. They argued that just because the value of sheep had doubled in a single year, there was no reason for wages to double as well. Instead, they agreed to pay shepherds the value of their traditional number of ewes on the basis of the previous year's prices.

This apparently small change transformed pastoralism in northern Afghanistan. Since spring and summer pastures were already privately owned, and the nomads raised sheep specifically for the meat market, paying shepherds in kind was the last barrier to a completely cash economy. As soon as the value of labor was no longer specifically tied to livestock, the real cost of wages fell as the price of sheep rose. For example, in 1975 an owner of a herd of 700 animals paid his shepherd crews wages totaling 40,000 afghanis ($800) over the course of a year, while the cost for the same labor in ewe payments under the old system would have amounted to the cash equivalent of 70,000 afghanis ($1,400). Not only that, but by retaining all of their ewes, owners of contract herds experienced a much higher rate of growth than previously. Formerly subsistence-based, employing family labor, and dependent on both cash sales and milk production, pastoralism swiftly evolved into a form of commercial ranching in which sheep were valued only for the price they brought at market. Wealthy pastoralists sedentarized their families, abandoned milk production as an economic activity, and hired teams of shepherds to move their sheep through the migration cycle. While this opened up many more opportunities for shepherds, they soon found themselves trapped permanently as pastoral laborers because cash wages could not reproduce like ewes. Shepherds found it difficult both to support their families and acquire the animals needed to become owner-operators, an important stabilizing element in the old system. Shepherd families without their own sheep were therefore also forced to sedentarize.

Perhaps one of the keys for determining whether pastoralism has become commercially oriented is the degree to which outside investors attempt to enter the pastoral economy. In Iran, city merchants, taking advantage of high sheep prices because of the oil boom there, began to invest in pastoralism in the 1970s, hiring their own shepherds and running sheep on tribal land that had been nationalized by the Shah. One of the initial consequences of the Iranian Revolution was that the nomads took back control of much of their pasture land and excluded these outsiders. In northern Afghanistan, city-based merchants, attracted by the new markets and high prices for sheep, began to invest in sheep even though they had no previous experience in the business. Excited by the prospect that their herds (and profits) could potentially grow geometrically, they found that there were a number of ways to run their animals. Small herd owners would pay a nomad family an inexpensive fixed fee to take their sheep to the mountains for the summer. Many poor nomad families found that by doing this, they could not only make money, but keep all the milk and wool for themselves. Families that did not have enough animals to support themselves could therefore maintain their traditional lifestyle and avoid sedentarization. Other merchants struck deals with rich nomads, agreeing to pay the cost of a shepherd in order to run their sheep together. Since up to a certain point, between about 300 to 800 sheep, the number of shepherds remained the same, this was an attractive proposition. Finally, truly entrepreneurial merchants combined their animals, hired their own shepherds, rented pastures, and ran the entire operation themselves. This most commercial of enterprises had a disadvantage in that hired shepherds felt few obligations to the owners. They were often accused of slaughtering a disproportionate number of "dying" sheep to eat.

The rise of sheep as investments increased the degree of economic stratification among pastoralists. Whereas in the past, even the poorest nomad could hope to become the owner of a substantial flock through shepherd contracts and good herding luck, the new cash payments made this practically impossible. Formerly, at the other end of the spectrum, even the wealthiest nomads could be reduced to poverty by a spring blizzard or an epidemic. But new profits in commercial sheep raising, invested in agricultural land or trading ventures, could almost permanently secure their wealth. The profits from the land could also be used to maximize the return on wethers. Full-grown animals brought twice the price of immature ones, but only families with considerable resources could afford to wait. More significantly, the commercialization of pastoralism and the sedentarization of families reduced the importance of women's labor. In subsistence pastoralism, women's labor was a key component in milk production, but the high price of sheep made it possible to abandon this resource. With a less important role in the production cycle, and no longer taking part in the migration, sedentarized nomadic women lost much of their autonomy and became subject to such restrictions as veiling, which they had ignored as nomads.

THE VIABILITY OF CONTEMPORARY NOMADIC PASTORALISM

National governments in southwest Asia have traditionally thought of pastoral nomadism as an archaic form of production that would vanish with economic development. In particular, they have tended to view nomads as "homeless" people whose lives can only be improved by settlement. This belief was most pronounced in Iran where nomadism itself was banned by Reza Shah as an affront to his vision of a modern society. Yet nomadic pastoralism will undoubtedly continue to persist into the twenty-first century, not because people are too poor to do anything else, but because pastoralism often provides a higher standard of living than subsistence farming and contributes significantly to national economies. Indeed, as Table 4.3 indicates, in the mid-1980s the number of sheep and goats in Turkey, Iran, and Afghanistan alone was estimated at around 125 million animals.

In looking to the future, nomadic pastoralists are most likely to continue where they fill a niche that cannot be filled by others. Of course, as long as there is a high market demand for sheep and goats, or their milk products, wool, and skins, pastoralism itself will never disappear. The question is whether traditional *nomadic* pastoralism will disappear. Thus in areas such as Turkey, where arable land greatly exceeds permanent pasture land, animal husbandry has been largely integrated into village agriculture. The number of nomads there has thus declined dramatically over the past few centuries. Those remaining, such as the Yörük, have

TABLE 4.3 *Estimated Livestock Production in Southwest Asia, 1985* (in millions)

	PEOPLE·	ARABLE LAND (IN HECTARES)	PASTURE (IN HECTARES)	SHEEP	GOATS
Afghanistan	16.5	8.1	27.4	20.0	3.0
Iran	44.6	14.8	44.0	34.5	13.6
Turkey	49.2	27.4	9.0	40.4	13.0

Source: FAO Production Yearbook. Vol. 39, (1985).

Ewes are tied together at the neck to facilitate milking by the women of the camp. When family labor is replaced by hired shepherd teams such milk processing is abandoned.

been marginalized to the point where they must rent alpine pasture rights from local villagers.[32] In more arid and semi-arid regions, however, only mobile pastoralism can effectively exploit the vast areas of seasonally available grassland. For example, in Iran and Afghanistan the amount of permanent pasture land is three times greater than arable land and nomads retain a comparative economic advantage over farmers who cannot possibly undertake the long-distance migrations required to maintain large flocks. Here the absolute number of nomadic pastoralists (estimated at about two million in each country) has remained approximately the same over the past two centuries even though their percentage of the total population, and therefore their apparent importance, has declined dramatically.

This is not to say that pastoralism can remain unchanged. In many regions, the pastoral economy may thrive but become more commercial, depending less on families and more on hired shepherds. Where resources are too limited or too irregular to encourage such market-oriented herding, familial pastoralism will likely continue as before, but the differences between subsistence and commercial pastoralism will become so marked that no single model will adequately explain them both. Nevertheless, with their traditional market links, herding skills, and substantial investment in livestock, sheep-raising pastoralists will continue their annual migrations from lowlands to highlands in an eternal quest for greener pastures long after the pages of this book have turned to dust.

NOTES

1. Marion C. Cooper, *Grass, An Account of the Migration of a Bakhtiari Tribe in Search of Pasture* (New York: Putnam, 1925).

2. C.G. Feilberg, *La Tente Noir* (Copenhagen: Gyldendal, 1944).

3. Fredrik Barth, "The Land Use Pattern of Migratory Tribes of South Persia," *Norsk Geografish Tidsskrift*, 17 (1959), 1–11.

4. Richard Tapper, *Pasture and Politics: Economics, Conflict and Ritual among the Shahsevan Nomads of Northwestern Iran* (New York: Academic Press, 1979).

5. Thomas Barfield, *Central Asian Arabs of Afghanistan* (Austin: University of Texas Press, 1981).

6. The importance of evaluating the position of a family in its development cycle was first elaborated in a study of the Fulani of west Africa, but has generally been employed in all studies of pastoralists. cf. Derrick Stenning, "Household Viability among the Pastoral Fulani," in *The Development Cycle* in *Domestic Groups*, ed. Jack Goody (Cambridge: Cambridge University Press, 1965).

7. Tapper, *Pasture*, p. 241.

8. William G. Irons, 1975, *The Yomut Turkmen: A Study of Social Organization among Central Asian Turkic-speaking Population* (Ann Arbor: Anthropological Papers of the Museum of Anthropology, 58, University of Michigan, 1975).

9. Fredrik Barth, *Nomads of South Persia* (Boston: Little, Brown, 1961), p. 125.

10. Barth, *Nomads*, p. 124.

11. Barth, *Nomads*, pp. 108–9.

12. Marshall Sahlins, *Tribesmen* (Englewood Cliffs, NJ: Prentice-Hall, Inc., 1968), pp. 24–27.

13. Charles Issawi, *The Economic History of Iran: 1800–1914* (Chicago: University of Chicago Press, 1971), p. 20.

14. Joseph Fletcher, "Turco-Mongolian Monarchic Tradition in the Ottoman Empire" in *Eucharisterion: Essays Presented to Omeljan Pritsak*, edited by Ihor Sevcenko and Frank Sysyn. Harvard Ukranian Studies 3–4 (1979–80): part 1: 236–51.

15. John Woods, *The Aqquyunlu: Clan, Tribe Confederation* (Minneapolis: Bibliotheca Islamica, 1976).

16. John Perry, "Forced Migration in Iran during the 17th and 18th Centuries," *Iranian Studies*, 8 (1975), 199–215.

17. There are now a number of specific studies on nomadic confederations in southern Iran: Lois Beck, *The Qashqa'i of Iran* (New Haven: Yale University Press, 1986); Gene Garthwaite, *Khans and Shahs: a Documentary Analysis of the Bakhtiari in Iran* (Cambridge: Cambridge University Press, 1983); Pierre Oberling, *The Qashqa'i of Fars* (The Hague: Mouton, 1974).

18. Ibn Khaldun, *The Muqaddimah*, trans. Frans Rosenthal, ed. N. Dawood. (Princeton: Princeton University Press, 1967), pp. 120–21.

19. Beck, *Qashqa'i*, p. 163.

20. William Irons, "Nomadism as Political Adaptation: The Case of the Yomut Turkmen," *American Ethnologist*, 1 (1974), 635–58; G.C. Napier, "Memorandum on the Condition and External Relations of the Turkomen Tribes of Merv," in *Collection of Journals and Reports from G.C. Napier on Special Duty in Persia 1874* (London: Her Majesty's Stationery Office, 1876).

21. Vincent Cronin, *The Last Migration* (New York: Dutton, 1957), p. 10.

22. Thomas R. Stauffer, "The Economics of Nomadism in Iran," *Middle East Journal*, 19 (1965), 284–302.

23. Barfield, *Central Asian Arabs*, p. 116.

24. Jacob Black-Michaud, *Sheep and Land: The Economics of Power in a Tribal Society* (Cambridge: Cambridge University Press, 1986).

25. Jacob Black, "Tyranny as a Strategy for Survival in an 'Egalitarian' Society: Luri Facts versus Anthropological Mystique," *Man*, 7 (1972), 614–34.

26. Barth, *Nomads*, pp. 13–14, 17, 99.

27. Black-Michaud, *Sheep and Land*, pp. 105–8.

28. Black-Michaud, *Sheep and Land*, p. 62.

29. Black-Michaud, *Sheep and Land*, p. 107.

30. A.V. Chayanov, *The Theory of Peasant Economy*. Madison: University of Wisconsin Press, 1986.

31. Barfield, *Central Asian Arabs*, pp. 165–70.

32. Daniel Bates, *Nomads and Farmers: A Study of the Yoruk of Southeastern Turkey* (Ann Arbor: Anthropological Papers of the Museum of Anthropology, 52, University of Michigan Press, 1973).

FURTHER READINGS

Azoy, Whitney, *Buzkashi: Game and Power in Afghanistan*. Philadelphia: University of Pennsylvania Press, 1982.

Beck, Lois, *Nomad: A Year in the Life of a Qashqa'i Tribesman in Iran*. Berkeley: University of California Press, 1991.

Bradburd, Daniel, *Ambiguous Relations: Kin, Class and Conflict among the Komachi Pastoralists*. Washington, D.C.: Smithsonian Institution Press, 1990.

Digard, Jean-Pierre, *Techniques des nomads baxtyâri d'Iran*. Cambridge: Cambridge University Press, 1981.

Glatzer, Bernt, *Nomaden von Gharjistan*. Weisbaden: Franz Steiner Verlag, 1977.

Khoury, Phillip and Joseph Kostiner, eds., *Tribes and State Formation in the Middle East*. Berkeley: University of California Press, 1990.

Michaud, Roland and Sabrina, *Caravans to Tartary*. New York: Viking, 1978.

Pehrson, Robert N., *The Social Organization of the Marri Baluch*. New York: Wenner Gren, 1966.

Shahrani, M. Nazif, *The Kirghiz and Wakhi of Afghanistan*. Seattle: University of Washington Press, 1979.

Szabo, Albert and Thomas Barfield, *Afghanistan: An Atlas of Indigenous Domestic Architecture*. Austin: University of Texas Press, 1991.

Tapper, Nancy, *Bartered Brides: Politics, Gender, and Marriage in an Afghan Tribal Society*. Cambridge: Cambridge University Press, 1991.

CHAPTER FIVE

*T*HE HORSE RIDERS: NOMADS OF THE EURASIAN STEPPE

Of all the world's pastoralists, none left a more indelible historical impression than the horse-riding nomads of the Eurasian steppe. With an economy based on a mobile form of animal husbandry that scattered people across a vast landscape, they lived under the sky's great blue dome in tents of felt, consuming milk and meat as the central part of their diet, and glorifying military adventure and heroic personal achievement. These horse-riding peoples stood in stark contrast to neighboring sedentary civilizations. Though relatively few in number and seeming to lack even the basis for state organization, for more than 2,500 years they nevertheless managed to create great empires that continually terrorized and periodically conquered powerful sedentary states in northern China, Iran and Afghanistan, and Eastern Europe.

The invasion of the Roman Empire by Attila the Hun and his followers in the fifth century and the immense conquests of Chinggis Khan and his successors in the thirteenth are perhaps the best-remembered nomadic incursions. But these were but two of a string of successive nomadic empires: Scythians, Sarmatians, Huns, Khazars, Kipchaks, the Golden Horde, and Kalmuks along the European frontiers; Massagetae, Sakas, Yüeh-chih, Tocharians, Hephalites, Turks, Chaghatai Mongols, Timurids, Uzbeks, and

Kazaks north of the Iranian Plateau; and Hsiung-nu, Wu-sun, Hsien-pi, Jou-jan, Turks, Uighurs, Mongols, Oirats, and Zunghars on the borders of China. Yet our understanding of them has long been clouded by prejudice because sedentary historians tended to treat nomadic attacks as a form of natural history, like a plague of locusts. In ancient China for example, court officials argued that it was impossible to maintain civilized relations with people who moved to and fro like birds and beasts. Medieval Christian and Muslim commentators, on the other hand, explained invasions by nomadic peoples such as the Huns or Mongols as God's punishment for sinful societies. Even in more recent times it was argued that nomads invaded sedentary areas primarily in response to drought. The truth is far different. The nomads of Central Eurasia had their own distinct political and economic organization that was logical and coherent but, because it was based on such different principles than agricultural civilizations, its unique dynamic was rarely recognized.

HORSE DOMESTICATION AND THE RISE OF STEPPE PASTORALISM

Archaeological evidence indicates that the horse was domesticated around 4000 B.C. on the steppes of southern Russia, much later than sheep, goats, or cattle. Recent research has also detected microscopic evidence of bit wear on horse teeth from this period, indicating that horseback riding may have been intimately associated with the animal's domestication, although this is still subject to debate.[1] However, it would be until around 1000 B.C. before horse-riding nomadic pastoralists would make an appearance on the stage of world history. Before that time, horse raising was part of a mixed economy associated with farmers who also raised livestock. They inhabited permanent villages located along the banks of the rivers that flowed through the steppe. The presence of pig bones recovered from archaeological sites is an indication of their sedentary life, for no nomadic tribes raise pigs.

Horses were uncommon outside the steppe region in early times and their adoption by peoples in other regions was initially associated with the use of chariots, not horse riding. While early horse-drawn chariots were slow and clumsy, little more than glorified carts, by 1700 B.C. the introduction of the spoked wheel and sophisticated bridling systems made possible new lightweight designs capable of fast movement. First appearing in the areas bordering the steppe lands, the light horse-drawn chariot spread quickly to regions such as Egypt and Mesopotamia where horses had to be imported. The Hittite and Assyrian empires in particular depended on light chariots to overwhelm enemy foot soldiers. Although the transmission links are not yet fully known, chariot technology had entered China

The small but hardy steppe horse provided the nomads of Central Eurasia with an un-precedented mobility that was a key element of their military power.

by 1200 B.C. where it became an integral part of the region's military organization.[2] In all these sedentary societies, chariots were not only weapons of war, but became symbols of power for their ruling aristocracies.

The world of the steppe nomad came into existence as a result of a series of changes in economy, horse technology, and weaponry. Taking advantage of mobility provided by carts pulled by horses or oxen, some groups became more nomadic. Leaving the protection of river valleys, they began to migrate across the grasslands with large herds of animals. The Bronze Age invasions of Iran and India by Indo-Europeans around 1200 B.C. displayed such mobile pastoral economies. But the people fought on foot or from chariots. Contemporary illustrations show no evidence of cavalry; the few horse riders shown are mounted clumsily on the rump as if they were riding a donkey.[3] Around 900 B.C., the nascent steppe nomads made two dramatic innovations. The first was a form of horse riding that gave the rider more control over his animal, including a saddle and an improved system of bits and bridling. The second was mounted archery. Using the compound bow, mounted archers now formed a cavalry that was both swift and deadly, able to attack an enemy at a distance or even while retreating (the famous "Parthian shot"). The steppe nomads now combined a mobile economy with a powerful mobile military. This new culture soon displaced the semi-nomadic, riverine agricultural settlements and even began to threaten neighboring sedentary civilizations.

In the west, the first historically known nomads were the Cimmerians and Scythians who descended on the kingdoms of the Near East at the end of the eighth century B.C. Later, the Scythians allied themselves with the Assyrians in 674 B.C., but then helped to destroy their erstwhile allies and raided from northern Iran to the borders of Egypt. The nomads of Mongolia underwent a similar transformation, although they did not enter the Chinese historical record until much later. Sun Tzu's classic *Art of War* (dating from the middle of the fourth century B.C.) made not a single mention of cavalry, yet within a few decades of its completion, tribes of horse-riding nomads known as Hu were raiding along China's whole northern frontier. In response, the border Chinese states themselves quickly adopted cavalry troops into their own armies.

> ...King Wu-ling of Chao (325–299 B.C.) changed the customs of his people, ordering them to adopt the barbarian dress and practice riding and shooting, and led them north in a successful attack on the forest barbarians and the Lou-fan.[4]

This new steppe nomadic world formed a distinct culture that simultaneously disdained alien customs while coveting foreign goods which were often imported over great distances. Its famous "animal style" of art, with leaping stags and fighting animals executed in gold, carved wood, or boldly colored felt appliqué, certainly displayed a cultural ethos strikingly different from that of their sedentary neighbors.[5]

We find our most vivid account of these ancient mounted nomads in the writings of the Greek traveller and historian Herodotus, who visited the Scythians in the middle of·the fifth century B.C. Herodotus described them as heavy drinkers of imported wine who also smoked hemp and worshiped a pantheon of gods. They built elaborate tombs stocked with rich goods and sacrifices (some human) for their dead. Many of these details were dramatically confirmed by discoveries of frozen tombs in the Siberian borderlands of Mongolia dating from this period which produced some of the oldest examples of feltwork, carpet weaving, and horse decorations in the world. Indeed, the bodies resting in the tombs were so well preserved that their vivid tattooing remained intact.[6]

In a display of Kazak horsemanship and physical strength, each rider competes to pull his opponent from his horse. Such scenes have impressed sedentary visitors to the steppe from the time of Herodotus.

But it was in war, Herodotus explained, that the Scythians were most feared, a characteristic that would be noted in later Chinese accounts of the nomads in Mongolia:

> In what concerns war, their customs are the following. The Scythian soldier drinks the blood of the first man he overthrows in battle. Whatever the number he slays, he cuts off all their heads and carries them to the king; since he is thus entitled to a share of the booty, whereto he forfeits all claim if he does not produce a head. ...The skulls of their enemies, not indeed of all, but of those they most detest, they treat as follows. Having sawn off the portion below the eyebrows, and cleaned out the inside, they cover the outside with leather. When a man is poor, this is all that he does; but if he is rich, he also lines the inside with gold: in either case the skull is used as a drinking cup.[7]

The uniformity in nomadic material culture and other customs across the Eurasian steppes was quite striking. Yet, as Owen Lattimore has argued, it was not the spread of a single people that brought about this change but the embrace of a new technology and way of life by many previously distinct societies along the fringes of the steppe. Marginal farmers from China, forest hunters from Siberia, and the more sedentary inhabitants of the steppe itself all adopted a fully nomadic style of life to more effectively exploit the Central Eurasian grasslands, and in the process created a common culture of their own.[8] That such profound changes could occur rapidly was seen much later in history when the horse was reintroduced to the plains of North America by the Spaniards. Only after neighboring tribes acquired the horse could Plains Indian culture develop. Within a century, a wide variety of tribes with heterogeneous origins had all adopted similar cultural practices based on horse riding and bison hunting.[5] So natural did this style of life appear to outsiders that in the popular imagination it became the stereotype for all North American Indian cultures, even though it did not exist in the precontact period.

NOMADIC PASTORALISM IN CENTRAL EURASIA

Horse-riding pastoralists historically occupied the grasslands and mountain pastures of Central Eurasia, those rolling plains of grass, scrub land, and semi-desert punctuated by high mountain ranges which extend from the Hungarian Plain and the Black Sea in the west across the Kazak steppe and Mongolian Plateau to the borders of Manchuria and the Pacific Ocean. On the north, this region is bounded by the thick forests of Siberia and Russia, while its southern frontier confronted the ancient urban civilizations of Anatolia, Iran, Turkestan, and China.

The steppe lands are divided into two distinct geographical zones: the Mongolian Plateau in the east, and the Russian and Kazak steppes in the west. The eastern zone, averaging 1,500 meters or more in elevation, is much higher than the western steppe which lies at around sea level. They are separated by the Pamir, Tien-shan, and Altai mountain ranges. This division is more than topographic, for it has long marked a significant political and cultural frontier. Those nomads on the Mongolian Plateau have always focused their attention on China, while those on the Kazak and southern Russian steppe have had closer connections with the Near East and Europe. Historically, even religions and languages often changed at this point. In the seventeenth and eighteenth centuries, for example, Buddhist Mongols occupied the east, while Muslim Turks dominated the west, a pattern that has continued in modified form down to the present day. For this reason, nomadic empires typically had their borders at this point and those that spanned the whole steppe zone invariably split into at least two parts along this fault line.

Pastoral nomadism was the dominant way of life in Central Eurasia throughout most of its known history because the steppe zone itself was inhospitable to agriculture. This may come as a surprise to those who think of the American Great Plains or Russian steppe as ideal grain-growing areas, but until the introduction of steel plows and steam-driven tractors in the late nineteenth century, it was difficult or impossible to break the thick sod of these permanent grasslands. In addition, the steppe's severely cold winter, short growing season, and relatively low average rainfall (punctuated by cycles of drought) made agriculture less dependable than pastoralism. Therefore, except along the flood plains of major rivers or in sheltered mountain valleys, permanent farming communities were rare. Even in those regions, farming villages were particularly vulnerable to destructive raids by their nomadic neighbors. Many were abandoned in times of political disorder and not reestablished for many generations, if ever.

The history of the nomads of Central Eurasia and their relationships with surrounding regions is, of course, predicated on what the nomads themselves took for granted: their cycles of movement, the demands of stock raising, economic constraints, and basic political organization. While often denigrated as primitive by outside observers, steppe nomadic pastoralism is in fact a sophisticated economic specialization.

THE FIVE ANIMALS

Nomadism in Central Eurasia depends on the exploitation of extensive but seasonal steppe and mountain pastures. Since humans cannot digest grass, raising livestock is an efficient way of exploiting the energy of a grassland's ecosystem. The herds consist, as the Mongols say, of the *five animals*: sheep, goats, horses, cattle, and camels. Of these, sheep and horses are the most important, but the ideal is to have all the animals necessary for both subsistence and transportation so that a family or tribe can approach self-sufficiency in pastoral production. There was never any specialization in the production of a single species (such as developed among the camel-raising Bedouin of the Near East and North Africa), although the proportion of each species within a herd always reflects the constraints imposed by local ecological conditions: a higher percentage of cattle in wetter regions, an increased percentage of goats in areas of marginal pasture, and larger numbers of camels along desert margins. As Table 5.1 illustrates, herd composition is basically similar whether the nomads use the open steppe or mountain pastures.

More than in any other pastoral area, the nomads of Central Eurasia take full advantage of multiple uses of their animals. The relatively rigid distinction between transport animals and subsistence animals that is common elsewhere is unusual here. If an animal can be used for both, it will be used for both. Steppe nomads not only ride horses but also milk mares, eat horse meat (and sometimes blood), and use their skins for leather. Similarly, while the camel is used primarily as a baggage animal, it is also milked, used as a source of hair, and occasionally eaten. Oxen, which are exclusively subsistence animals elsewhere, are also employed to pull carts or carry loads. A Chinese history of the second century B.C. even claimed that a young child first learned to ride a sheep before graduating to a horse!

The horse has always held cultural pride of place among steppe nomads. Indeed, from its inception, traditional steppe pastoralism has been defined by the preeminence it gives to horse raising and horse riding. For

TABLE 5.1   Herd Composition on the Eurasian Steppe by Region

NORTHERN MONGOLIA, 1940S
(PERCENTAGE OF TOTAL LIVESTOCK)

REGION	SHEEP	GOATS	CATTLE	HORSES	CAMELS
Eastern Steppe	58.6	14.0	11.7	12.8	2.9
Khanghai Forest-Steppe	57.7	17.0	13.0	11.1	1.2
Gobi Desert Steppe	51.1	27.6	4.5	9.2	7.6
Altai Mountain Steppe	56.0	29.1	5.7	6.5	2.7
Total	55.8	21.9	8.7	9.9	3.6

TURKESTAN
(PERCENTAGE OF TOTAL LIVESTOCK)

REGION	SHEEP	GOATS	CATTLE	HORSES	CAMELS	DONKEYS	PIGS*
Xinjiang, 1933	71.0	10.0	12.0	6.0	few	--	--
Kuldja, 1877	75.0	6.0	7.0	11.0	1.0	--	--
Kazakhstan, 1920s	51.0	8.4	24.4	12.0	2.2	--	2.0
Kirghizia, 1920s	55.0	13.6	17.0	11.4	1.0	--	1.8
Turkmenia, 1920s	--- 74 ---		12.8	3.8	6.3	3.1	--

(*Pigs are an indication of Russian settlement as they are not found among steppe nomads.)
Source: Lawrence Krader, "The Ecology of Central Asian Pastoralism." Southwestern Journal of Anthropology (1955), 11: 301–326, p. 313.

just as camels transformed the deserts of the Near East from barriers into highways, so horse riding has permitted rapid movement of nomads across vast distances, allowing communication and cooperation among peoples and tribes that are of necessity highly dispersed. The horse figures most prominently in the military exploits of the nomads because it gives them the mobility and power in battle to defeat much larger opponents. The oral epics of steppe peoples have always sung praises to the horse, and its sacrifice was an important ritual in traditional steppe religions. Indeed, the man on horseback is the very symbol of steppe nomadism and, as a metaphor for military and political power, has passed into the cultures of neighboring sedentary societies. Your own city probably has at least one statue (collecting pigeon droppings) of a great man astride an oversized bronze horse. However, while some anthropologists have labelled these nomadic pastoralists "horse cultures," horse raising was never the exclusive focus of any steppe tribe in spite of the animal's cultural and military importance. For although there are no great sheep epics, they are the foundation of the steppe economy, with horse raising only an important adjunct to this more essential task.[10]

Kazak girl getting the sheep in line for milking. Although the steppe nomads have always given pride of place to their horses, their economy is based primarily on sheep raising.

    Sheep and goats are by far the most important subsistence animals and are the mainstay of steppe pastoralism because they reproduce more rapidly than cattle or horses and can consume a wider variety of grasses. They are also the main source of milk and meat for food; wool, hair, and hides used to produce felt, rope, clothing, and storage bags; and dried dung which can be used as fuel. Large stock such as cattle, camels, and horses also provide a secondary source of milk and meat. Fermented mare's milk (*kumiss*), in particular, has been the favorite drink of the steppe nomads for thousands of years.

On the Mongolian Plateau, sheep historically accounted for between 50 and 60 percent of all animals raised, although their numbers declined in regions where the pasture was poor in grasses, such as in the arid deserts, at high altitudes, or in the forest margins. The proportion of sheep reached its maximum among nomads who were engaged in significant trade with urban markets. For example, under the same ecological conditions in nineteenth-century Kuldja (Ili Valley), sheep constituted 76 percent of the flocks among the Kazaks, for whom the sale of lambskins was very important, as compared with 54 percent among the more subsistence-oriented Kalmuks.[11]

The number of horses and cattle are highest in those parts of the steppe with access to abundant pasture and water. Steppe horses are particularly well adapted to the harsh conditions of the region. Although small in size, they are very hardy and capable of living on the open range throughout the winter without fodder, conditions that would kill other breeds of horses. Herds of horses and cattle must be grazed separately from the sheep and goats because the latter crop the grass too closely for large stock to graze after them. Therefore special pastures are reserved for grazing large stock or they are pastured ahead of the sheep and goats when a single area is used.

Camels found on the Eurasian steppe are primarily of the two-humped variety known as Bactrian. In addition to providing transport for nomadic families, camels were the mainstay of the overland caravan route for more than 2,000 years. Unlike their one-humped relatives in Arabia, Bactrian camels have a thick wool coat that enables them to survive cold winters. Camel's hair is highly valued for making cloth and continues to be an important export to the world market today. The percentage of camels is highest in arid areas where it is more difficult to raise horses and cattle. For example, in the desert region between the Caspian and Aral seas, the Turkmen kept three times as many camels in their herds than the steppe-dwelling Kazaks to their north. Similarly, the Mongols maintained more than twice as many camels in the Gobi Desert than on the Eastern Steppe, and six times more than in the Khanghai Forest Steppe (Table 5.1).

THE MIGRATORY CYCLE

Here, as elsewhere, the nomadic life is based on the ability of people to move with their animals throughout the seasonal migration. Shelter and household goods must be portable. In this respect, nothing is more striking than the yurt used throughout the Eurasian steppe. It consists of a series of folding wooden lattice frameworks that are set in a circle around a door frame. Curved wooden spokes are tied onto the top of the lattice frame and linked to a round wooden crown to form a hemispherical or conical dome, depending on the angle at which they are bent. The resulting framework is lightweight yet exceptionally strong and cannot be easily blown down. In the winter, the yurt is covered by thick mats of wool felt which provide insulation against even bitter cold. In the summer, the side felts are removed and replaced by reed matting that allows air to circulate. In ancient times, yurts were erected on large carts and moved around as a unit, but by the Middle Ages this practice had become relatively rare. However, the use of wheeled carts pulled by oxen or horses to transport goods has always been characteristic of nomadic life in Central Eurasia, whereas in the neighboring regions of the Near East, nomads used no wheeled vehicles. Those families that could not afford yurts employed simpler felt-covered huts.[12]

The migratory cycle took two basic forms: horizontal movements across the steppe and vertical movements in and out of mountains. Those nomads who used the flat steppe made much longer migrations because they moved to more northern latitudes to find summer pasture, while their mountain-dwelling neighbors could accomplish the same feat simply by changing the altitude of their camps. The Kazak nomads who migrated across the steppe between the banks of the Caspian and Aral seas often travelled more than 500 kilometers round-trip, while the Kirghiz pastoralists in the Pamir Mountain region moved less than 100 kilometers because

Erecting a yurt frame which will be covered with panels of felt. The yurt can withstand the severe cold and high winds common to Central Eurasia in the winter.

their winter camps in lower-lying mountain valleys were close to their summer camps at the snow line.

Regardless of whether horizontal or vertical movements are involved, limited winter pasture has always been the key constraint on pastoral production. The range of choices for a winter camp is restricted because it must provide ready access to water, shelter from the wind, and sufficient pasture to last the season. Once selected, winter camps tend to remain fixed and families return to the same site each year. Winter camps have the highest population density, sometimes including many hundreds of yurts. Favored locations include lower-lying mountain valleys, river flood plains, and depressions on the steppe. Wind-swept areas free of snow are preferred, but if the ground is covered with snow, then the horses can be let loose to paw through the icy surface and uncover the pasture below. The pasture can then be used by other animals. Winter pastures provide only a bare minimum of subsistence, and under open-range conditions, the livestock lose considerable weight. As a somewhat sardonic Kazak proverb explains: "Sheep are fat in the summer, strong in the autumn, weak in the winter, and dead by spring." Winter herding is also a dangerous business, for shepherds freeze along with the animals if caught unprepared.

Aided by spring rains, steppe pastures bloom after the winter snows melt and camping groups disperse widely to take advantage of the newly abundant pasture. Moving deep into these grasslands, the nomads draw on seasonally available pools of melted snow in low-lying areas to water their cattle and horses. In such pasture the sheep do not have to be watered at all, getting the moisture they need from the grass and dew. Animals weak from the winter's cold and hunger begin to recover their weight and vitality. Lambing commences in the spring and fresh milk becomes available. Although normally considered one of the best of times, there is always the potential for disaster if the pastures fail to appear on time or the temperatures drop too low. The greatest danger is an unseasonable snowstorm that covers the steppe with snow or ice. In only a few days under these conditions, much of the livestock, particularly the newborn young, can die. Although such an event might occur but once a generation, it can cripple the pastoral economy for years.

Movement to the summer pastures begins when the spring grasses begin to dry out or are consumed by the animals. Households are most dispersed during this season in order to take advantage of all available pasture. In these summer pastures, the animals rapidly gain weight. To maximize production, the herd is often split so that the milking animals can remain near the camp while the other animals are taken to better grazing in more distant pastures. Women devote considerable effort to milk processing. Mares are milked separately to produce *kumiss*, but the milk from sheep, goats, and cows is mixed together to make butter, cheese, or yoghurt which can be dried into rocklike balls (*qrut*) for later use. The

Kazak women and girls spend most of the summer processing sheep and cow's milk into dried yogurt which can be stored indefinitely. The milk is first boiled and then set overnight to ferment into yogurt. The fresh yogurt is then put in a porous bag to separate the solids from the liquids. The resulting soft paste is then rolled into balls and set to dry in the sun until it becomes as hard as rock.

summer pastures are abandoned at the onset of cooler weather when the nomads begin the return migration to their winter quarters. The sheep are normally sheared at this time. Most of the wool is reserved for making felt which is produced by first beating the wool, pouring boiling water on it, and then rolling it back and forth until the fibers lock to create the fabric. Felts are often decorated by applying a layer of dyed wool to the surface before rolling. Heavy felt panels made of coarse wool are used to cover yurts, while the more delicate wool sheared from the lambs is used to make cloaks, winter boots, or saddle blankets. Wool may also be spun into thread, dyed, and woven into rugs, saddlebags, or knotted carpets. Hair from goats is used to make ropes and coarse cloth, while camels' hair is collected for sale or for making fine cloth. Autumn is also traditionally the time to breed sheep in order to ensure a spring lambing, for lambs dropped out of season on the open steppe have a high mortality rate.

Pastoralists who employ stored fodder cut it in the fall, but the more traditional strategy is to graze the animals away from the winter encampment as long as possible to preserve the nearby pasture for the hardest times. While pastoralists attempt to maintain as many live animals as possible, they must also carefully calculate how many animals they can reasonably support through the winter. Where nomads cannot sell their animals to sedentary markets, surplus livestock is slaughtered and the meat smoked for use during the winter. Before Central Eurasia was incorporated into the expanding Russian and Chinese empires in the seventeenth and eighteenth centuries, autumn was also traditionally the time when nomads preferred to raid sedentary areas because their horses were strong, the work of the pastoral cycle was largely done, and the farmers had their harvests completed. Such raids provided grain to help the nomads through the winter.

CONTROL OF RESOURCES

In steppe societies, pasture was held in common by extended kinship groups. Nomadic migrations were not random, but within a defined range of pastures to which a group had access. Where pasture was dependable, nomads tended to have only a few fixed camping sites to which they returned each year. This was particularly true in the forest steppe zone where pastoralists might establish permanent winter villages with barns for their animals and cultivate nearby fields for grain and fodder. Where only marginal pastures were available, the migratory cycle displayed both more frequent movement and greater variation in the location of camps. In the absence of state control, a pastoralist's range was defined by the power of his kinship group. The strongest tribes and clans laid claim to the best pastures at the best time of year; weaker groups could use them only after they had moved on. Right of transit through another's territory was a generally accepted principle, although disputes could easily arise when migrating groups were accused of moving too slowly in order to graze their animals. While nomads defended proprietary rights in such fixed investments as wells or scarce winter campsites (particularly if they had built barns or houses), the concept of exclusive land ownership was poorly developed.

The nomads' ability to readily transport their herds and families had considerable political importance. In particular, it made them practically invulnerable to conquest by neighboring sedentary states until modern times. For, unlike farming communities, when steppe nomads were threatened with invasion they could move their entire population and pastoral economy out of harm's way. Attackers encountered nothing but an empty plain with dust on the horizon, and with only abandoned campsites to occupy, they were invariably forced to leave. The nomads would then harass a retreating army all the way back to the frontier, often inflicting such heavy losses that they would not think of returning any time soon. The Persian king Darius the Great lost much of his army when he attempted to chase the Scythian nomads across the steppes of southern Russia in 514 B.C. The Chinese also complained of the same tactics four centuries later during their wars with the Hsiung-nu of Mongolia. No match for China's large armies, the Hsiung-nu made it a point to retreat before they were attacked:

> If the battle is going well for them they will advance, but if not, they will retreat, for they do not consider it a disgrace to run away. Their only concern is self-advantage, and they know nothing of propriety or righteousness.[13]

On the other hand, attacks by other pastoral peoples who sought to occupy key pasture areas permanently could not be resisted by strategic retreats. If successful, these groups could occupy vital winter campsites and thereby take control of the whole area. Given a choice between submitting or fleeing, many defeated tribes maintained their autonomy by emigration. The history of Central Eurasia is therefore replete with examples of whole peoples periodically relocating themselves hundreds, even thousands, of kilometers away, where they then established new migratory ranges. Such mass movements necessarily displaced other tribes in their turn, eventually leading to invasions of sedentary areas by those nomads occupying the margin of the steppe. Such large-scale emigrations were exceptional, however, the results of political decisions by tribes to find a new home range rather than fight for their old one. They were not the product of hungry sheep seeking new pasture.

SOCIAL ORGANIZATION

THE FAMILY CAMP GROUP

Throughout Central Eurasia, pastoralists shared similar principles of organization. The minimal social unit on the steppe was the household, usually measured by the number of tents, and the minimal economic and political unit was the camp group (*aul*, Turkish; *ayil*, Mongolian). The term was applied both to the small, mobile camping groups consisting of only a dozen yurts and to the hundreds that might occupy a single large winter camping area. Ideally, it was composed of patrilineal relatives who shared common pasture and camped together when possible. This description of the Kalmuk pattern was typical of the ideal:

> An extended family may consist of several generations of consanguine male relatives, connected more or less closely by patrilineal descent, together with wives and immature children, and headed by the senior male of the senior family. After marriage a son may demand his livestock and move away, but ideally he should remain with his father and brothers. Moving away is a sign of trouble between kin. There is a tendency for extended family herds to be held in common as long as possible.[14]

Camping groups composed of extended families were well adapted to pastoral production. As we saw in the last chapter, they could supply all the labor needed to maximize herding without having to regularly hire outsiders. Because pasture was held in common and a herdsman could efficiently look after hundreds of animals, individually owned livestock could be combined to create a single large herd. Similarly, camping as extended family groups made it easier for the women to carry out their cooperative tasks like milk processing or felt making. But a man was always responsible for his livestock and, as noted above, if he disagreed with their management he had the right to remove them and go elsewhere. Large groups of kin also provided protection against theft and served as allies in disputes with other groups.

MARRIAGE ALLIANCES AND THE ROLE OF WOMEN

Women in steppe nomadic pastoral societies had more authority and autonomy than their sisters in neighboring sedentary societies, or pastoral nomadic societies in other regions for that matter. Women played a key role in daily economic life. Although the details cannot be confirmed for the entire history of Central Eurasia, most visitors made comments similar to those of Johann de Plano Carpini, the Pope's envoy to the Mongols in the thirteenth century:

> The men do nothing but occupy themselves with their arrows and to a small extent look after their herds; for the rest they go hunting and practice archery....Both men and women stay in the saddle for a long time....All the work rests on the shoulders of the women; they make the fur coats, clothes, shoes, bootlegs and everything else made from leather. They also drive the carts and mend them, load the camels, and are very quick and efficient in all their work. All the women wear trousers, and some of them shoot with the bow as accurately as the men.[15]

Although in formal terms these societies were strongly patrilineal, in many groups steppe nomadic women participated in tribal politics and sometimes even war. Herodotus stated that while among the Scythian nomads of the Black Sea steppe, women were generally secluded, among the neighboring Sarmatian tribes, women participated in raids and could not marry until they had killed an enemy in battle. He also noted that these tribes were occasionally led by queens, one of whom had defeated an invading Persian army and killed its emperor. Later Chinese accounts also regularly depicted elite women in critical positions, especially during conflicts over royal succession. Medieval Arab and Persian writers were continually astounded at the freedom of steppe nomadic women and the prominent role they played in court politics. The best-documented example of this was seen in the early Mongol empire in the thirteenth century when the senior wife of the "Great Khan" was the normal choice for regent during the interregnum following the death of her husband.

Marriage rules throughout Central Eurasia stress the importance of clan exogamy; that is, partners should always come from a group that is not patrilineally related to them in the previous five, seven, or even nine generations. This is not to say they married strangers; the preferred choice of a bride was from a man's mother's clan, so that over time reciprocal marriage alliances would bind the two groups together.[16] Such reciprocal alliance patterns gave women an important structural role linking tribes together. So daughters, while lost to their natal families, still bound them to other groups. For example, the Unggirad, the clan of Chinggis Khan's wife Börte, were fond of proclaiming that their political power lay in the strength of their marriage alliances and not on their military prowess:

> They are our daughters and daughters of our daughters, who, become princesses by their marriage, serve as shields against our enemies and by the petitions they present to their husbands obtain favors for us.[17]

Marriage involved the payment of a large brideprice in livestock, generally collected from a large group of agnates, although a man might live with his prospective in-laws and do brideservice instead. Among the nineteenth-century Kazak, this amounted to between 50 and 100 animals, preferably horses, measured in groups of nine (an auspicious number). However, a woman also brought a significant dowry to the marriage, sometimes equal to the brideprice, that included both household furnishings and luxury goods. (Chinggis Khan, for example, made his first political alliance by giving a valuable sable skin he received as dowry to the powerful khan of a neighboring tribe.) Marriage created a new household and a man could then demand his share of the herd. The youngest son not only got his own share but also eventually inherited the remaining property of his father. This practice, ultimogeniture, was a form of social security, since the youngest son was expected to support his elderly parents. Rank, as opposed to personal property, generally went to the eldest son upon his father's death although a man could legally appoint any son as his heir.

CLAN AND LINEAGE ORGANIZATION

The household and camp group were the most important units in the daily life of the Central Eurasian nomad, but to deal with the world it was necessary to organize into larger units. Within the nomadic world, political and social organization was based on a model of nested kinship groups, the *conical clan*. The conical clan was an extensive patrilineal kinship organization in which members of a common descent group were ranked and segmented along genealogical lines (Figure 5.1). This genealogical charter was important because it justified rights to pasture, created social or military obligations between kinship groups, and established the legitimacy of local political authority. When nomads lost their autonomy to sedentary governments, the

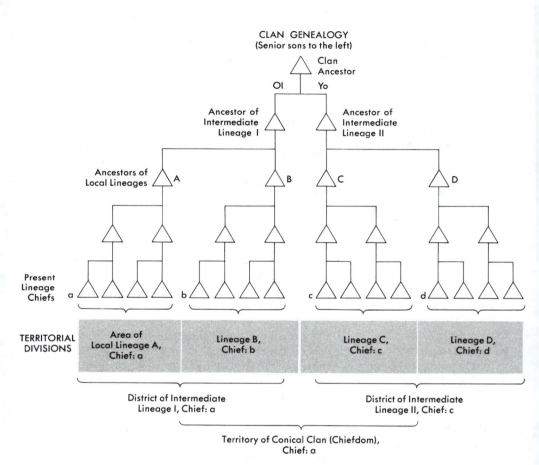

FIGURE 5.1 Schematic model of chiefdom integrated on conical clan lines.
Marshall Sahlins, *Tribesmen.* Englewood Cliffs, NJ: Prentice-Hall, Inc., 1968, p. 25.

political importance of this extensive genealogical system disappeared and kinship links remained important only at the local level.[18]

This segmentary structure was more than a mental construct. It was reinforced by permanent chieftains who provided leadership and internal order for lineages, clans, and whole tribes. The idiom of kinship was the common currency for determining the legitimacy of leadership. Elder generations were superior in rank to younger generations, just as elder brothers were superior in rank to younger brothers. By extension, lineages and clans were hierarchically ranked on the basis of seniority. There were also hierarchical distinctions between noble lineages (white bone) and common lineages (black bone), but from the lowest to highest all members of the tribe claimed descent from a common ancestor. This meant that deviations from the ideal had to be disguised by manipulating, distorting, or even inventing genealogies that justified changes in the status quo. Powerful individuals saw ancestors retroactively promoted at the expense of declining elites and "structural amnesia" relegated genealogically senior (but politically weak) lines of descent to oblivion. This tradition produced ruling lineages of unparalleled duration. The direct descendants of the Hsiung-nu founder Mao-tun retained their authority for 600 years, the direct descendants of Chinggis Khan for 700 years, and a single unbroken Turkish dynasty (of Central Eurasian heritage) ruled over the Ottoman Empire for more than 600 years.

It would be a mistake, however, to assume that the conical clan was the true foundation of supratribal government. Though based on a kinship idiom, particularly in describing the organization of component tribes, the nomadic polities of Central Eurasia encompassed millions of people. For example, the Kazaks numbered well over four million in the nineteenth century, while the Chinese estimated the ancient Hsiung-nu and medieval Turks at one million each. This scale of organization was possible in part because "genealogical descent" in central Eurasia was more similar to what we would today label ethnic identity than to the sharply defined genealogical tribes of the Bedouin. With each reorganization of the steppe, new identities would emerge. For example, the Mongols began as a fairly small group, but after their great conquests many of the formerly distinct neighboring tribes began to identify themselves as "Mongols," often retaining their older tribal affiliation as a clan name.

Even so, such large empires went far beyond the needs of simple (or even complex) pastoralism. In fact, they were designed for something quite different: the permanent extortion of the world's great sedentary civilizations.

POLITICAL ORGANIZATION

Large-scale political organization among steppe nomads was designed to deal primarily with external relations. Indeed, it could only be financed by bringing in revenue from the outside because the pastoral economy was too extensive and undiversified to support a sophisticated state structure. Rulers of steppe empires therefore did not expect to support themselves by extracting revenue from their nomadic subjects, rather the reverse. They used the military might of their nomad followers to extract revenue from outsiders which could not only pay for the administration of the empire but also could be redistributed among the potentially rebellious component tribes to keep them happy. In the southern Russian steppe, this revenue came from the control of vital links in overland trade networks which supported such empires as the Scythians, the Khazars, and the Golden Horde. As an intermediary between different states, the nomad empires here could often set the terms of trade and grow wealthy in the process. Nomads on the Mongolian frontier, on the other hand, had to take a more active role because they faced a single state—China—which attempted to restrict trade and contact with the nomads.

THE IMPERIAL CONFEDERACY

The nomads of the Mongolian Plateau faced a difficult political and economic problem in dealing with China. How could a people who numbered only one million in total, were divided into many tribal groups, and were scattered across a vast distance deal effectively with the world's largest agrarian state? In particular, how could such a small number of nomads ever hope to stand as the political equal of a state fifty to one hundred times its own size in population, ruled over by a powerful centralized government with access to an immense revenue stream, and possessed of a standing army and Great Wall that said, Nomads Keep Out? By all theories of economics and government this should have been impossible, yet it was historically true.

Such organizational problems were successfully overcome by creating an *imperial confederacy*, that is, a confederation using the principles of tribal organization and indigenous tribal leaders to rule at the local level while maintaining an imperial state structure with an exclusive monopoly that controlled foreign and military affairs. It had three basic levels of organization. At the top, the imperial leadership of the empire was drawn from the ruling lineage of the tribe that founded the state. At a secondary level, collateral relations of the ruler were usually appointed as governors to supervise the indigenous tribal leadership in each region. These imperial appointees served as the key links between the central administration and the indigenous tribal leaders. The local tribal leaders constituted the third level of organization. They were members of the indigenous elites of each tribe and, although structurally inferior to imperial appointees, they retained considerable autonomy because of their close ties to their own people who would even follow them in revolt if the imperial commanders overstepped their authority.[19]

Imperial confederacies maintained levels of organization far in excess of any needed to handle tribal relations or livestock problems. They emerged in Mongolia as a structural response by the nomads to the problems of organizing themselves to manipulate China. No single tribe along the frontier could hope to deal effectively with a united China, but a single empire with an imperial administration could wield a power that even China could not ignore. Uniting the nomad tribes of Mongolia by conquest was only the first step in building an effective empire, because the nomadic state could not depend solely on the threat of military force to maintain cohesion, it also had to offer real economic benefits. In exchange for accepting a subordinate political position, the leaders of the confederacy's component tribes received access to Chinese luxury goods and trade opportunities they could not have gained themselves. Therefore imperial confederacies owed their continued financial success and political stability to their relentless exploitation of resources from outside the steppe, and exclusive control of foreign affairs was central to their power.

THE OUTER FRONTIER STRATEGY

The foreign policies of all imperial confederacies of Mongolia had a single aim: to extract benefits from China directly by raiding or indirectly through subsidies, and to establish institutionalized border-trade agreements. Without such revenue the imperial confederacy would collapse. Yet to succeed, they had to influence decision making at the very highest levels of government because foreign policy was made at court and not by frontier governors or border officials. To this end, the nomads implemented a terroristic *outer frontier strategy* to magnify their power. Taking full advantage of their ability to suddenly strike deep into China and then retreat before the Chinese had time to retaliate, they could threaten the frontier at any time. Such violence and the disruption it caused encouraged the Chinese to negotiate agreements favorable to the nomads.

The outer frontier strategy had three major elements: violent raiding to terrify the Chinese imperial court, the alternation of war and peace to increase the amount of subsidies and trade privileges granted by the Chinese, and the deliberate refusal to occupy Chinese land even after great victories. The threat of violence always lurked beneath the surface of even the most peaceful interactions. A Chinese defector working for the nomads once warned some Han dynasty envoys of the danger they faced in very simple terms:

> Just make sure that the silks and grainstuffs you bring the Hsiung-nu are the right measure and quality, that's all. What's the need for talking? If the goods you deliver are up to measure and good quality, all right. But if there is any deficiency or the quality is no good, then when the autumn harvest comes we will take our horses and trample all over your crops![20]

The Chinese had three choices when confronted with frontier violence: respond defensively and ignore the nomads' demands, fight them aggressively by attacking the steppe, or buy peace with expensive treaties. Each approach produced its own set of problems. If their requests were ignored, the nomads could continually raid the frontier, looting to get what they wanted and wreaking havoc with China's border population.

The Ming dynasty (1368 to 1644), which persisted longest with such a nonintercourse policy, suffered more nomad invasions than any other Chinese dynasty. The political and military pressure created by nomad attacks therefore eventually forced all Chinese dynasties to attempt the other solutions. The alternatives of aggressive military action or appeasement were, however, only slightly less problematic. Paying "tribute" to horse-riding barbarians violated the very essence of a Sinocentric world order in which the Chinese emperor was (in theory) paramount. Such payments were particularly galling, since from the beginning the Chinese recognized that in terms of population, military strength, and economic production, they were far more powerful than the nomads. Therefore, all Chinese dynasties attempted at least once to resolve their "nomad problem" by resorting to punitive campaigns against the steppe tribes.

But success in warfare always proved illusive. While the nomads could be driven away from the frontier, they could not be conquered because they were mobile and simply moved out of sight until the Chinese armies withdrew. Aggressive frontier warfare was also economically far more disruptive for the Chinese than for the nomads. It drained the treasury and strained the peasantry with ever-increasing demands for taxes and soldiers. For the nomads, war was cheap. Steppe households were always prepared to provide horses, weapons, and supplies on short notice; and the loot collected in China repaid this investment many times over. Finally, continuous military operations threatened the balance of power at the Chinese court by increasing the political influence of the military and the emperor at the expense of the civilian bureaucrats. Threatened with the loss of their hegemony, these officials argued that military campaigns were always far more expensive than simply paying the nomads to stay away. These bureaucrats constituted an important internal lobby for gaining peace by appeasing the nomads. Consequently, no native Chinese dynasty proved able to maintain an aggressive foreign policy against the nomads for longer than the reign of a single emperor. Although their military strategies differed, each dynasty was finally forced to conclude that war was not the answer to its nomad problem.

OF PREDATORS AND PREY

The relationship between China and the nomads of Mongolia had its own largely unrecognized logic. Because centralized empires on the steppe were economically dependent on exploiting a prosperous and united China, they were structurally linked to them. It is no accident that nomadic empires came into existence simultaneously with the unification of China and disappeared when China's political and economic organization collapsed. As Table 5.2 illustrates, there was a close correlation between native Chinese dynasties and imperial confederacies in Mongolia. This

TABLE 5.2   Cycles of rule: Major dynasties in China and steppe empires in Mongolia

			CHINESE DYNASTIES			STEPPE EMPIRES
			NATIVE		FOREIGN	
CYCLE 1	(1)		Ch'in and Han (221 BC–AD 220)			HSIUNG-NU (209 BC–AD 155)
	(2)		Chinese dynasties during the period of Disruption (220–581)			Hsien-pi (130–180)
		(3)			T'o-pa Wei (386–556) and the other foreign dynasties directly before and after	Jou-jan
CYCLE 2	(4)		Sui and T'ang (581–907)		FIRST TURKISH (552–630) SECOND TURKISH (683–734) UIGHUR (745–840)	
	(5)		Sung (960–1279)			
		(6)			Liao (Khitan) (907–1125)	
		(7)			Chin (Jurchen) (1115–1234)	
		(8)			Yüan (Mongol)--------- MONGOL (1206–1368)	
CYCLE 3	(9)		Ming (1368–1644)			Oirats Eastern Mongols
		(10)			Ch'ing (Manchu) (1616–1912)	Zunghars

Source: Thomas Barfield, *The Perilous Frontier*. Cambridge, MA and Oxford: Blackwell, 1989, p. 13.

was particularly true of the relationship of the Han dynasty and the Hsiung-nu and the T'ang dynasty and the Turks/Uighurs. For this reason, nomadic empires in Mongolia were intent on exploiting, not conquering, China. Native Chinese dynasties never feared their replacement by nomads, but the nomads' potential for disruption. Indeed, with the exception of the Mongol empire, foreign dynasties that established empires

This old Kazak man's traditional hat made of silk and sheepskin is a modern example of the historic links between the steppe nomads and China. From 2,000 years nomad demands for such luxury goods as silk presented succeeding Chinese dynasties with a key foreign policy problem.

in China were all from Manchuria, and products of a very different tribal tradition.

Although raids and crude extortion may have characterized the early interactions between nomad empires and native dynasties in China, they eventually evolved into a more symbiotic relationship. To maintain their lucrative trade relations and imperial subsidies, leaders of imperial confederacies would give military assistance to declining Chinese dynasties to protect them from domestic rebellions. The most prominent example was the importance of Uighur aid in putting down the An Lu-shan Rebellion against the T'ang dynasty when it was on the verge of extinction in the mid-eighth century. As leaders of a steppe empire, the Uighurs sent the cavalry troops who broke the back of the rebel army in battle and helped restore the dynasty to power. By 840, the Uighurs were collecting 500,000 rolls of silk a year in subsidies from China, although because they presented a few horses annually at court, the Chinese officially deemed them "tributaries," an unrivaled example of the literate sedentary world's ability to disguise embarrassing facts about its relationship with the steppe. But perhaps the best way to understand an imperial confederacy is to turn to the Hsiung-nu, the first and most stable nomadic empire the world has ever seen.

THE HSIUNG-NU EMPIRE

The Hsiung-nu empire was founded by their leader (*Shan-yü*) Mao-tun in 210 B.C., contemporaneous with the reestablishment of a unified China under the Han dynasty. Although the nomads on the steppe took no part in the civil war that followed the collapse of the Ch'in dynasty, they did threaten to devastate border regions by raiding, wreaking havoc, and stealing anything that could be carried off. They also intrigued with frontier commanders against the central government. Such raids and border intrigues induced the Han emperor to attack the Hsiung-nu in 200 through 201 B.C., but the war ended disastrously when the nomads encircled his army and he had to sue for peace to escape capture. It was the most humiliating defeat that the Chinese were ever to suffer at the hands of the Hsiung-nu, and the emperor sent envoys to the *Shan-yü* to negotiate peace and establish the *ho-ch'in* ("marriage alliance") policy as a framework for relations between the two states. The *ho-ch'in* policy had four major provisions:

1. The Chinese made fixed annual payments in goods to the Hsiung-nu (which at their maximum amounted to somewhat less than 100,000 liters of grain, 200,000 liters of wine, and 92,000 meters of silk);
2. the Han gave a princess in marriage to the *Shan-yü*;
3. the Hsiung-nu and Han were ranked as co-equal states;
4. the Great Wall was the official boundary between the two states.[21]

In exchange for these benefits the Hsiung-nu agreed to keep the peace.

As generous as the treaty provisions seemed to the Chinese, the Hsiung-nu were far from satisfied. After expanding their own power in Mongolia they renewed their raids on China and then sent envoys seeking peace. Pointing out that the Hsiung-nu were now the paramount power on the northern frontier, Mao-tun demanded a new peace treaty with more subsidies and frontier trade, stating:

All the people who live by drawing the bow are now united into one family and the entire region of the north is at peace. Thus I wish to lay down my weapons, rest my soldiers, and turn my horses to pasture, and forget the recent affair [of raiding China] and restore the old pact, that the peoples of the border may have the peace that they enjoyed in former times, that the young may grow to manhood, the old live out their lives in security, and generation after generation enjoy peace and comfort.[22]

The Han court decided the Hsiung-nu were far too powerful to attack and so agreed to renew the treaty and open border markets. Mao-tun died peacefully in 174 B.C., leaving his huge empire to his son.

After Mao-tun's death, the Hsiung-nu made border trade their key demand. Since the Chinese feared that closer economic links between their own frontier people and the nomads would inevitably weaken imperial control of the border region, they had erected barriers to prevent all contact with the steppe nomads, including trade. Now the ho-ch'in subsidy payments, although very profitable for the Hsiung-nu political elite, could not adequately compensate the larger number of ordinary nomads who were forced to forgo raiding. Unless they gained access to regular markets where they could trade live animals or other pastoral products for grain, cloth, or metal, the Hsiung-nu leadership could not keep the peace. The Shan-yü extorted trade rights the same way he had extorted subsidies: by raiding or threatening to raid China. Loot from such raids kept the Hsiung-nu tribesmen supplied until China finally agreed to open regular border markets. Once established, these border markets quickly became important trade centers to which the Hsiung-nu flocked. The whole relationship between China and the nomads became more stable and old hostilities were forgotten: "From the Shan-yü on down all the Hsiung-nu grew friendly with the Han, coming and going along the Great Wall."[23]

This peaceful situation lasted until 133 B.C. when, hoping to militarily defeat the Hsiung-nu, the Han court abruptly abandoned the ho-ch'in policy by mounting a surprise attack on the nomads, beginning more than a half century of frontier warfare. The wars failed. Although China threw massive armies against the Hsiung-nu, occasionally defeated them in battle, and encouraged the defection of some tribes, they found nothing to conquer but empty land. And lack of supplies forced Chinese armies to retreat within a few months of each campaign. The cost of these frontier wars in men, horses, and money proved so high that the dynasty practically bankrupted itself. So after decades of war, the Chinese concluded they had no more chance of conquering the nomads of the steppe than they had of governing the fish in the sea. By 90 B.C. they had abandoned their attacks on the steppe and adopted a completely defensive position, cutting off trade and repulsing raids.[24]

Ironically, it was this stalemate that badly undermined the Hsiung-nu imperial confederacy. With no subsidies, no trade, and borders too strong to raid, the Hsiung-nu sought to renew the old treaties, but China now insisted that any new agreement take place within the framework of the "tributary system" in which the nomads would be required to pay homage to the Han emperor, send a hostage to court, and pay tribute to China. It was a relationship the Hsiung-nu considered unacceptable:

> "That is not the way things were done under the old alliance," the *Shan-yü* objected. "Under the old alliance the Han always sent us an imperial princess, as well as allotments of silks, foodstuffs, and other goods, in order to secure peace along the border, while we for our part refrained from making trouble at the border. Now you want to go against old ways and make me send my son as hostage. I have no use for such proposals."[25]

The stalemate continued until 53 B.C. when, after splitting into factions during a bitter civil war, one *Shan-yü* agreed to accept the Chinese demands. Surprisingly, the tributary system proved a sham. In return for formal compliance, the Hsiung-nu received even larger gifts and better border markets. Once they discovered its true nature, the Hsiung-nu actively demanded the right to present "tribute" and send hostages to court because they profited so handsomely. They threatened the Chinese with invasion if not allowed to come. When the system was regularized around A.D. 50, it is estimated that the annual cost of direct subsidies to the frontier tribes amounted to about $130 million in goods which was equivalent to one-third of the Han government's payroll or 7 percent of the empire's total revenue.[26] Such a sum would still be considered significant today in Mongolia, but 2,000 years ago it represented an absolutely astounding amount of revenue, given the much smaller size of the ancient Chinese economy. Under the tributary system, the relationship between the Han dynasty and the Hsiung-nu became so close that nomads acted as "frontier guarding barbarians," protecting China from attacks by other tribes from the steppe such as the Wu-huan and Hsien-pi, and, not coincidentally, milking the dynasty for more subsidies. Even though the Hsiung-nu lost control of the other steppe because of a second civil war, they retained their importance by using Chinese aid to fend off other rivals.

So important was this relationship that the Hsiung-nu provided one of the Han dynasty's last bulwarks against domestic rebels when China fell into civil war in 180. But because nomad empires were dependent on revenue provided by a prosperous and stable dynasty, they could not survive its collapse. With its fall in 220, the nomads had no rich provinces to loot or governments to scare and their subsidy payments disappeared. Under such conditions, centralization proved impossible to maintain and the tribes in Mongolia reverted to anarchy. An empire as powerful and centralized as that of the Hsiung-nu would not emerge for another 300 years when the Turks were able to exploit a newly reunified T'ang China and establish a relationship structurally similar to that of the Han and Hsiung-nu.

THE NOMADS WHO CONQUERED THE WORLD

Of all the world's nomads, none are more famous but less understood than the Mongols who conquered most of Eurasia in the thirteenth century. Under the leadership of Chinggis Khan and his successors, Mongol armies annihilated every opponent they met in battle and created a world empire that ran from the Pacific Ocean to the Danube River, from the frozen forests of Siberia to the muggy shores of the Persian Gulf. Indeed, these conquests were so vast that it seemed that no land where a steppe pony could ride was safe from the Mongol onslaught. Even the parts of Eurasia that the Mongols did not conquer often seemed to have been saved more by chance than a stiff defense: Chinggis halted his armies on the banks of the Indus River in 1222 and refused to proceed further into India because he said it was "too hot." The Mongol armies that easily overran Russia and Eastern Europe during a series of campaigns between 1237 and 1242 only halted further attacks because their leaders decided that taking part in the election of a new Mongol khan was more important than wiping out the knights of Western Europe and sacking Rome. By the time the Mongol storm had abated at the end of the thirteenth century and the empire had divided into four successor states, the Mongols had achieved what no conquerors, ancient or modern, had ever accomplished before: uniting most of the Eurasian landmass in a single state. Who were these guys? And how did such a small group of nomads come to conquer most of the world?

THE RISE OF CHINGGIS KHAN

Temüjin, the future Chinggis Khan, was an unlikely aspirant for the title of world conqueror. At the time of his birth around 1167 the Mongols were only a minor power on the steppe, their confederation having been destroyed a generation earlier in attacks by rival nomadic tribes aided by the Jurchen rulers of northern China. Temüjin's father was only a minor Mongol chief, and his murder by an enemy tribe when Temüjin was still a young boy left the family in a precarious position. Deserted by even their own relatives and forced to flee into the mountains without livestock, they survived by hunting marmots and birds, fishing, and gathering wild plants. While this was not a very promising start for a career in steppe politics, Temüjin did at least have the proper descent to compete for Mongol leadership, and upon reaching maturity he began his rise by attracting followers as a successful warrior chief. His considerable talents were soon recognized by more senior Mongol leaders who, seemingly unable to abide one another, elected Temüjin their tribal khan around 1190. This position was one of little power, however, for the Mongols were not united and were prone to desert their khan at the first sign of trouble. But such a position did allow Temüjin to become an important leader in the Kereyid confederation as a subordinate to his political patron, To'oril Khan, the Kereyid chief.

Temüjin served To'oril Khan well, even helping to restore him to power in 1196 and aiding in the defeat of the rival Tatar tribe a little later. He also helped the Kereyid win victories against the Naiman, another rival confederation in Mongolia. Yet the same victories that raised him to prominence also incited jealousy. When Temüjin asked for a marriage alliance with To'oril Khan after a great victory in 1203, the Kereyid leader refused and then attempted to poison his former client. Anticipating his swift demise, most of the Mongol clans deserted Temüjin. He retreated to Lake Baljuna with only 4,600 loyal troops. Then Temüjin's fortune suddenly turned for the better, for when an envoy reported the Kereyid were busy feasting—meaning mostly drunk—he immediately used the opportunity to attack them. After three days of fierce fighting, To'oril Khan was forced to flee and lost his head soon thereafter. Temüjin became ruler of the very Kereyid confederation which months before had been on the verge of destroying him.

This sudden change in fortune inspired an alliance of his enemies led by the Naiman. After reorganizing his army, Temüjin met them in battle a year later (1204). Had he lost, it would have ended his career, but he won a major victory, defeating the Naiman and scattering their allies. While many campaigns would follow, from this point he was master of Mongolia. At a great meeting of the steppe tribes in 1206, a *khuriltai*, Temüjin's leadership was confirmed and he was proclaimed Chinggis Khan, a title by which the rest of the world would come to know him.

MONGOL POLITICAL AND MILITARY ORGANIZATION

More than half of Chinggis Khan's adult life was consumed by the tribal politics and steppe warfare necessary to unite the nomads under his rule. Having finally become master of the Mongolian steppe at the age of forty, he would spend the remaining twenty years of his life laying the basis for the largest and most powerful empire the world had ever seen.

Chinggis's bitter experiences with steppe politics and the fickleness of tribal military units influenced his ideas about military strategy and political organization and gave the Mongol empire a unique structure. It was not an imperial confederacy, but an autocratic state that deliberately broke up tribes and redistributed their people into new military units. No man, under pain of death, was allowed to move to another unit without permission. Chinggis also refused to employ his patrilineal relatives in high office, preferring to appoint personal followers, *nökör*, and loyal household servants to the highest ranks in the empire. Chinggis also expanded his bodyguard, the *keshig*, to create a military elite of ten thousand men whose officers outranked all the older traditional tribal leaders. The early Mongol state was therefore run by men who were personally appointed by Chinggis Khan on the basis of their talent and loyalty, not their kinship ties to him or their rank in the previously existing tribal order. So effective was this strategy that as the empire expanded, the older tribal divisions became insignificant. Mongolian political organization under Chinggis Khan was not the culmination of a long evolving steppe tradition but a deviation from it. While it was more effective than any previous steppe empire, it was also unique. After the fall of the Mongol empire, the nomads would revert to their older and less centralized imperial-confederacy model of organization.

The Mongol army grew from 95,000 in 1206 to 129,000 at the time of Chinggis's death in 1227. Of mixed tribal background, it was organized into decimal units of 10, 100, and 1,000, with divisions of 10,000 (*tümen*) the largest tactical unit. The *tümen* were under the control of Chinggis's most trusted friends and *tümen* leaders had direct command of about half the troops in the army. The army was strictly disciplined, subject to central authority, and trained to fight as a group rather than as individuals. Those who broke ranks to loot or who engaged in personal combat without regard to orders were severely punished. Campaigns were carefully planned in advance so that the Mongols put their mobility to best advantage. In one key respect, however, Chinggis Khan differed from previous nomadic leaders: he had a penchant for fighting decisive battles. The traditional nomadic strategy when confronted with a large, well-organized force was to withdraw or delay giving battle until the enemy was exhausted and had begun retreating. Of course, Chinggis Khan was experienced at using the tactical retreat to lead an enemy into ambush—the most common Mongol trap—but he never employed the strategic retreat of withdrawing long distances to avoid the enemy. Instead, he sought the best tactical position and attacked.

The Mongol aim in battle was to overwhelm and then destroy the enemy. Their pursuits of defeated armies were legendary, often lasting for days over scores of kilometers in order to prevent the enemy from regrouping. And Chinggis had commanders that could do this with a superb but terrible efficiency, for the Mongols had superior organization, more discipline, and better tactics than any previous steppe army. In addition—and this was critical to their later success—the Mongols ultimately acquired the skills of siegecraft. Other steppe armies only raided around walled cities; the Mongols learned to destroy them. By recruiting skilled military engineers from China and Central Asia, the Mongols could breech fortifications, divert rivers to flood an enemy position, or build roads and bridges to speed the army's passage. The Mongol army's combination of speed, striking power, and technical ability put it centuries ahead of any contemporary rivals. Indeed, it is difficult to consider the Mongol conquests in the context of medieval warfare, for their blitzkrieg strategy displayed many unique features that would not be replicated until the twentieth century. Their campaigns are still studied by modern military strategists as the basis for mobile tank warfare.

THE MONGOL CONQUESTS

Like all nomad leaders before him, Chinggis Khan was dependent on revenue from outside the steppe to support his nomadic state. Like them, he initially employed the outer frontier strategy of terroristic raiding against northern China to extract revenue and persuade the governments there to establish peace treaties which would guarantee trade and funnel tribute to Mongolia. Chinggis's first attacks on a sedentary state, the Tangut Kingdom of Hsi Hsia in 1207 and 1209, quickly produced favorable results. After having his capital besieged, the Tangut king secured a peace treaty by pledging to send troops to aid the Mongols in future wars and by marrying his daughter to Chinggis Khan. He also provided the Mongols with large numbers of camels, bolts of woolen cloth, and hunting falcons for which the Tanguts were famous. Since the Mongols had no intention of directly governing such a sedentary area, the Tangut king retained his sovereignty.

Following these events, Chinggis began the much greater task of extorting the Jurchen, rulers of the Chin dynasty in northern China. Descendents of Manchurian tribes that had conquered most of northern China a century earlier, the Jurchen were a formidable opponent, possessing a state with a population of 50 million, a powerful army, and strong frontier fortifications. But at the Battle of Huan-erh-tsui in 1211, the Mongols attacked and routed a much larger Jurchen force to gain control of the key passes into China. Over the next three years, the Mongols mounted ever deeper invasions of China, but at the end of each campaign season they returned to the frontier and abandoned most of the land they had overrun. The third Mongol invasion in the autumn of 1213 was the most devastating. The Jurchen capital of Chung-tu, on the site of today's Peking, was surrounded but proved too strongly fortified to be taken. Instead, the Mongols turned south, devastating the towns and villages all over the north China plain. Chinggis then returned to Mongolia but left his commanders to maintain the siege of Chung-tu.

By the winter of 1214, the Jurchen court had become so desperate that a court faction favoring accommodation with the Mongols surrendered the capital and negotiated a peace treaty. The emperor gave the daughter of his predecessor in marriage to Chinggis together with horses, gold, and silk. The Mongol army, loaded with this and the loot seized in the south, then withdrew from China: "Our soldiers lading [their beasts with] satin and goods as many as they could carry, tied their burdens with silk and went away."[27] Unlike native Chinese dynasties, however, the Jurchen were not content to buy off the nomads, and soon resumed the war. This was to prove disastrous both for the Jurchen and the economy of northern China. For while Chinggis Khan would never again personally return to China, he left a permanent force to do battle there. Twenty years of warfare followed and led to the ultimate destruction of the Chin dynasty by the armies of his son Ögödei in 1234. However, in both his wars with the Tanguts and the Jurchen, Chinggis's goal was never conquest but extortion. A true son of the Mongolian steppe, he had no interest in becoming a Chinese emperor. Northern China came under direct Mongol rule by default only because the Mongols had killed the victims they initially intended to extort and were then forced to take on the responsibilities of administration themselves.

Chinggis Khan's campaigns into other sedentary areas showed a similar lack of interest in permanent occupation. Content with the conquest of the steppe nomadic tribes, he initially attempted to strike peaceful agreements with the more distant states of western Asia. The most important was with the Khwarazm Shah, ruler of the lands that today make up Central Asia, Iran, and Afghanistan. Unlike the extortionate Mongol ultimatums presented to the Hsi Hsia and Chin states in China, this accord only required that the Khwarazm Shah, Ala' al-Din Muhammad, accept the diplomatic equality of the two empires and provide for the free movement of Mongol envoys and trade caravans. In Mongol eyes such an agreement had a sacred quality to it and any deliberate treaty violation, particularly one that insulted Mongol honor, was viewed as sufficient cause for a war of annihilation. It was a severe but effective way to ensure that agreements were not broken.

The Khwarazm Shah had contempt for this new Mongolian ruler's pretensions of superiority (Chinggis had even had the gall to refer to him as "my son" in diplomatic exchanges), and was determined to put him in his place. In 1218, 450 Muslim merchants who had just left Mongol territory were murdered and their goods seized by Khwarazm Shah's uncle, the governor of Utrar. When Chinggis demanded redress, the Khwarazm Shah responded by murdering his envoy, a heinous breach of diplomacy. Leaving some troops behind to continue the fight in China, Chinggis Khan mobilized the main Mongol army for an invasion of the west in retaliation. An army of 150,000 descended on Central Asia. In 1219, Utrar was destroyed.   In 1220, the great cities of Transoxania—Bukhara, Samarkand, Tirmidh, and Urgench—all fell with great loss of life. The following year, the Mongols overran Khorasan, eventually destroying the cities of Merv, Balkh, Herat, and Nishapur. By 1222, the Mongols had reached the banks of the Indus. A separate Mongol force sent in pursuit of the fleeing Khwarazm Shah rounded the Caspian Sea in 1223. The Mongols returned the way they had come and arrived home in 1225.[28]

This was the first time that a major nomadic power direct from the Chinese frontier had invaded the sedentary states of the west. The outer frontier strategy of devastation and terror wreaked havoc with the more fragile ecology of the region. China might replace large population losses and regain economic productivity within a few generations, but here the damage was more long lasting. Cities whose populations numbered in the many hundreds of thousands were completely destroyed and irrigation systems were ruined, severely hampering economic recovery. Writing about conditions in the region one hundred years later, one observer still spoke of the:

> ...ruin (in the present day) as a result of the eruption of the Mongols and the general massacre of people which took place in their days.... Further there can be no doubt that if for a thousand years to come no evil befalls the country, yet it will not be possible to repair the damage, and bring the land back into the state it was formerly.[29]

Chinggis Khan withdrew his troops from most of the areas he overran. Only Khwarazmia was put under Mongol control, with government in the hands of non-Mongol administrators. Thus as puzzling as the severe harm done to the area was its quick abandonment. We saw in the last chapter that the Turkish nomads who had previously entered southwestern Asia from the steppe had always attempted, usually successfully, to found new dynasties and become rulers. However, under Chinggis Khan, the Mongols, with their Chinese frontier heritage, still preferred extortion and raiding to conquest.

It was not until decades after the death of Chinggis that the Mongols began to take real responsibility for administration. It was only after the collapse of the Jurchen in 1234 that Ögödei's prime minister, Yeh-lü Ch'u-ts'ai, was able to set up a proper government in China. He was particularly concerned with curbing destructive Mongol policies towards peasants that lowered agricultural production. Considered unfit to be soldiers and possessing no special skills that were of direct value to the Mongols (as did artisans, merchants, or scholars), it had been proposed to Ögödei that these useless people be exterminated and their land allowed to revert to pasture. Yeh-lü Ch'u-ts'ai argued strongly against the proposal, explaining that if he were allowed to set up a system of taxation and let the peasants work in peace, he could produce annual revenues of a half million ounces of silver, 400,000 bags of grain, and 80,000 pieces of silk. Only the tribes of the northern steppe with no personal experience of the realities of sedentary civilization would have failed to understand that the surpluses they demanded were based on peasant production. As the goods flowed into the Mongol capital of Karakorum, the talk of eliminating peasants ceased.[30]

But if Chinggis Khan retained the old nomadic principle that extortion was superior to conquest, his immediate descendents did not. The Mongol armies were too powerful, too dominant, to stay put on the steppe. At first by default, and then by design, the successors of Chinggis Khan began to see the value of occupying sedentary territories themselves. Following the final conquest of northern China in 1234, Chinggis's son, the Great Khan Ögödei, sent the Mongol army to conquer Eastern Europe. The Great Khan Möngke, Chinggis's grandson, began the conquest of Sung China in 1251, a task that was finally completed by his brother Khubilai in 1279. Möngke also ordered the permanent occupation of Iran and dispatched an army there under the command of his brother, the redoubtable Hülegü, in 1253. Hülegü not only conquered Iran by 1256 but went on to Mesopotamia where he destroyed the city of Baghdad in 1258, killing over 200,000 people, including the last Abbassid Caliph (the titular head of Sunni Islam) which ended a dynasty that had lasted for five centuries.

With these conquests, Mongol leaders finally recognized that possessing a nomadic cavalry supported by the wealth of sedentary farmers and artisans produced the most powerful political and military base. This became obvious when, during a civil war following Möngke's death in 1259, Khubilai Khan used his control of northern China to cut off all supplies to the Mongol capital of Karakorum which lay deep in the steppe. His younger brother and rival, Ariq Böke, discovered that without supplies his occupation of the Mongol heartland was strategically worthless. Khubilai soon defeated his brother and became ruler of China. The Mongol world empire then split into four successor states: the Yüan dynasty in China and Mongolia, the Il-khanate in Iran, the Chaghadai khanate in Transoxiana, and the Golden Horde on the southern Russian steppe.

THE MONGOL DEVASTATION

Why were the Mongol invasions so destructive? Some modern historians argue that it was because the Mongols hated sedentary civilization and took the opportunity to destroy it, a typical example of nomad "savagery." On the other hand, some modern Mongol apologists have argued that their destructiveness was exaggerated and they were not much worse than anybody else. Neither of these explanations is very satisfactory.

There is little evidence that Chinggis ever displayed a particular hostility to sedentary civilization *per se*. Though he did consider the nomad way of life superior, he recognized sedentary civilization as the source of the goods he so desired and employed many of its skilled administrators to run the empire. But while there is little evidence he hated cities, unfortunately for Mongol defenders, the evidence is overwhelming that Chinggis wrecked havoc on a scale that would not be repeated until modern times (and then only with the help of labor-saving machines). In China, the scale of devastation is apparent just by comparing a Jurchen census of 1195 which enumerated a population of about 50 million people in northern China with the first Mongol census of 1235 to 1236 which counted only 8.5 million. Even accepting the possibility of a large undercount, clearly the population and productivity of northern China had been severely damaged. And, as noted earlier, the situation was, if anything, proportionately worse in western Asia where a policy of destruction as a form of military terrorism expanded beyond any practical purpose.[31]

A prime (but hardly unique) example of the Mongol destruction was the treatment of the city of Herat in northwestern Afghanistan. The city initially surrendered and its population was left unmolested, but it later rebelled after receiving word of a Mongol setback. An angry Chinggis dispatched an army of 80,000 with these instructions: "The dead have come to life again. This time you must cut the people's heads off: you must execute the whole population of Herat." After an eight-month siege, Herat fell and contemporary accounts placed the number of inhabitants massacred during the next seven days at over a million (an exaggeration perhaps but indicative of the scale of the disaster). The Mongols then left for good but, fearing that some people might have escaped by hiding, Chinggis ordered a small force to return a few days later. They discovered and killed the city's remaining 2,000 people who had miraculously survived the initial holocaust.[32] That Chinggis Khan did not approve of the torture of captives, but instead coldbloodedly ordered their massacre by the hundreds of thousands, was of little comfort to his victims.

Such behavior was inexplicable to sedentary historians for whom the conquest of productive populations was the goal of warfare. But it fell well within the pattern of relationships that had evolved over the centuries along the Sino-Mongolian frontier. In their relationship with China, the steppe tribes of the north had only indirect ties with agricultural producers. They traded at border markets and got gifts directly from the Chinese court. To the nomads, China became known as a fabulous storehouse of wealth. But how this wealth came to be produced, or how the Chinese organized its administration and the taxation of millions of peasants and artisans, was of no interest to the nomads. Peasant production, the basis of the Chinese economy, was belittled by nomads who considered peasants to be no more a part of a political universe than were the domestic animals of the steppe. Peasants fell into the category of useless people who, as individuals, could provide no special service to the Mongols. They were used as human shields in wave attacks on cities, displaced from their homes, and prevented from returning to productive farming.

Perhaps the only satisfactory explanation is that this Mongol strategy of extortion, of the use of terror and violence to induce the surrender of cities and the submission of foreign rulers, was a policy that had outlived its usefulness. Though an old steppe tactic, the Mongols carried it to excess and killed the victims they initially had only intended to extort. Since the outer frontier strategy that previous nomadic groups had used so effectively against China depended on having a government in China to extort, Mongol strategy under Chinggis Khan aimed at destroying the power of leaders to resist Mongol demands, not the occupation of their territory. Extremely conscious of their small numbers and fearful of rebellion, Chinggis often chose to annihilate a region's entire population if it appeared too troublesome to govern. This was particularly true of cities or governments that surrendered and then revolted. That this was not an inherent characteristic of Mongol warfare could be seen in Khubilai Khan's conquest of Sung China, where maintaining the region's productivity and population base received a high priority. Better yet is this admonition by Ghazan Khan, the Mongol Il-khan ruler, to his unruly nomad subjects:

> I am not on the side of the Tazik *ra'iyyat* [Persian peasant]. If there is any purpose in pillaging them all, there is no-one with more power to do this than I. Let us rob them together. But if you wish to be certain of collecting grain and food for your tables in the future, I must be harsh with you. You must be taught to reason. If you insult the *ra'iyyat*, take their oxen and seed, and trample their crops into the ground, what will you do in the future? ...The obedient *ra'iyyat* must be distinguished from the *ra'iyyat* who are our enemies. How should we not protect the obedient, allowing them to suffer distress and torment at our hands.[33]

Running a sedentary state and extorting it were two very different propositions. The Mongols eventually learned this lesson, but not before a massive amount of destruction was wrought on their neighbors.

THE DECLINE OF THE STEPPE

It is often assumed that following the dissolution of the unified Mongol empire that the steppe nomads immediately entered a period of steep decline. In fact, the Mongol successor states dominated Eurasia well into the fourteenth century. The Mongol dynasty of Il-khans lost control of Iran in 1335 and the rulers of the Yüan dynasty were driven out of China in 1368, but the Golden Horde ruled Russia (the infamous "Tatar yoke") for another century. The empire of Tamerlane dominated Central Asia during the fifteenth century and was succeeded by the nomadic Uzbeks in the sixteenth century. Similarly, the nomads in Mongolia retained considerable power on the steppe even after their expulsion from China. Reverting to their older imperial confederacy organization, they pillaged the frontiers of Ming China (once capturing an emperor), and raided to the

gates of Peking before a satisfactory peace was established in the late sixteenth century.

Beginning in the seventeenth century, the nomads began encountering
a new type of state that put their traditional strategies at risk. In the east, a
new Manchurian dynasty established itself in Peking in 1644 and soon conquered all of China. Using a policy of alliances, it had incorporated the old
Mongol leadership of southern Mongolia (the descendents of Chinggis Khan)
under its control even before invading China. With these Mongols as allies,
the Ch'ing government later won control of northern Mongolia. This put
them in conflict with the Zunghars, the last of the independent nomad empires which was based in the Ili Valley at the heart of Central Eurasia. For
the next century, the Ch'ing emperors and Zunghar khans engaged in a
deadly duel over who was to control Central Eurasia. After a series of wars
that ranged over Mongolia, Tibet, and Turkestan, the Zunghars were finally
defeated and then annihilated by the Ch'ing armies in 1757. The situation in
the western steppe was similar. Beginning in the late sixteenth century, the
expanding Russian empire first seized the steppe lands of the Black Sea, the
traditional center of nomadic power since the time of the Scythians. The Russians also claimed large tracts of Siberia, which lay just north of Mongolia,
and by the nineteenth century were expanding rapidly eastward across the
steppe, defeating the Turkish-speaking Kazaks and finally incorporating all
their territory after the capture of Tashkent in 1865.

Caught between the two expanding world empires that divided Central Eurasia between them, the nomads had no place to run, no place to rebuild their independent power. Their traditional military superiority of
mounted archery was lost to new weapons (cannons, muskets, and later rifles) which gave better-organized sedentary armies an advantage. Reduced to the status of political intermediaries within large multinational
empires, the authority and power of Kazak and Mongol khans were severely restricted. As a result, the significance of the tribal political structure itself declined when it could no longer provide such basic functions as
ensuring rights to pasture, resolving disputes among rival factions, or even
legally punishing wrongdoers. The use of elaborate genealogies which so
carefully preserved distinctions among clans soon disappeared among
many steppe nomadic peoples once they lost their autonomy.[34]

The nineteenth century was therefore a time of true political and military decline of the steppe peoples, and accounts by western travellers
paint a stark picture of both the poverty and weakness of the nomads
under imperial rule. In northern Mongolia, Chinese merchants who extended goods on credit extracted compound interest on unpaid balances
and made immense profits, draining the wealth of Mongolia into China.
These paper debts eventually far exceeded the value of the goods imported (a process not unfamiliar to the holders of bank credit cards who
pay only their minimum balance).[35] Earlier independent chieftains would

have forbidden such exploitation and set the terms of trade to benefit the nomads, but after centuries of Ch'ing rule, the Mongol princes had become a conservative class of rulers dependent on this system to preserve their own power. They were unwilling to upset a situation from which they personally benefited.

While uneven terms of trade put northern Mongolia at a disadvantage, its basic economy remained intact. Elsewhere, nomads inhabiting areas of the steppe suitable for agriculture found themselves displaced by waves of immigrants seeking new lands to farm. In southern Mongolia, Chinese peasants began to settle on tribal pasture land, which was often sold to them by unscrupulous Mongol leaders. On the Kazak steppe, Russian farmers, assisted by the Czarist government, acquired the best land for themselves to grow grain. The pace of settlement in both regions vastly increased when the introduction of railroads in the late nineteenth century made it possible to move goods and people overland inexpensively. Not only did these settlement policies make pastoralism more difficult because the nomads were restricted to what had been marginal lands, they eventually resulted in the Kazaks and Mongols becoming minorities in what had been their own lands. Today, only the Mongolian People's Republic has maintained both a pastoral economy and its Mongol population. In China, the Mongolian Autonomous Region has a population that is 80 to 90 percent ethnically Han Chinese, while in newly independent Kazakhstan, Kazaks make up less than half of the total population.

CENTRAL EURASIAN PASTORALISTS TODAY

During the twentieth century, all the nomads of Central Eurasia experienced similar attempts to transform their social and economic lives by revolutionary socialist governments. While the Kazaks, Kirghiz, and Turkmen were all granted republic status within the Soviet Union, in practice, policy was set in Moscow. Similarly, northern Mongolia (which had sought Russian protection after it broke away from China following the collapse of the Ch'ing dynasty in 1911) was also closely tied to Moscow after the Soviet troops occupied the country in the 1920s. Its policies mirrored those of the Soviet government and, though nominally independent, had little more freedom than an ethnic republic. When the People's Republic of China came to power in 1949, it too created ethnic republics for non-Chinese regions such as southern Mongolia and Xinjiang, but set policy in Peking. The policy of collectivization in particular had a pervasive impact on the lives of the nomads in these regions. It both tied them into the larger national economies of the Soviet Union and China and subjected them to their dominant ideology far more intensely than any other place in the world.

THE RISE OF COLLECTIVIZATION

The emergence of a socialist Soviet Union did not have a profound impact on pastoralists until the 1930s when Joseph Stalin implemented a radical scheme of universal collectivization. Designed to bring the entire agricultural econ-omy under direct state control, the plan attempted to incorporate all farmers and pastoralists into centralized collectives or state farms by confiscating their assets and putting them under communal management. The private ownership of such basic resources as land, animals, and equipment was pro-hibited. At the same time, the traditional elites were condemned as "class en-emies" which often resulted in their imprisonment, death, or deportation. Symbols of the old way of life, including religion, dress, and such customary practices as wedding and funeral feasts, were declared obsolete and publicly forbidden.

The disruption caused by forced collectivization had a dramatic im-pact on both everyday life and tribal social organization. However, unlike Iran under Reza Shah, Stalin's primary target was not the nomads but the Russian peasantry and its traditional village life; sedentarizing pastoralists was only a secondary goal. But the path to collectivization was neverthe-less extremely destructive to the pastoral economy because, unlike peas-ants, the nomads had one powerful option open to them in resisting these new state demands: they could destroy their animals rather than surrender them. This they did on a large scale, and even those animals that were seized often died from neglect under collective management. Although the range of estimates for the loss of human life and livestock during collectiv-ization varies, all researchers agree that the Kazaks, as the largest popula-tion of pastoralists, suffered some of the worst abuses:

> From 1929 to 1933 the number of livestock in Kazakhstan was reduced by a factor of ten, from 36–40 million to 4 million (specifically the number of cows dropped from 6.5 million to 965,000; sheep from 18.6 million to 1.4 million; horses from 3.5 million to 315,000 and camels from 1 million to 63,000). ...According to an estimate by Kazakh scholars, 1.75 out of 4.12 Kazakhs perished from famine and typhoid.[36]

Collectivization of pastoralists in other parts of the Soviet Union had similar consequences, although the loss of life was not quite as great. In Kirghizstan, the total number of sheep and goats declined from approxi-mately 3,100,000 to 949,000 between 1930 and 1932, while the number of cattle was reduced from 876,000 to 315,000. The Soviet Union did not re-cover from these losses until the 1960s.[37]

In Mongolia, which followed Soviet policy in lock step, attempts at full-scale collectivization during the same period resulted in a 30 percent loss of livestock and produced a revolt in the western part of the country that was suppressed only with the aid of Soviet troops. However, perhaps because the Mongolian economy was almost entirely dependent on pastoral production, the policy was drastically scaled back and people were once again allowed to control at least some of their own animals.[38] Chinese communists later followed the Soviet Union's lead in establishing pastoral communes after their victory in 1949, but they never attempted to control pastoralists as severely. China's leaders did not want to provoke a repeat of the Stalinist disasters and they also feared the consequences of political unrest among the pastoral Turkish and Mongol ethnic minorities who inhabited sensitive border regions.

With some modifications to allow restricted ownership of domestic animals and small private plots, state farms and collectives eventually became the exclusive form of rural organization in the socialist bloc. Some idea of how a pastoral collective works in practice can be seen in Caroline Humphrey's detailed study of Buryat collectives during the 1960s and 1970s.[39] The Buryats are Mongol-speaking people located in the Barguzin region of Lake Baikal in the Soviet Union, a region perhaps best known as the source of the world's finest sable furs. They too initially experienced widespread livestock losses during the early period of collectivization, but lost far fewer people than groups such as the Kazak. Indeed, of all the region's nomads, they may have been the most receptive to the new policy because local Buddhist monastic orders held large animal holdings that were available for expropriation and the Buryat elite had earlier produced a surprising number of radical politicians who were able to represent their interests within the new socialist system.

Humphrey stresses that the collectives were multifaceted institutions. With an average population of 336 households, the Buryat collective served a dual role as a primary social community and economic production unit. Although they all had foreign names in keeping with Soviet ideology (Karl Marx, Great October, Red Banner, etc.) most disguised an older social organization based on clan relations, since kinsmen tended to join together when the collectives were first founded. And because the right of travel and the possibility of changing jobs were tightly restricted, these ties were unintentionally reinforced over time. While schools stressed the importance of following national norms in preference to local customs for generations, much of Buryat culture has remained intact: belief in shamans and animistic spirits, the importance of Buddhist burial rites, and the conviction that kinsmen were the primary social group.

Central planners rejected traditional forms of pastoralism as unscientific and even the use of yurts was attacked as "unhygienic" and "old-fashioned." Instead, they expected collective farms to employ a factory-style division of labor in order to meet production schedules. Buryat collectives were also designed to encourage a more sedentary way of life by building permanent houses around the collective's center. Other innovations included the assigned allocation of labor for milk production, transport, or

Women's fashions have dramatically altered because of Chinese influence on the Kazaks in Xinjiang as can be seen in this picture of three generations of a single extended family.

other activities by an office manager who was responsible for all major decisions; the creation of large herds of a single species tended by professional shepherds; and compensating workers through a system of points on collective farms or with a salary on state farms. The collective's management was held responsible for meeting production schedules and delivering fixed quotas to the central government. The vagaries inherent in pastoralism meant that such arbitrary goals were rarely met, so collective managers were often fired and replaced.

Collectives put severe restraints on all forms of private production, including the size of private plots which were used to grow fodder for family-owned animals and the sale of labor or the exchange of goods for profit. Nevertheless, these private plots and animals were highly productive and constituted an important resource. Yet because the accumulation of property was so severely restricted, such earnings could not be invested to increase the size of private herds or acquire land. The surplus was therefore devoted to reinforcing kinship ties by contributing to ritual events and, more important in a system where personal connections are vital to success, to a system of reciprocal gifts between collective officials and ordinary workers. Only by gaining people's cooperation could a leader get anything done, and only officials had access to such things as scarce consumer goods, important services, advanced education, and job placement.

While such gift giving had strong roots in older Mongol culture and played an important role in Buryat social life, this new system depended less on demonstrating success in pastoralism than success in politics. In particular, the sought-after jobs of "specialist" in the collective's center, which required at least some education and party affiliation, were often given to those people least connected with the pastoral economy. The actual work of shepherding, dirty and difficult jobs in distant pastures, was to be avoided. As Humphrey notes, this led to the irony of awards for meeting real production goals always going to backward-looking shepherds who least fit the ideal of a progressive Soviet worker. What they did know well was pastoralism.

THE DEMISE OF COLLECTIVIZATION

Throughout the socialist world, the organization of the rural economy into collectives came under increasing criticism during the 1980s because it was held responsible for the underproductivity of the agricultural economy. Quotas of hectares to be plowed or potatoes to be dug often resulted in poor use of land or harvested crops left to rot for lack of storage or timely transport. Pastoralism under collectivization was even more problematic because animal husbandry, a risky enterprise in any economic system, was particularly ill suited to the fixed targets of five-year plans and centralized administration. Successful animal husbandry demands that decisions be made on the spot because delay may result in catastrophic losses: the consequences of a lack of water, a sudden freeze, or the need to move outside of the normal schedule cannot be resolved by a distant manager if the widespread death of animals is to be avoided. The problem is compounded when the workers have no stake in the livestock and suffer few consequences if there are losses. (This is something that private absentee owners in Iran and Afghanistan also complain about, but they can at least fire the negligent workers or tie their pay to a split in the herd's increase.) Whatever the defects of traditional pastoralism in Central Eurasia, its dependence on households as the basic units of production at least provided both the necessary flexibility to adapt to sudden changes and made efficient use of labor and resources.

Collectives were first abolished in the People's Republic of China during the 1980s as part of a nationwide policy of economic reform. Previously under the *iron sheep* policy, those whose herds increased did no better than those whose herds lost animals (equivalent to the *iron rice bowl* policy on farming communes). With no personal responsibility for losses or gains, it was recognized that under collectivization the rural economy was stagnating. To increase production, the Chinese government introduced the *dual responsibility system*. In the first phase, households were made responsible for their own production and labor. After they met a minimum quota in goods or money, they could keep the rest. In the second phase, communal property was divided up and each household received a long-term lease to land and pasture for its exclusive use, a form of private ownership. Production soared.

Just how profound these changes were could be seen among the approximately 300,000 Kazak pastoralists of the Altai Mountains, part of the larger Kazak Autonomous Region in Xinjiang. The communes there were dismantled in 1984 through 1985, and their property was sold to member families by means of interest-free loans to be repaid over a ten-year period. The specialized animal herds were broken up so that a family received a mix of all types of animals, a reversion to the traditional form of Kazak pastoralism. In the Altai, the average family of five or six people received 70 sheep, 7 horses, 9 cattle, and 3 camels. Seasonal pasture areas were also divided into plots and distributed by lot. Families had exclusive-use rights on their plots but could not sell them. The right of transit between pastures was guaranteed. A similar distribution of farmland was made when it was part of the commune's resources. Tractors and trucks were sold to their drivers. They were expected to rent their services to others and use the money to pay off their loans and maintain the equipment. To keep the level of production high, the government prices paid to producers were designed to assure a profit even when they used purchased fodder. To increase the use of fodder, they encouraged its private production for family use or sale. The pastoralists were also provided with wheat at subsidized prices which was trucked to the mountain pastures in the summer. By making grain regularly available and a basic component of the Kazak diet, there was less pressure to slaughter animals for food.

The Kazak response to these changes was very positive. Keeping a mix of animals allowed people to manage their own resources and resume the pattern of migration they traditionally preferred. However, while in comparison with the commune system this looked like a reversion to an older form of pastoralism, it was in fact something new because the Kazaks were more closely connected with the market than previously and because there was a greater integration of agriculture with animal husbandry. The extended family became the key economic unit. Members cooperated to get the best mix of resources by sending one or more households to the mountains with the animals while the rest grew grain and fodder crops. The women with the pastoral groups stayed in the lower pastures with the milking animals while the men took the rest of the herd to high mountain pastures. The care of the animals markedly increased herd totals, rising almost 18 percent in the first two years of the policy, although much of this increase may have been due to new ways of accounting rather than true gains. More telling was the response to severe winter conditions during 1986 and 1987, the worst in many years. The herds declined by less than 2 percent, whereas under similar conditions in 1960, the herds had suffered catastrophic losses of between 30 percent and 50 percent. Kazaks attributed the difference to the new level of protection they were willing to provide their own animals as opposed to those that were collectively owned.

Under private control, pastoralism became more profit oriented. In some families, women's milk production from herds, which had previously been restricted to domestic consumption, began to be sold to increase income. Butter and *kumiss* (fermented mare's milk) were shipped to urban areas for sale. Since a mare could produce about 3 kilograms a day, a family with a sizable herd had the potential to earn 2,000 to 3,000 yuan (1 yuan = $.35) a season—an enormous new source of potential income. The biggest source of wealth was, however, the rise in the underlying value of the livestock families had acquired from the communes. Sheep acquired for 18 yuan ($5) rose to 150 yuan ($43) in value within three years. In addition to the traditional fat-tailed sheep, families began adding new varieties of sheep for wool production. Some herders also began to add goats for the cashmere wool they produced. The sale of meat and hides was open to both state industries and private buyers.

Although the profits have been high, Kazak herders complain that they are cheated by more experienced Uighur merchants who come into the steppe to buy animals at a discount. While Kazaks consider it undignified to haggle over the price of an animal, oasis merchants have been famous for thousands of years for their ability to bargain. And without contacts or experience in the cities, few rural Kazaks feel capable of selling their animals in oasis markets.

It is important to stress that not all families, or even a majority, took advantage of all these possibilities, but by Chinese standards, the Kazaks in the Altai became much more prosperous. Their per capita income rose from 300 yuan in 1984 to 450 yuan in 1987, a 50 percent increase. Even more startling after years of income leveling under the iron sheep policy was the emergence of 10,000 yuan families whose annual income of that amount or more made them models of the new system's opportunities.

The greatest dissatisfaction with the new system was from party members who had been extremely powerful in the commune system and found their authority greatly eroded when they lost their monopoly on the distribution of commune jobs and property. Formerly subservient commune members now ignored these officials and they complained it was becoming difficult to recruit young people for the government jobs that

A Kazak family on the move to its mountain pastures in the Altai Mountains. The policy of decollectivization in China put control of livestock back into the hands of families who resumed the older pattern of migration with whole families to the summer pastures with mixed herds of animals.

previously had been sought after. Officials who held administrative jobs in towns also found themselves economically worse off because their salaries did not keep pace with inflation or provide the opportunity for wealth that animal ownership did. Ironically, some pastoral Kazaks argued that now that these officials were out of the economic production cycle, government services such as schools and medical clinics improved as officials attempted to create a new niche for themselves.

Until 1991 changes among nomadic pastoralists in Central Eurasia were products of planning by socialist governments which, like China, desired to increase economic productivity while maintaining tight political control. The collapse of the Soviet Union and the transformation of its ethnic republics into independent states have opened an entirely new era in history in which these areas are now free to set their own policies. No longer remote parts of a large centralized empire, the new states of Central Eurasia have begun to rediscover their own national past—a past in which pastoral nomads are now heroes rather than villains. Of the five new states that formerly constituted the Central Asian Republics of the Soviet Union, three (Kazakhstan, Turkmenistan, and Kirghizstan) are now run by descendants of tribal groups that were pastoral nomads before the revolution in 1917. The new Kirghizstan flag even uses the round wooden crown of a yurt frame as its central motif. And in neighboring Mongolia the banner of Chinggis Khan has once again been raised as a national symbol of greatness.

Economic changes are also occurring rapidly. The Mongol government has sold the state's assets to individuals so that pastoralists once again control their own land and animals. They will now determine their own strategies of economic production and, as among the Kazaks in Xingjiang, are likely to return to older patterns of family based production. While the economic policies in each of these new states is developing differently, in all of them animal husbandry will take on a more important role. Pastoralism that was formerly perceived as marginal by the distant central planners in Moscow is now considered vital by officials of national governments with capitals in Alma Ata, Ashkabad, and Bishkek. They need to increase pastoral production of all types in order to feed the local population and as a way to generate revenue by exporting pastoral products to neighboring countries.

Whatever the final results of the changes in these countries, it is clear that the nomads of Central Eurasia, with access to the world's largest grasslands, will continue to be important to the economy of the region. Overland trade is once again reviving the region's economic life. Railroads and highways, a new silk route of iron and asphalt, permit the export of pastoral products to distant cities where they fetch high prices. Similarly, goods from around the world now find their way into the heart of Asia. In the Altai it is not uncommon to see TV antennas rising from Kazak winter camps. (Indeed, during my own visit in 1987 to one distant valley, accompanied by a producer from Kazak television, community leaders demanded to know when they would get a satellite dish like their neighbors!) But with these new links, pastoralism is likely to become more similar to cattle ranching in the United States, a business with explicit standards of profit and loss. But no matter how the economy changes, nomadic pastoralists will remain key symbols of Kazak or Mongol ethnic identity, even as the majority of Kazaks and Mongols settle into the region's growing cities. Like the camel-raising Bedouin, the cultural identity of the descendants of Chinggis Khan is so closely tied to the history of great deeds by men on horseback that even as their number declines, their role as symbols of a proud way of life will grow.

N O T E S

1. David Anthony, and Dorcas Brown, "The Origins of Horseback Riding," *Antiquity*, 65 (1991), 22–38.

2. K.C. Chang, *Archaeology of Ancient China* (New Haven: Yale University Press, 1977), pp. 279–80; Edward Shaughnessy, "Historical Perspectives on the Introduction of the Chariot in China," *Harvard Journal of Asiatic Studies*, 48 (1988), 189–238.

3. James Downs, "The Origin and Spread of Riding in the Near East and Central Asia, *American Anthropologist*, 63 (1961), 1193–1203.

4. Burton Watson, trans., *Records of the Grand Historian of China*, translated from *The Shih-chi of Ssu-ma Ch'ien* (New York: Columbia University Press, 1961), II, 159.

5. cf. Karl Jettmar, *The Art of the Steppes* (New York: Crown, 1964).

6. Sergei Rudenko, *Frozen Tombs of Siberia: The Pazyryk Burials of Iron Age Horsemen* (London: Dent & Sons, 1970).

7. Herodotus, *The History*, trans. David Grene (Chicago: University of Chicago Press, 1987), Book IV, Chapters 64–65.

8. Owen Lattimore, *Inner Asian Frontiers of China* (New York: American Geographical Society, 1940), pp. 58–66.

9. Preston Holder, *The Hoe and the Horse on the Plains* (Lincoln, NB: University of Nebraska Press, 1970).

10. Elizabeth Bacon, "Types of Pastoral Nomadism in Central and Southwest Asia," *Southwestern Journal of Anthropology*, 10 (1954), 44–68.

11. Lawrence Krader, "The Ecology of Central Asian Pastoralism," *Southwestern Journal of Anthropology*, 11 (1955), 313.

12. Peter A. Andrews, "The White House of Khurasan: The Felt Tents of the Iranian Yomut and Goklen," *The Journal of the British Institute of Iranian Studies*, 11 (1973), 93–110; cf. Richard Bulliet, *The Camel and the Wheel* (Cambridge: Harvard University Press, 1977).

13. Watson, *Records*, II, 155.

14. David Aberle, *The Kinship System of the Kalmuk Mongols* (Albuquerque: University of New Mexico Press, 1953), p. 9.

15. Bertold Spuler, ed., *History of the Mongols: Based on Eastern and Western Accounts of the Thirteenth and Fourteenth Centuries* (Berkeley: University of California Press, 1972), pp. 80–81.

16. Charles Lindholm, "Kinship Structure and Political Authority: The Middle East and Central Asia," *Journal of Comparative History and Society*, 28 (1986), 334–55.

17. Francis Cleaves, trans., *The Secret History of the Mongols* (Cambridge: Harvard University Press, 1982), p. 16, note 48.

18. Lawrence Krader, *Social Organization of the Mongol-Turkic Pastoral Nomads* (The Hague: Mouton, 1963).

19. Thomas Barfield, "The Hsiung-nu Imperial Confederacy: Organization and Foreign Policy," *Journal of Asian Studies*, 41 (1981), 45–61.

20. Watson, *Records*, II, p. 172.

21. Ying-shih Yü, *Trade and Expansion in Han China: A Study in the Structure of Sino-Barbarian Economic Relations* (Berkeley: University of California Press, 1967), pp. 41–42.

22. Watson, *Records*, II, p. 168.

23. Watson, *Records*, II, p. 176.

24. M.A.N. Loewe, "The Campaigns of Han Wu-ti," in *Chinese Ways in Warfare*, eds. Frank Kierman and John Fairbank (Cambridge: Harvard University Press, 1974).

25. Watson, *Records*, II, p. 186.

26. Yü, *Trade*, pp. 61–64.

27. Cleaves, *Secret History*, §248, p. 185.

28. V. V. Barthold, *Turkestan Down to the Mongol Invasion* (London: Gibb Memorial Series, 1968), pp. 381–462; John A. Boyle, trans., *The History of the World Conqueror* (Manchester: Manchester University Press, 1958), provides a translation of the most important contemporary account by the Persian historian Ata Malik Juvaini.

29. Guy Le Strange, *The Lands of the Eastern Caliphate* (London, 1905), p. 34.

30. Igor de Rachewiltz, "Yeh-lü Ch'ü-ts-ai (1189–1243): Buddhist Idealist and Confucian Statesman," in *Confucian Personalities*, eds. A. F. Wright and Denis Twitchett (Stanford: Stanford University Press, 1962).

31. Thomas Barfield, *The Perilous Frontier: Nomadic Empires and China* (Cambridge, MA and Oxford: Basil Blackwell, 1989), p. 204.

32. John A. Boyle, "Dynastic and Political History of the Il-Khans" in *Cambridge History of Iran, vol. 5: The Saljuq and Mongol Period*, ed. John Boyle (Cambridge: Cambridge University Press, 1968), p. 316.

33. I.P. Petrushevsky, "The Socio-economic Condition of Iran under the Il-khans," in *The Cambridge History of Iran, vol. 5: The Saljuq and Mongol Period*, edited by J. A. Boyle (Cambridge: Cambridge University Press, 1968), p. 494.

34. Krader, *Social Organization*, pp. 332–33.

35. M. Sandorj, *Manchu Chinese Colonial Rule in Northern Mongolia* (New York: St. Martins Press, 1980).

36. Olga B. Naumova, "Evolution of Nomadic Culture under Modern Conditions: Tradition and Innovation in Kazakh Culture," in *Rulers from the Steppe: State Formation on the Eurasian Periphery*, eds. Gary Seaman and Daniel Marks (Los Angeles: Ethnographics, 1991), pp. 291–307.

37. Elizabeth Bacon, *Central Asians under Russian Rule* (Ithaca: Cornell University Press, 1980), pp. 116–50; Martha Brill Olcott, *The Kazakhs* (Stanford: Hoover Institution Press, 1987), 184–87.

38. Charles Bawden, *The Modern History of Mongolia* (New York: Praeger, 1968), pp. 290–327.

39. Caroline Humphrey, *Karl Marx Collective* (New York: Cambridge University Press, 1983).

FURTHER READINGS

Basilov, Boris, ed., *Nomads of Eurasia*. Seattle: University of Washington Press, 1989.

Cammann, Schuyler, *The Land of the Camel: Tents and Temples of Inner Mongolia*. New York: Roland Press, 1951.

Hudson, Alfred E., *Kazak Social Structure*. New Haven: Yale University Press, 1964 [1938].

Jagchid, Sechen, and Paul Hyer, *Mongolia's Society and Culture*. Boulder: Westview, 1979.

Jagchid, Sechin, and Van Jay Symons, *Peace, War, and Trade along the Great Wall: Nomadic-Chinese Interaction through Two Millennia*. Bloomington: Indiana University Press, 1989.

Lattimore, Owen, *The Desert Road to Turkestan*. Boston: Beacon Press, 1929.

Lattimore, Owen, *High Tartary*. Boston: Beacon Press, 1930.

Lattimore, Owen, *Mongol Journeys*. London: Jonathon Cape, 1941.

Lattimore, Owen, *The Mongols of Manchuria*. New York: H. Fertig, 1969 [1934].

Lattimore, Owen, *Nomads and Commissars*. New York: Oxford University Press, 1962.

Lattimore, Owen, *Studies in Frontier History: Collected Papers 1929–58*. Oxford: Oxford University Press, 1962.

Morgan, David, *The Mongols*. Cambridge, MA. and Oxford: Blackwell, 1987.

Ratchnevsky, Paul, *Genghis Khan: His Life and Legacy*, trans. and ed. Thomas Haining. Cambridge, MA and Oxford: Blackwell, 1991.

Saunders, J.J., *The History of the Mongol Conquests*. London: Routledge & Kegan Paul, 1971.

Schwarz, Henry, ed., *Bibliotheca Mongolica, Part I: Works in English, French and German*. Bellingham, WA: Western Washington, 1978.

Sinor, Denis, ed., *Cambridge History of Inner Asia*. Cambridge: Cambridge University Press, 1990.

Vainshtein, Sevyan, *Nomads of South Siberia: The Pastoral Economies of Tuva*. Cambridge: Cambridge University Press, 1980.

Vreeland, H.H., *Mongol Community and Kinship Structure*. Westport, CT: Greenwood Press, 1973.

CHAPTER SIX

THE YAK BREEDERS: HIGH ALTITUDE PASTORALISM IN TIBET

Nomadic pastoralism is primarily an adaptation to environments where the mobile grazing of natural pasture land by domestic animals is more sustainable than agriculture. In previous chapters, we have seen that such habitats are most often generated in arid and semi-arid regions where precipitation is the critical variable. However, aridity is not the only condition that can create a grassland ecosystem. High-altitude environments also produce distinct ecological zones which can support extensive tracts of pasture land. Here, pastoral nomadism has long been the dominant, even exclusive, economic activity because severe conditions at high altitudes (frost, short growing seasons, hailstorms, and the like) have made other uses difficult or impossible.

High-altitude pastoralism is generally defined as year-round animal husbandry in regions that lie above 3,000 meters. The permanent occupation of a high-altitude zone by nomads is of critical importance. While nomads in many places take advantage of high-mountain pastures in the summer, very few are equipped to live there year-round. Even if they were, there are in fact very few places in the world with extensive tracts of land above 3,000 meters. In Eurasia, high-altitude pastoralism is therefore restricted to areas of the Tibetan Plateau and adjacent mountainous regions which lie above the upper limits for the farming of barley and below the

The Tibetan Plateau is too high for agriculture but provides extensive pastures for herds of yaks, sheep and goats even though the climate makes living there a challenge.

permanent snow line. These limits vary by latitude. In more northerly areas of Tibet and neighboring Qing-hai (along the edge of Mongolia and Xinjiang), agriculture stops at 2,800 meters, while at the southern border of the Tibetan Plateau with India, crops may be found growing as high as 4,500 meters. Similarly, the permanent snow line is located at higher elevations in the south than in the north. The absolute size of each highland pasture area depends on the local topography: in steep terrain the grassland zone comprises just a few mountain slopes, but where the land is flat or rolling it may encompass thousands of square kilometers.

The most extensive highland plateau areas lie in central Tibet where altitude and topography have combined to produce large open tracts of pasture. Unlike the steppe regions of Eurasia, these grasslands are not continuous, but are broken up by sharp mountain ridges, lakes, and extensive tracts of barren rock or sand. Here, pastoralism has thrived in part because it has no competition. Neighboring farmers, for example, cannot possibly encroach upon the grasslands because their crops will not grow at such high altitudes. Like the Bedouins of the Arabian Desert, the nomads of the Tibetan Plateau therefore inhabit a region that others would label a wasteland. It is a wilderness which is singularly unattractive to outsiders because of its high winds and hail-storms, frequent fluctuations in the weather, and sudden extreme temperature changes even during the course of a single day. The sun's ultraviolet rays are particularly strong at high altitudes and will burn unprotected skin. The sun's glare, reflected from rocks and snow, can also cause temporary blindness. Although direct solar radiation provides much warmth in bright sunlight, the region's climatic regime is more similar to the Arctic than to the temperate zone. Temperatures average well below freezing most of the year and nightly lows of -40°C (-40°F) during the winter are not uncommon. As if these conditions were not difficult enough, the low atmospheric pressure encountered at high altitudes reduces the capacity of the lungs to transport oxygen, producing altitude sickness in visitors from the lowlands and making even simple exertion exhausting. It is not without reason then, and a certain degree of pride, that the *drokba*, the high-pasture nomads of Tibet, claim that only they can live and even thrive in an environment that would destroy lesser mortals.

T H E   *D R O K B A*
O F   N O R T H W E S T E R N   T I B E T

In Tibet, the ethnic label *drokba* is confined exclusively to the nomads of the high pastures. Like the Bedouin of Arabia, they form a distinct society that is separate from neighboring sedentary communities with whom they share a common language and Buddhist religion. They are concentrated in the Changtang, or Northern Plateau, region of Tibet. Perhaps the term concentrated is misleading, for the area is of immense size. Stretching over 1600 kilometers from east to west and encompassing more than two-thirds of Tibet's territory, it supports millions of head of livestock and about 500,000 people, a quarter of Tibet's population. Until crude roads were built following the Chinese occupation, transport in and out of the region was by yak caravan on treks that often required thirty or sixty days to complete. Although much richer in resources and population, its isolation is only comparable to the deserts of Arabia or the Sahara. Yet in spite of its physical size, the *drokba* have closer political ties with the region's sedentary rulers than nomads elsewhere and lack the autonomous tribal structure found in Mongolia, Iran, or Arabia. Indeed, Tibet provides a case study of the encapsulation of nomadic pastoralists into a larger state system which provides overall administration. To explain this seeming paradox, we must first understand how pastoralism is organized in Tibet and the unique relationship it has developed with its sedentary neighbors.

Until recently, the high-altitude pastoralism of Tibet was one of the least well-known. With the country's physical isolation and restrictions on dealings with the outside world, Tibet had won a reputation as a hermit kingdom. This situation was compounded when the region was incorporated into the People's Republic of China in 1959 following an invasion by Chinese troops which forced its ruler, the Dalai Lama, to flee to India along with many thousands of refugees. In the 1980s, the situation began to change because of a series of economic reforms in China and the government's attempt to encourage foreign investments. Tibet was initially opened only for tourism, but within a few years Chinese authorities began to allow some limited independent research. At this time, anthropologists Melvyn Goldstein and Cynthia Beall, who had worked with ethnic Tibetan communities in neighboring Nepal, received permission to conduct the first long-term field study of nomadic pastoralists in Tibet. The results of their research in 1986 through 1988 among the *drokba* living in Pala, a district of about 650 square kilometers in western Tibet with a population of 263 people, have provided a rich and detailed picture of contemporary Tibetan pastoralism and its historical struggles over the past forty years.[1]

THE ANIMALS

The herds of high-altitude pastoralists in Tibet consist mostly of yaks, sheep, and goats. Horses are highly valued but few in number, while camels are nonexistent except in a few districts bordering Mongolia. Cattle are considered village animals because they cannot survive the cold at high altitudes, although some cattle-yak hybrids (*dzo*) are found among pastoralists.

High-altitude pastoralism is uniquely dependent on the yak, a native of the highlands that will not reproduce at lower altitudes. Like the camel in the desert or the horse on the steppe, the yak is so essential for high-altitude life that it is the key animal by which the Tibetans identify their pastoralism. Indeed, the Tibetan term for yaks in general, *nor*, is also commonly used to mean "wealth." The wild yak is indigenous to the high Tibetan Plateau. Just when it was domesticated is unknown, but the genetic difference between wild and domestic yaks is not all that great because they still interbreed easily. The wild male yak (*drong*) looks like something out of the last Ice Age, standing 2 meters tall with a shaggy wool coat and huge horns. Domesticated male yaks are smaller, standing 1.2 to 1.5 meters in height and weighing between 200 and 250 kilograms. Female yaks (*dri*) are about three-quarters the size of the males. With the exception of a few bulls kept for breeding, male yaks are castrated for ease of management. Even so, they are dangerous to handle because of their size and sharp horns.

Yaks provide transport, milk, meat, and hair to the *drokba*.

What gives the domesticated yak its significance is its ability to thrive at high altitudes. With their heavy coats of hair and wool, and thick layers of fat, yaks are well adapted to the cold. They can graze contentedly on the short vegetation at 6,000 meters even in the winter. In fact, male yaks are not actively herded, they are simply let loose to graze and rounded up when they are needed. Pastoralists in central Tibet take advantage of the yak's preference for high places by locating their own camps at altitudes of between 5,000 and 5,500 meters. Domesticated yaks supply a variety of products for household consumption. They are the source of fine belly wool used to make tent cloth, produce milk through most of the year, can be slaughtered for meat, and their dung is used as fuel. The horns of large yaks even make good beer mugs. In addition to their important role in subsistence, yaks also provide transportation. A yak can be ridden or packed with about 90 kilograms of baggage and is essential for moving the nomads' heavy tents and household baggage from one campsite to another. The yak also makes long distance trade possible, for only it can cross the high mountain passes fully loaded and plow its way through snowdrifts without assistance.

In addition to yaks, some pastoralists make use of a *dzo*, the hybrid offspring of yak and common cattle. Cattle cannot survive at high altitudes and so are restricted to Tibetan villages, while yaks pine away if taken below 3,000 meters. By crossbreeding the two, a *dzo* hybrid is obtained which is superior in many ways to either of its parents. It straddles the altitude range of both and it is at home at much higher elevations than village cattle but can still move easily into lower altitudes. The *dzo* is much larger than a cow, produces more milk than a yak, and makes an excellent pack animal because it follows in line, while yaks tend to bunch together, a liability on narrow mountain trails. The *dzo* is particularly attractive in regions where farmers and nomads are close to one another and move in and out of each other's territory. For this reason, it tends to be associated with village-based pastoralists who run herds of surplus animals for their relatives in nearby uplands. The *dzo* is relatively rare among the high pasturage nomads of central Tibet because conditions there are too cold and the pastures too high. Unlike the mule, which is a sterile hybrid, the *dzo* is fertile but has never established itself as a separate breed because its genetic characteristics are unstable beyond the first cross.[2]

The sheep and goats raised by the *drokba* are unique to the region. Particularly adapted to high altitudes, with much longer coats of wool and hair to protect them from the cold, they are a distinctly different breed than those raised at lower elevations. For example, the fine, thick undercoat of insulating wool produced by Tibetan goats is the source of the world-famous (and extremely expensive) cashmere. The metabolism of sheep and goats on the Tibetan Plateau is also adapted to cope with the lack of oxygen by means of more hemoglobin in their blood, larger lungs, and faster rates of respiration than lowland stock.

While high-altitude pastoralism and yak breeding are synonymous in Tibet, it is a mix of species (as in other pastoral regions) that makes the economy viable. As among the steppe nomads, it is the sheep and goats that are the economic mainstay of pastoralism and they constitute the vast majority of livestock raised. For example, although the *drokba* measure wealth in terms of yaks (with one yak equal to six sheep or seven goats), Goldstein and Beall found that in Pala, the small stock constituted more than 85 percent of the total livestock. Historically, herders maintained twice as many sheep as goats, but recent demand for the Tibetan goat's valuable cashmere has increased its value so much that flocks are now composed of about equal numbers of both. It is the small stock that provide the bulk of milk in the summer, dried dung for fuel, wool used to make felt, and skins for coats. Wool and live animals are the main items of exchange in trade with farming villages by which the nomads acquire the grain that makes up the bulk of their diet. The small stock also play a unique role as transport animals in the salt trade. Caravans of sheep and goats, laden with packages of salt weighing about 10 to 15 kilograms apiece, make incredibly long journeys of forty or sixty days to distant markets! One advantage of using sheep and goats is that they are packed at the beginning of the journey and not unloaded until the end, which saves considerable labor.

Tibetan horses, like those of the Central Eurasian steppe, are small but sturdy ponies. However, in sharp contrast with the horse-raising nomads of

Salt collected by nomads is packed in small bags which will be strapped to the backs of goats and sheep for transport to distant markets.

the steppe, the *drokba* keep very few horses and use them only for transportation. As among the Bedouin, horses in Tibet are expensive luxuries (costing 5 yaks or 40 to 50 sheep apiece) which require constant care. In the winter, they must be protected against the bitter cold by covering them with felt blankets and feeding them stored fodder. For these reasons, Goldstein and Beall found that only a quarter of the households in Pala even owned a horse, not surprising, since they comprised less than .001 of 1 percent of the community's total livestock (28 out of 9,000 head). The high altitude also puts a physical strain on horses and Tibetan riders must take care not to exhaust them. Indeed, there is a saying that "a horse is not a horse if it does not carry uphill, and a man is not a man if he does not walk downhill."[3] In the past, the horse played an important role in warfare, but today their value is mainly as a marker of status.

The Tibetans keep two varieties of dogs. The first breed is a mastiff that is used to protect the small stock from predators like wolves and snow lions. The second breed is a highly valued hunting dog which is used most often in the pursuit of wild sheep or gazelles. A few nomads also keep cats as pets.

PASTURES AND MIGRATION

There are striking differences between the migration cycles of arid-zone pastoralists and those of nomads who live at high altitudes. At high altitudes, the pastures are more dependable because they receive regular precipitation.

However, they lack the seasonality that determines patterns of nomadic movement elsewhere because throughout the region there is only a single growing season. Depending on the latitude, pastures begin to green in late spring and mature rapidly in summer before dying off by the autumn. No matter which pasture is chosen, the livestock will still have to forage on dead vegetation for eight months out of the year. One pasture is therefore very much like another, so the nomads shift camps not to take advantage of differences between ecological zones, but to exploit more distant pastures in order to preserve the supply of grass around their home base. This requires only a limited set of short moves which, like those of the Central Asian Arabs, take place between a set of fixed pastures. In central Tibet, each family has a home base which they inhabit during the winter, spring, and summer. In the fall, most migrate a day or two's journey to previously unused pastures so that their animals can put on as much weight as possible before the winter begins, although some family members may choose to stay at the base camp. This almost stationary pattern of pastoralism highlights a point made often in earlier chapters: the degree of nomadism in any pastoral community depends on the productivity and dependability of its pastures. For example, in neighboring Qing-hai, at the headwaters of the Yellow River, Tibetan nomads have less productive pastures and consequently make many more moves, particularly in the spring and summer, than their cousins on the central plateau.[4]

The extremely cold temperatures make shelter essential. For this reason, it may seem surprising that a form of black tent is employed rather than a yurt. But since a yurt requires an expensive engineered wooden frame, the lack of wood and skilled carpenters (and comparative cost involved) have precluded its use here. Even if yurts were readily available, the black tent is such an important symbolic marker of nomadic Tibetan cultural ethnic identity that the people are loath to abandon them. In the areas bordering Mongolia, for example, yurts were often used as portable temples, while the black tent was retained for habitation. Although a Tibetan black tent may seem superficially similar to those found in Arabia or Afghanistan, it is sturdier. In contrast, its panels are made of woven yak hair rather than goat hair. Since the belly hair of a yak is similar to cashmere in fineness, the resulting cloth has a much tighter weave and provides more insulation than the black tents of the arid zones. In addition, to protect themselves from the cold and winds, the *drokba* often pitch their tents over deep foundations that employ rock walls to create a semi-subterranean dwelling. Animal shelters are also constructed at the base camp to provide protection for the small stock or to store fodder.

The determination of pasture rights is of critical importance in all pastoral societies. In spite of the *drokba*'s clear separation from neighboring farming communities, historically, the nomads were under the political control of large Buddhist monasteries to which they were bound. These monastic estates (Pala was part of the Panchen Lama's domain) claimed legal title to all the neighboring grasslands. The pastures themselves were named and their boundaries listed in registration books along with their capacity. Sets of families were granted the exclusive right to use specific pastures in return for a fixed tax payment. The amount of allocated pasture was determined by the size of a family's livestock holdings and was redistributed by the estate managers every three years. Right of transit, including a day's grazing, was permitted but there were no common pastures open to all. This management system worked particularly well, since the gross number of animals in a region was relatively stable over time, even though individual families might experience large gains or losses.

PASTORAL PRODUCTION AND TRADING RELATIONS

The *drokba* are exclusively pastoral. Managing their herd demands that they maximize the production of their livestock products in order to produce enough to meet the household's direct consumption needs along with a surplus for trade with sedentary communities, for without a grain supply they could not survive.

Milk is the most important subsistence product. It is never consumed fresh but instead is first boiled and turned into yoghurt. Some yoghurt is consumed directly, but most of it is churned into butter and the remaining solids dried for storage. (The liquid whey is sometimes boiled down to a blackish paste used as a form of face makeup by the women.) Milking, yoghurt making, and butter churning are exclusively women's work. For this reason, all the milking animals must be grazed close to camp. The work is particularly heavy in the summer when all the animals are giving milk, while in the winter, only the *dri* (female yaks) are still producing. In measuring the production of one herd of 155 sheep and goats and 11 yaks, Goldstein and Beall found that at the height of the season they produced around 32 liters daily, while in the winter, the *dri* production amounted to only about 3 liters daily.[5]

Wool and hair are collected in the summer. As we mentioned above, the goat's cashmere wool has recently become the most valuable product for international trade, but sheep's wool has always been in greater demand in trade with farmers. Each sheep produces about a half kilogram of wool which is used primarily to make felt (that material of a thousand uses) or reserved for trade with farmers. Since Tibetan pastoralists do not use yurts which consume large quantities of felt, they have proportionally larger surpluses of wool available for trade. Yak hair, which has less value in trade, is used domestically for weaving tent panels.

The slaughter of animals for skins and meat plays a larger role in Tibetan pastoralism than elsewhere. In Pala, the average household of five

Freshly made cheese is laid out in the sun to dry so that it can be stored for later use.

slaughtered twenty-two animals, wealthy households more than twice that number. Most of the animals are butchered all at once just before the start of winter because they are in the best physical condition. Deciding exactly how many animals to cull is an important decision. While pastoralists try to maximize their herds' size, they must also take into account their households' need for meat, the likelihood that the animals will not survive the harsh winter season, and the alternative uses for nonreproductive animals. Since a single winter coat requires ten tanned sheepskins or goatskins, and meat is a staple of the winter diet, the annual demand is substantial. The number of live animals to be exchanged with farmers for grain must also be taken into account. Unlike the passive management of your insured bank account, Tibetan pastoralists cannot just let their assets sit. Since all animals will die at some point, herders must determine the optimum time to trade or eat their animals, and their choice of how many and what types of animals to cull often spells the difference between economic success and failure.

The actual slaughter of animals puts the Buddhist *drokba* in a quandary because of their strong belief in reincarnation. Buddhism holds that the killing of any sentient being creates a debt of bad karma that may eventually result in an unhappy rebirth. But since the nomads can hardly be expected to be vegetarians and survive, they attempt to avoid this fate by delegating the actual killing to a small number of men who have made this activity an economic specialization or to others who simply need the work (women were traditionally forbidden to kill animals). Those readers who think this avoidance is hypocritical (the bad karma only attaches to the actual killing, not to the eating) are gently reminded that the average consumer of hamburgers, personally incapable of slaughtering a live cow, has no qualms about eating the meat after it has been ground and packaged by someone else. The cold mountain air provides a natural deep freeze so that it is not necessary for the meat to be smoked or dried; it is simply stacked in piles and used as needed through the winter and spring.

The direct production of pastoral commodities represents only one part of the economy. The staple diet on the high plateau is *tsamba*, roasted barley, which accounts for three-quarters of all calories consumed by the *drokba* (about 80 kilograms annually for an adult). Tea, brewed with butter and salt, is also consumed at every meal. Both these staples must be obtained in trade. Raiding farming areas, historically common elsewhere, was rare in Tibet both because these communities were strongly fortified and because the demand for pastoral products was so great that the terms of trade generally favored the nomads, particularly for wool and live animals. In 1987, Goldstein and Beall found that a kilogram of wool could be exchanged with farmers for 6 kilograms of barley, so that the wool of 45 sheep could be exchanged for the grain necessary to support an adult for a year. Live sheep were also in great demand by villagers and each could be exchanged with farmers for 23 to 34 kilograms of barley. Farmers also work for the nomads during the summer, particularly to tan hides (which the nomads refuse to do themselves) and to construct storage buildings for which they are paid in sheep.

In addition to pastoral products, the nomads in central Tibet play a key role in the international salt trade. Until recently, they were the exclusive source of salt for neighboring regions of Nepal, Bhutan, and Sikkim. To obtain salt (which is free to anyone who wishes to gather it), the nomads form work parties which travel to the distant salt flats in the spring. There, they collect the salt and package it for transport. Using sheep, goats, and yaks as pack animals, the loaded caravan then returns home. While some of the salt is consumed by the nomads and their animals, the bulk is transported during the fall and winter to distant villages where it is exchanged for grain. The investment in time and animals is considerable, since the entire process of extraction and the round-trip caravan journeys can consume three or four months. For this reason, the number of pastoralists participating in the trade fluctuates, depending on the price of salt and a household's needs. Thus a poor family anxious to preserve its livestock could meet its needs through the salt trade, while a more wealthy family would consider the work involved too great to be worthwhile.

One unique aspect of the relationship between pastoralists and sedentary villagers is the incorporation of a small but steady flow of farmers into pastoralism. As we have seen in previous chapters, this is the very opposite of the normal pattern of sedentarization where nomads become villagers. Pastoralists in Tibet consider their way of life easier than that of farmers, odd as that may seem to outsiders, and even an impoverished pastoralist can support his family by working for someone else or engaging in the salt trade. Therefore there are none of the inexorable pressures to leave the pastoral economy that we saw among the Basseri of Iran. On the contrary, agricultural land is so limited in these alpine regions that there is little demand for outside labor. The pastoral economy, on the other hand, is more expansive, employing seasonal laborers from the valleys as well as herding excess livestock owned by the villagers. The farming families that send their surplus livestock to high pastures either contract with a pastoral household to do the work or assign a son or brother to the task. Over time, as such a man picks up the necessary skills and begins to specialize in pastoral production, he may attach himself permanently to *drokba* society by marrying a nomad woman, eventually cutting his ties to his old extended family.[6]

SOCIAL STRUCTURE

The basic unit of Tibetan pastoral society is the household, normally a nuclear or stem family. These combine together to form small camp groups which share nearby pastures. The upper levels of lineage or clan organization are not well developed on the northern plateau because the nomads were all under state control and turned to the agents of the landed estates or to monastic officials to resolve disputes. In other areas where political control was more diffuse, such as the northeast, the nomads appear to have maintained larger organized kinship units.[7]

A new household is brought into existence by marriage, at which time a man receives his inheritance and a woman her dowry. Together this creates the nucleus for an autonomous household and, since each woman expects to be the mistress of her own tent, extended families are difficult to maintain although relatives continue to camp together and share the work. The parents retain one child to support them in old age who, in return, receives their shares in the remaining livestock and tent. Unlike the Mongols, Tibetan parents are not restricted in their choice of a residual heir. While it might be the youngest son, they are free to choose among the most promising of their children. A particularly popular choice is to designate a daughter as heir and attract an in-marrying son-in-law. In the past, children might also have been dedicated to service in a monastery.

Tibetan social structure displays more structural flexibility than in any other pastoral society. While the vast majority of marriages are monogamous, both polygyny and polyandry are permitted. As among other Eurasian pastoral societies polygyny was generally restricted to the wealthy because it meant that a man must support two autonomous tents. However, unlike any other nomadic pastoral society, the Tibetans also permitted polyandry, the marriage of one woman to two or more husbands. Although it was not common, when it did occur always took the form of fraternal polyandry, the marriage of a woman to two or more brothers. The debate about the reasons for such an unusual marriage practice has attracted considerable attention in the anthropological literature, but most researchers agree that it is highly unstable. Eventually each of the brothers wants his own wife and the polyandrous unit splits.[8]

The position of women among Tibetan pastoralists is stronger than in other pastoral societies. In particular, because all siblings inherit equally, a daughter's rights in the paternal estate are just as strong as a son's. Thus we do not find a system of brideprice, but rather dowry. Each woman has her own marriage fund which will form the core of her own household. And unlike other dowry systems (those of nineteenth-century Europe and America, for example) a woman never loses control of this asset. Should she divorce her husband, she is entitled to the return of her dowry and a share of any increase of the herd under her management.[9] Women also play a key economic role in maintaining the household because they do most of the work. After observing what seemed to be a system of hardworking women and lazy men around the encampment, Goldstein and Beall were surprised to discover that the women in Pala considered the division of labor fair, for as one commented:

> But of course I don't resent having to do all the milking and my other tasks. The men have their work as well and I wouldn't want to change with them. I'm always here by my children and tent and do not have to undergo the hardship of long-distance travel as the men do when they go on their journey to collect salt from distant lakes, or when they go to trade in the winter with villagers a month away.[10]

TRADITIONAL POLITICAL ORGANIZATION

Before 1959, the government of Tibet was primarily in the hands of Buddhist religious leaders. Often described as a theocracy, the clergy in Tibet managed large estates and religious endowments which supported a large network of monasteries. In some ways this system may seem very archaic, reminiscent of feudal Europe or ancient Egypt, but in other ways it was quite sophisticated. A key part of their organizational power lay in the fact that these institutions were permanent, in the same sense that a modern corporation is permanent. It was the institution that owned the land and ruled the people, not individuals or their families. Such foundations could therefore concentrate wealth and power over many generations and not suffer the periodic dispersal of property through inheritance. Indeed, in harmony with the Buddhist concept of reincarnation, not only was the monastic institution theoretically immortal, so was its leadership. Upon the death of a religious leader, officials would begin a search for his new incarnation and, upon discovery, reinstall him in his old estate. Officials would then act as regents in his name until he again reached the age of majority and ruled directly.[11]

In other parts of the world, such wealthy religious endowments fell victim to expropriation by secular rulers (witness the confiscation of monastic wealth in England by Henry VIII) or were vulnerable to the perils of roving armies or bandits who would loot and burn such targets of opportunity. Tibet, however, was so remote and difficult to reach that it rarely fell victim to hostile invaders who in any event could not occupy any more than a fraction of its immense plateau. Similarly, after the fall of the last Tibetan king around 840, the religious establishment faced no internal secular rivals strong enough to challenge their dominance. By the seventeenth century, Buddhist religious leaders, most notably the Dalai Lama, not only controlled Tibet but had successfully converted the Mongols to their faith and established a close relationship with the Manchu Ch'ing dynasty (1644 to 1911) in China.

Within Tibet, the nomads were considered part of large monastic estates which legally owned their land and had rights to their labor. Because of these legal obligations, the inhabitants of such estates are often referred to as serfs, which technically they were. But our conception of serf (a medieval wretch who was poor, landless, and abused by the Sheriff of Nottingham or an evil baron) is misleading when applied to the *drokba*. The *drokba* might not have been the legal owners of their pasture, but they were the private owners of their animals, which in a pastoral society is of more importance. In addition, "feudal obligations" were reciprocal: the administrators of landed estates could not evict the nomads from their hereditary pastures. Thus there was a considerable variation in wealth among the nomads and many were quite prosperous. For those who were poverty-stricken, the monasteries offered a source of aid, either through direct alms or as a source of wage labor. Unlike the nomads of Mongolia under the Ch'ing administration who were restricted to their banner territory, once they had met their obligations, Tibetan nomads were free to travel and to trade for personal profit.

The political encapsulation of the nomads within a state structure always has a profound effect on their political organization. The elaborate systems of consanguinity and descent, so important in autonomous pastoral nomadic societies, tend to fall into disuse when nomads lose their autonomy to a state because they rely on outsiders to adjudicate important disputes and ensure their access to resources. In central Tibet, disputes were settled by local administrators whose decisions could be appealed to higher authorities, even to the Dalai Lama in Llasa. Raids were uncommon because the rustlers could be captured and tried. Even the triennial redistribution of pasture, since it was based on the size of a household's livestock holdings, was an excellent management tool which prevented conflicts from arising between neighboring pastoral groups. As long as the rate of taxation was not viewed as unreasonable, the system had benefits as well as obligations. For example, compared with the endemic raiding that occurred in Qing-hai which was nominally under China's control, the degree of security in central Tibet was quite striking.[12]

TIBET   UNDER   CHINESE   RULE

The relationship between China and Tibet was historically ambiguous. The close relationship between the Ch'ing emperors and the Dalai Lamas was at once religious and political. While China did not administer Tibet directly, it did have considerable influence there; and while Tibet saw itself as autonomous, the country had not developed an independent presence in the world community. With the establishment of the People's Republic of China in 1949, the communist regime claimed legal sovereignty over Tibet as an autonomous region but recognized the Dalai Lama as its legitimate ruler. The odd combination of an atheistic Marxist government in Peking working with a Buddhist clergy in Llasa lasted only ten years. In 1959, the Chinese army invaded Tibet, forced the Dalai Lama to flee, and ruled directly.

The Chinese invasion brought an end to the old Tibetan political system. Monasteries were abolished and their wealth was confiscated. Political control fell into the hands of secular officials appointed by the Chinese. Initially, the changes had little impact on the *drokba*, but when rebellions against Chinese rule broke out, many nomadic groups got caught up in the fighting before it was suppressed by Chinese troops. At the local level, they continued to pasture their animals as before. As with the Kazaks in Xinjiang, in the early days of their rule, the Chinese were anxious to maintain pastoral production and therefore did not make many demands on the nomads. Families remained the basis of economic organization and animals remained private property. Organized religion was prohibited but not its private practice. This policy of accommodation changed radically with the inauguration of the Cultural Revolution in 1966. The Cultural Revolution was an attempt to tighten the implementation of revolutionary socialism in China proper and introduce it in those ethnically autonomous regions that had previously escaped its implementation. It was particularly hostile to traditional culture of all types and was determined to destroy all vestiges of the old order. The Cultural Revolution arrived in Tibet in 1970 with the establishment of communes. Wealthy pastoralists were declared "class enemies" and had all their assets seized. The communes then collectivized most of the animals, seized tools such as churns and buckets, and assigned the communes' members to jobs. The *drokba* were

Chinese rule in Tibet has created a series of roads that the nomads use to transport sheep and goats to markets.

forbidden to practice Buddhism and religious articles such as books, images, and shrines were destroyed. Although each commune member technically owned a share of the community's assets, in reality the situation was much more serflike than under the Buddhist clergy. Whereas under the old system only the distribution of pasture was controlled by the estate, now all aspects of economic and social life were fixed by state policies.

As in other socialist countries, pastoral communes attempted to rationalize production by creating specific job categories and assigning work on a factory model. Instead of carrying out a variety of tasks, people were now expected to become full time herders or milk processors. Labor was compensated by a system of points assigned for each day's work which was recorded in a workbook, a cumbersome mechanism for a largely illiterate population. While each member received at least the bare minimum for subsistence and extra money based on the number of accumulated points, the majority saw their standard of living drop precipitously. This was both because the level of taxation by the government was much higher than that collected by the monasteries and because the Chinese forced the communes to make forced sales of wool and meat to the government at low prices. This transfer of wealth out of the local community was compounded by an overall drop in production because the communal herds did not receive the level of care that had been devoted to privately owned stock.

Reorganizing the economic structure of Tibetan society was only part of the Cultural Revolution's agenda. Chinese policy also attempted to destroy Tibetan culture by ruthlessly suppressing all aspects of religion and ridiculing local cultural traditions. "Class struggle sessions" were conducted by party cadres to inculcate the new values and condemn the persistence of overt symbols of cultural identity such as braided hairstyles for men. To overturn both Buddhist values and the traditional sexual division of labor, women were required to participate in animal slaughter. The damage such actions did in small pastoral communities should not be underestimated. There were no anonymous victims in face-to-face communities where "class struggle" demanded the persecution of friends, kinsmen, or even family members. It was as if an alien political blizzard had struck at the very core of cultural life.

Like a blizzard, however, the storm passed. The damage done by the Cultural Revolution throughout China, and particularly in minority areas, was condemned when new leadership in Peking abandoned radical socialism in 1976. The commune system was abolished in central Tibet in 1981. As among the Kazaks of the Altai, Tibetan commune assets were divided among its members. Each individual in Pala received 37 animals so that the average family of five started with a herd of 25 yaks, 125 sheep, and 35 goats, plus an additional 30 to 40 goats which families had previously acquired as private stock during the commune period. Taxes and forced sales to the government were also suspended for the rest of the decade. After a short period of suspicion that the reforms would be short-lived, the pastoralists in Pala returned to the economic organization they had practiced before the communes were instituted.

Cultural life was also revived as people once again openly practiced Buddhism, restored their household shrines, and donated money to rebuild the local monasteries that had been destroyed during the Cultural Revolution. Reestablishing this religious identity appears to have taken on much greater significance than among steppe nomads such as the Kazaks or Mongols. Historically, the Tibetan pastoralists have viewed themselves as an integral part of a larger Tibetan society for which Buddhism is one of the most important defining characteristics. While the practice of Islam is important to the Kazaks in Xinjiang, with decollectivization, they have put more emphasis on the reestablishment of a pastoral and tribal identity than on any religious revival. Similarly, in Mongolia, where Tibetan Buddhism was once universal, shamanistic practices and cultural revitalization through a nationalist cult of Chinggis Khan have taken on more prominence than organized religion.

The economic changes after reform included an increase in the number of goats raised in order to profit from the cashmere trade and a decline in the number of pastoralists engaged in the export of salt. The restoration of private ownership also provides striking evidence of the dynamics of

An old nomad reading from a Buddhist prayer book hand printed from wooden blocks. During the Cultural Revolution the Chinese government attempted to suppress Buddhism in Tibet, but belief remained strong in spite of persecution. Today religious practice has revived and is practiced openly.

risk in pastoralism. Within less than ten years of restoring private owner-ship of livestock in Pala, its economic structure had once again become stratified. Although they all started with 37 head of livestock per capita, by 1988 38 percent of the households in Pala owned less than 30 head per ca-pita, while 12 percent owned over 50. Such rapid changes in growth and decline demonstrate how risky pastoralism is, and why nomads have al-ways realized that good management must be combined with good luck to ensure success.

   After decollectivization, livestock census figures appeared to show rapid increases in livestock in Tibet. While such figures were heralded as evidence for the success of the new policy, the government also feared that the pastoralists desire for the exponential growth of their livestock might devastate the natural grasslands and therefore force the *drokba* to cull their herds in order to reduce the overall number of animals. As in other coun-tries that have large pastoral populations, the fear that nomadic pastoral-ists will fall victim to the "tragedy of the commons" and destroy their own economic base is an article of faith among Chinese officials and researchers. In fact, as Goldstein and Beall have argued, in Tibet this problem is vastly overstated mostly both because short-term data is used to make long-term projections and because the statistics themselves may be misleading. They note that since individual pastoralists have always attempted to maximize production (sometimes with spectacular success), if it were possible to radically increase herd size with no new changes in the existing technology or environment, then the northern plateau would have become saturated with enormous numbers of yaks and sheep long before the Chinese began counting them. Yet historically, the overall number of livestock in Tibet has remained remarkably stable on a regional basis, even though individuals might lose or gain substantially. This is apparent in the fact that the monasteries registered pastures on the basis of how many livestock each could support. Statistics that show spectacular increases in areas where pastoralism has been long established therefore need to be examined carefully. The high growth rates seen in recent Chinese figures are often the result of choosing an unusually low base year (initial counts after a long period of civil unrest, for example); or are the result of unacknowledged changes in accounting procedures (some figures include only a commune's own livestock, while others count privately owned animals as well); or are simply bogus (attempts by officials to inflate their success with invented rates of increase).[13]

One reason for misunderstanding between nomadic pastoralists and sedentary planners or officials is the very different ways they interpret pastoral assets. To the sedentary official, whether he be in Africa or Tibet, a herd is like a bank account: a fixed sum that grows by accumulating interest over time. Calculate the rate of increase and you can determine the exact size of the asset in the future as it grows toward infinity. (We leave aside "extraneous" factors such as bank failures, hyper-inflation, wars, and revolutions that make such a model less than satisfactory and have historically prevented the small savers from dominating the world economy.) To the pastoralist, on the other hand, a herd is more like a risky "common stock" investment (no pun intended) that both pays a dividend and has a variable underlying value. Dividends do not automatically compound and, as many an investor has learned the hard way, the value of a holding can fluctuate as dramatically downward as upward. Thus while the holder of a bank account can say exactly how much money he has at any point, a stock investor can only say how much money he has if he were to liquidate the investment today. Because pastoralists are in the business for life, the potential value of their assets is purely theoretical. Since cycles of exponential growth are usually closely related to cycles of exponential decline, pastoralists understand that in the real world they cannot begin to approach infinite herd growth. This truth may be obscured in frontier regions where livestock are introduced for the first time, such as Texas, Australia, or Argentina, and seem to reproduce without limit; but where pastoralism has long been established and its upper limits have been reached, herd growth is ultimately a zero-sum game. The gains in one herd are generally offset by losses in another.

T H E   F U T U R E
O F   P A S T O R A L I S M   I N   T I B E T

Pastoralism is likely to thrive in Tibet to a degree unmatched elsewhere in Eurasia. Its vast pastures can be effectively utilized in no other way and they cannot be converted to farmland. The local economic demands for wool and meat, and the export of cashmere to world markets make it economically viable. In addition, there are none of the pressures that induce nomads to leave the pastoral economy such as the attraction of wage labor in the cities and oil fields of the Middle East, the pressures of high population growth in East Africa, or the destruction of the pastoral economy that occurred in Kazakhstan.

In spite of the harsh climatic conditions, Tibetan nomads believe that their way of life is easier than that of farmers, so they have no desire to switch places with them. They may, however, remain pastoral and become less nomadic. In the northern plateau where only a few moves are necessary to take care of the livestock, the *drokba* have begun to replace their tents with permanent houses. This has become possible because trucks can now bring in the wood beams needed to erect them. In the time of yak caravans, the importing of such building materials to the high pastures was almost impossible. As we saw earlier with the Central Asian Arabs who abandoned yurts for permanent houses in their winter region, in areas where the pasture is dependable there is no contradiction between a pastoral economy and a permanent base. Indeed, from the animals' point of view there is no change at all, since they continue to move between the same pastures.

One change that is likely to occur is the evolution of Tibetan pastoralism away from subsistence and more toward commercial production. With China's enormous population, the demand for pastoral products is quite high, and under the new economic reforms Tibetan pastoralists can now personally benefit from the rising value of wool, meat, and cashmere. This, of course, was impossible under the commune system, and under the old regime in Tibet the difficulty of transport made it difficult to build trade networks for pastoral products beyond neighboring farming areas. Yet as their monopoly of the salt trade and participation in overland caravans demonstrated, the *drokba* have long been skilled long-distance caravan traders renowned for their sharp business sense. Unlike the Altai Kazaks in the neighboring province of Xinjiang who complain of being cheated by oasis merchants, Tibetan pastoralists are so at home in the rough and tumble of business that it is the sedentary merchant who is in danger of being skinned. Thus the slaughter of meat for household consumption, which is much higher than in other pastoral societies, may begin to decline as the value of meat as a commodity rises. If this occurs, then Tibetan pastoralists may begin to resemble ranchers for whom pastoralism is a cash business, although unlike commercial animal husbandry elsewhere,

Cashmere has become one of the nomads most valued items of trade. The hair combed here from the belly of the goat may ultimately end up in an expensive scarf or coat sold in an exclusive store in Paris, New York or Tokyo.

the ability of the Tibetans to combine meat and wool production for exchange with milk production for domestic use will continue because the family rather than hired shepherds will remain the key productive unit.

NOTES

1. Melvyn Goldstein, and Cynthia Beall, *Nomads of Western Tibet: The Survival of a Way of Life* (Berkeley: University of California Press, 1989).

2. Robert B. Ekvall, *Fields on the Hoof* (New York: Holt, Rinehart and Winston, 1968).

3. Goldstein and Beall, *Nomads*, p. 72.

4. Goldstein and Beall, *Nomads*, pp. 58–65; Ekvall, *Fields*, pp. 32–34.

5. Goldstein and Beall, *Nomads*, pp. 87–95.

6. James F. Downs, "Livestock, Production and Social Mobility in High Altitude Tibet," *American Anthropologist*, 66 (1964), pp. 1115–1119.

7. Ekvall, *Fields*, p. 29.

8. Ekvall, *Fields*, pp. 26–27.

9. cf. Nancy C. Levine, *The Dynamics of Polyandry: Kinship, Domesticity, and Population on the Tibetan Border*. Chicago: University of Chicago Press, 1988.

10. Goldstein, and Beall, *Nomads*, p. 95.

11. Franz Michael, *Rule by Incarnation: Tibetan Buddhism and Its Role in Society* (Boulder, CO: Westview Press, 1982).

12. cf. Robert B. Ekvall, "Peace and War among the Tibetan Nomads," *American Anthropologist*, 66 (1964), 1119–48.

13. Melvyn Goldstein, and Cynthia Beall, "The Impact of China's Reform Policy on the Nomads of Western Tibet," *Asian Survey*, 29 (1989), 619–41.

FURTHER READINGS

HIGH ALTITUDE ASIA

Aziz, Barbara, *Tibetan Frontier Families*. Durham, No. Carolina: Carolina Academic Press, 1978.

Ekvall, Robert, *Tibetan Skylines*. New York: Farrar, Straus & Giroux, Inc., 1952.

Huc, Evariste-Régis and Joseph Gabet, *Travels in Tartary, Thibet and China 1844–1846*. New York: Dover Publications, 1989 [1853].

Mathias, Hermanns, *Die Nomaden von Tibet*. Vienna: Verlag Herold, 1949.

Shahrani, M. Nazif, *The Kirghiz and Wakhi of Afghanistan*. Seattle: University of Washington Press, 1979.

HIGH ALTITUDE PASTORALISM IN SOUTH AMERICA

Baker, P.T. and M.A. Little, eds., *Man in the Andes: A Multi-Disciplinary Study of High-Altitude Quechua*. Stroudsburg, PA: Dowden, Hutchinson & Ross, 1976.

Browman, David Ludvig, "Pastoral Nomadism in the Andes," *Current Anthropology*, 15 (1974):188–196.

Flannery, Kent, and others, *The Flocks of Waimani: A Study of Llama Herders on the Punas of Ayacucho, Peru*. San Diego: Academic Press, 1989.

Flores-Ochoa, J.A., *Pastoralists of the Andes: The Alpaca Herders of Paratia*. Philadelphia: ISHI, 1979.

THE ENDURING NOMAD: PERCEPTIONS AND REALITIES

And some of our men just in from the border say
there are no barbarians any longer.

Now what's going to happen to us without barbarians?
Those people were a kind of solution.

Constantine Cavafy
"Awaiting the Barbarians"

In the previous chapters we have examined nomadic pastoralism as a way of life in different parts of the world largely from the nomads' perspective. But popular images about nomadic life, both positive and negative, are rarely the products of direct observation or experience. Instead, they are filtered through a series of legendary histories and folk beliefs that are deeply ingrained among sedentary people. These impressions are often so strong that facts alone cannot overcome them. Why should nomads be so difficult to demystify? To understand this we must leave the world of nomadic pastoralism as a way of life and instead examine the role nomads have played in the imagination of sedentary writers (of whom anthropologists are only a small minority), an imagination often aided and abetted by the nomads themselves for their own purposes.

Nomadic pastoral peoples, in spite of their relatively small numbers, have attracted more than their fair share of attention because they have always represented the classic "other," a social construction of a society and culture that appears to be the very antithesis of the observer's, that is simultaneously both attractive and repellent. Historically, these differences were expressed by the image of the nomad as a savage force of nature, as a cunning and dangerous barbarian, and as a free agent who, as in Cavafy's famous poem, quoted in part above, may represent some kind of answer to the ills of civilization.

The image of the nomad as a savage has very deep roots. Herodotus's hair-raising accounts of Scythian headhunting, blooddrinking, and cloaks of human skin in the fifth century B.C. placed them beyond the pale of Greek civilization. Similarly, many Han Chinese officials of the second century B.C., found the nomadic way of life so alien they declared that it was inappropriate to have a foreign policy toward them, and that nomadic tribes should be "regarded as beasts to be pastured, not as members of the human race."[1] The fourteenth-century North African scholar Ibn Khaldun similarly argued that what he termed "Bedouin civilization" was the incompatible precursor to a more advanced sedentary civilization. While Bedouin peoples had many admirable virtues such as bravery, generosity, and high standards of personal honor, as societies their behavior was incompatible with the maintenance of sedentary life:

> The Bedouins are a savage nation, fully accustomed to savagery and the things that cause it. Savagery has become their character and nature. They enjoy it, because it means freedom from authority and no subservience to leadership. Such a disposition is the negation and antithesis of civilization... For instance, they need stones to set them up as support for their cooking pots. So, they take them from buildings which they tear down to get the stones, and use them for that purpose. Wood, too, is needed by them for props for their tents and for use as tent poles for their dwellings. So, they tear down roofs to get wood for that purpose. The very nature of their existence is the negation of building, which is the basis of civilization. This is the case generally with them.[2]

Such savage nomads were a danger to sedentary society because they respected no rules. Like a cloud of locusts or a herd of elephants, they descended upon their neighbors and took what they wanted, not out of malice but because they made no distinction between the natural and social world. This view has survived into modern times in two forms. First, it is still casually asserted that nomadic pastoralism is but a primitive survival, a stage of evolution that lies between hunting and agriculture. This oft-cited claim is not supported by the archaeological record nor by the overwhelming evidence that nomadic pastoralism is an economic specialization as complex as agriculture. Second is the belief common among many government officials and development planners that movement is pathological, a belief that civilized life is only possible with a fixed address and a respect for bureaucratic boundaries (a concept particularly dear to tax collectors and others in the resource extraction business).

The fear of nomads as barbarians took a slightly different tack. Barbarian nomads were fully cultural, that is, they could reason and plan. But what they planned, from a sedentary perspective, was evil and destructive. Nomads, in the historian Gibbon's words, were "bold in arms and impatient to ravish the fruits of industry."[3] They stood ready to plunder their neighbors and overrun weak civilizations if given the opportunity. Such is the ferocious image of the Huns painted by Saint Jerome, a Roman historian of the fifth century A.D.:

> Lo, suddenly messengers ran to and fro and the whole east trembled, for swarms of Huns had broken forth from far distant Maeotis between the icy Tanais and the monstrous peoples of the Massagetae, where the Gates of Alexander pen the wild nations behind the rocks of the Caucasus. They filled the whole earth with slaughter and panic alike as they flitted hither and thither on their swift horses... May Jesus avert such beasts from the Roman world in the future! They were at hand everywhere before they were expected: by their speed they outstripped rumor, and they took pity neither upon religion nor rank nor age nor wailing childhood. Those who had just lived were compelled to die and, in ignorance of their plight, would smile amid the drawn sword of their enemy.[4]

A similar specter haunted the opposite end of Eurasia where it was widely believed that only the Great Wall of China kept the flood tide of barbarians at bay.

As we have seen, the horse-riding nomads of the steppe did have a powerful military force that could threaten their neighbors, and they deliberately cultivated a reputation for fierceness. They were also active purveyors of fear so that their very appearance on the frontier was designed to strike terror among their neighbors. But their military power was normally used to extort subsidies or favorable trade relationships from their neighbors, not to conquer them. The Huns, for example, were always prepared to withdraw from territory that they had overrun upon the payment of large sums of gold. In fact, nomads were generally too weak in numbers to hold extensive sedentary territory and became conquerors only when their neighbors collapsed from internal problems and created a vacuum. Even Ibn Khaldun laid the blame for the victory of nomadic conquerors at the feet of corrupt sedentary rulers who lost their thrones through bankruptcy and incompetence.

Yet the idea of the nomad as a permanent threat was nevertheless powerfully planted in the minds of sedentary observers for whom they represented a powerful anticivilization. In both the Koran and the Bible, the hordes of Gog and Magog are described as penned behind mountainous walls, waiting to strike the sinful societies of the south. Even today, visitors trek to China's Great Wall and look northward seeking to imagine the days when horse-riding nomads on a sea of grass lapped up against this last bulwark of civilization. It is a vision so overwhelming that, as the historian Arthur Waldron has shown, the Great Wall itself long ago left the pages of history for a grander mythic existence. In actuality, the Great Wall existed only sporadically during a few dynasties and even then never constituted much of a barrier to nomad incursions. Yet today, it has become a primary symbol of Chinese civilization, the cultural dyke that resisted the flood tide of barbarians who were always lurking just beyond the horizon (or in the imagination) of its defenders.[5]

If the image of the nomad as a savage or a barbarian was long the bogeyman of sedentary societies, the nomad as a free agent, as the repository of virtues lost in peasant society or urban civilization, presented an attractive face. The very tents of the nomads are a sign of their ability to move at will and take their mobile livestock economy with them, throwing off old constraints and relationships. This, of course, is the reverse image of an agricultural village with its fixed plots of land, permanent houses, and seemingly fixed relationships. Yet the price of this freedom is high, for to the villager such mobility also represents rootlessness and a lack of connection to a specific piece of land. Is it not the sentence of a wandering exile to do without luxuries and property? Nomads were therefore best admired at a distance because their freedom was purchased with sacrifices few sedentary people were prepared to tolerate.

Ironically, the romantic image of nomads is strongest in lands where there are no nomads today. Perhaps the idealization of their life is easiest to sustain if their goats are not eating from your garden, or if your country did not fall prey to the Mongol empire. For societies that stress individualism, self-reliance, and personal autonomy, the nomad would seem to provide a perfect role model. But this too is largely an illusion created by focusing on only certain aspects of nomadic culture. For while individuals in nomadic societies are confronted with a wide range of choices and held responsible for their decisions, they are still tied closely to larger social groups which set standards of personal behavior and responsibility and bind individuals tightly to cultural norms that they cannot ignore. The Bedouins camped alone in the deserts of Arabia do not see themselves as isolated individuals, but as communities united by kinship even when separated by distance. For the nomad, exile is the separation from the community by social rejection, not by physical distance. Thus though nomads may seem to have the freedom to get up and go, to start life anew at will, they are in fact much more constrained by a permanent web of relationships than residents of modern urban societies. It is the anonymous city dweller, alone in a sea of people with whom he has no permanent ties, who is the true social nomad, changing identity by flitting from one community to another or one job to another.

Historically, it did not matter much what sedentary people thought of nomads because they were in no position to dominate them. But when the balance of power changed and the nomads lost most or all or their autonomy, they became vulnerable to policies set by distant governments and

Stereotypes about pastoral nomads have ranged from the peaceful shepherd, such as this man watching his flock graze in northern Afghanistan to the fierce warrior, an image recalled by a Kazak man in the Altai Mountains proudly displaying his hunting eagle.

implemented by officials who had no conception of their way of life. Deeply seated beliefs about pastoral nomadism, such as those outlined above, therefore became the unexamined basis of policy. The negative attitude toward nomads in particular has underlain most attempts by governments to sedentarize nomads in order to put an end to a troublesome way of life. But even where nomads were viewed more positively, or where their economic importance could not be denied, a question still remained: Did nomadic pastoralism have a future in the modern world?

THE PROBLEMS AND PROSPECTS FOR NOMADS IN THE MODERN WORLD

In each of the preceding chapters we have seen that animal husbandry continues to play an important regional economic role in semi-arid grassland areas. Governments and international agencies have laid great stress on developing such pastoral resources to fulfill domestic needs and to provide exports. Yet the role of the nomadic pastoralist in this endeavor is less clear. It is not a simple problem, for it involves at least three basic questions:

1. Has the historic shift of power that led to the domination of pastoral societies by centralized sedentary governments made it impossible for them to compete effectively with other groups in nation-states? The legal status of pastoral land claims, the growing competition over the development of semi-arid lands for agricultural use, and the political role of nomads in the state all hinge on power relations in which the nomads often find themselves at a severe disadvantage.

2. Has nomadic pastoralism changed in any ways that make it more competitive in the modern world? The focus by anthropologists, and many nomads themselves, on "pure" forms of pastoralism may disguise the extent to which pastoralists have adapted to political and economic changes, and the historic importance of sedentarization as a normal aspect that has sustained the long-term viability of nomadic pastoralism.

3. Is nomadic pastoralism economically viable and environmentally sustainable? In sub-Saharan Africa in particular, there is the fear that pastoralists may be degrading the environment, hastening the process of desertification, and that nomads in general are a classic example of a self-defeating "tragedy of the commons" situation.

SHIFTS OF POWER

One of the key changes affecting the organization of nomadic pastoralism in the modern world has been the nomads' loss of autonomy after incorporation into sedentary states. Historically, nomads controlled their own pastures, administered their own justice, made peace and war, and moved as they pleased. Sedentary powers found it impossible to rule people who could remove themselves and their animals beyond the range of effective control. The Bedouins could escape into the deep desert with their camels where they could not be found, and many sedentary armies came to grief chasing the elusive horse-riding nomads of the steppe. Not only could nomads flee domination, their very mobility could be employed militarily to threaten their neighbors. Raids by nomads from Mongolia deep into China and wars along the steppes of Russia forced many neighboring states to treat the nomads as their diplomatic equals even when nomadic populations and economies were much smaller. In some cases, invasions even led to the conquest of weak sedentary states and the establishment of nomadic tribes as a political elite, a recurring cycle first described by Ibn Khaldun in his history of the rise and fall of dynasties in the Near East. Of course, not all nomads maintained such a high degree of autonomy. The sheep-raising tribes on the margins of the deserts in Arabia and North Africa, and those with permanent bases in sedentary areas, such as the Central Asian Arabs, always accepted the control of neighboring regional states because such an accommodation allowed them to invest in agricultural land and retain access to good pastures near urban centers and markets.

The rise of modern states with new weapons, technologies, and means of communication spelled the end to nomadic autonomy and military power. This decline was earliest and sharpest among the nomads who had previously been the most powerful, the horsemen of Central Eurasia. A major threat to their agricultural neighbors for two millennia, and one-time conquerors of most of the medieval world, the steppe nomads first found themselves at a disadvantage when their enemies acquired heavy cannons and muskets that reduced the effectiveness of mounted archery. This was the beginning of a technological revolution that, with the introduction of rifles and light cannons, brought devastating firepower to bear on nomad armies on the steppe. As a consequence, the balance of power in the border areas shifted and traditional bastions of nomad strength, such as the Black Sea steppe and southern Mongolia, were annexed by Russia and China in the seventeenth century. For the next two centuries, the nomads continually lost ground to these two powers until there were no more independent nomad tribes in Central Eurasia. With the spread of motor vehicles and aircraft in the twentieth century, even the vast deserts of Arabia and the Sahara could not offer protection against the armies of modern states. Sheer distance or lack of resources were no longer impenetrable barriers to movement or state control. In rapid order, previously autonomous nomads in sub-Saharan African, Iran, Afghanistan, Arabia, and North Africa all fell under direct state control, often for the first time.

This military advantage of sedentary states was also accompanied by a revolution in transportation technology during the past century and a half. The major innovation was the railroad which could move people and goods across vast distances economically. In the wake of military conquests and the establishment of colonial regimes, these railways brought immigrant farmers who settled on what had been prime land for grazing and pushed the nomads into more marginal territory. The Kazak steppe was settled by the Czars with grain farmers from the Ukraine whose descendants now constitute about 40 percent of the population, while in China, nomads of southern Mongolia progressively lost most of their land to Chinese settlers who now make up 80 to 90 percent of the region's population. In East Africa, the Masai lost the highlands to British farmers who established plantations for growing coffee and other cash crops. Railways also facilitated the development of mineral resources such as coal, iron, and oil that had previously been unexploited. Not all of these innovations were disadvantageous to pastoralists. Rail networks, and later truck and air transport, have made it possible for livestock breeders to sell their hides, wool, milk products, and meat to distant markets for high prices.

The incorporation of nomadic societies by sedentary state administrations had a profound political impact, but the structure of such relationships varied widely depending on the cohesion of the nomads' political organizations, whether they were perceived as allies or enemies of the central government, and whether they occupied strategic areas or played an important role in the national economy.

The nomads who were able to deal most effectively with state administrations were those that had effective supratribal political leadership with established ties to urban areas. In regions where nomads had long dealt with state authorities as unified groups, they retained considerable influence even after they lost autonomy. For example, the khans of the important tribal confederations in Iran were well-educated members of the national elite who were based in the cities where they represented their followers' interests and served as brokers at both the regional and national levels. Even though they lacked an official role in government, the fact that they often represented hundreds of thousands of followers in strategic parts of Iran gave them considerable influence. Similarly, prominent families among the Bedouin tribes in the Near East, such as the Rwala Bedouin, have been involved with complex negotiations to preserve the rights of their people to cross the borders of the region without documents or restrictions. The fact that the region's remaining monarchies have historically recruited their troops from Bedouin tribes has also given them a continuing political role.

Nomadic pastoralists without such supratribal organizations were the least effective in confronting state authorities. In East Africa, where age sets and petty chiefs had been the rule, pastoralists found they had little leverage with officials appointed by colonial regimes and the independent states that succeeded them. Among most nomadic groups, there was no single recognized leader or ruling dynasty that could bridge the gap between government officials and ordinary pastoralists. Without such representation, nomadic pastoralists have had little success in influencing national states to consider their needs when planning for national parks that exclude grazing livestock; nor have they been able to shift the focus of development planning away from its preoccupation with expanding agricultural productivity at their expense. However, the rise of the Zulu state in southern Africa during the nineteenth century and the important role Dinka pastoralists have taken in the long-running civil war in Sudan over the past thirty years demonstrate that this situation is far from static, and that as governments rise and fall, nomadic pastoralists may be in a position to restructure relationships more to their advantage.

Falling between these extremes were groups like the Mongols, Kazaks, and other Central Eurasian nomads who had powerful indigenous leadership and cohesive political structures which were destroyed after their incorporation into the empires of China and Russia. During the nineteenth century, local leaders were stripped of real authority, which left their followers vulnerable to oppression by government officials, often men of dubious competence and honesty who resented being exiled to such remote posts. In the twentieth century, the collectivization policies of succeeding communist regimes destroyed most of what remained of the nomads' traditional leadership structure. In spite of these vicissitudes, however, the recent economic reforms in China and Mongolia and the independence of former Central Asian republics of the Soviet Union have reinvigorated local ethnic nationalism and a new class of indigenous leaders has risen. These officials see pastoral production as an important part of a developing economy, and for some, the glorification of an imperial nomad past has become a key element of national pride, particularly among the Mongols who have practically deified Chinggis Khan.

PASTORALISM AND ECONOMIC DEVELOPMENT

Regardless of what sort of relationship nomads have established with the nations in which they reside, they all face the difficulty of overcoming the prejudice that mobile pastoralism is incompatible with economic development. Mobile pastoralism is all too often viewed as an archaic mode of production that, while colorful, has no future in the modern world. This debate revolves around the two distinct features of nomadic pastoralism: the mobility of populations and the economic organization of pastoral production.

Mobility

All the customary activities of the Bedouin lead to wandering and movement. This is the antithesis and negation of stationariness, which produces civilization.[6]

Two old Kazak women in conversation outside yurt during a wedding feast. Such feasts were forbidden as "wasteful" by the Chinese government during the period of collectivization but were quickly restored when the Kazaks regained control of their own livestock after economic reform in the mid-1980s.

Ibn Khaldun, and sedentary people in general, have generally viewed the nomadic life as inimical to civilization—which finds its ultimate expression in the development of cities. If pastoral nomads are to be brought into the modern world, they must first be settled. Only then can they receive education, health care, and raise their standard of living. Officials in many countries therefore proclaim that while they have nothing against pastoralism, and would even like to encourage it, the nomads must first agree to stay put like regular people. That this is often technically impossible may explain the nomads' lack of enthusiasm for such proposals. Indeed, since pastoralism is often a more dependable (and more profitable) way of making a living than subsistence agriculture on the semi-arid steppes of Central Eurasia, the mountains of Iran, or the African savanna, settlement might well mean a loss of wealth. With some justification, nomads have considered policies of sedentarization to be motivated primarily by the state's desire to control their populations better, not to do them any favors.

All governments have an innate antipathy toward people without a fixed address which extends even to those with multiple residences in different jurisdictions. The reason is political, not economic. Such people are difficult to command because they can move across borders to avoid taxes, smuggle goods, or escape conscription. Their loyalties are often tied to a social group rather than rooted to a single place. This is true whether they happen to engage in pastoralism or in some other occupation. The City of New York would dearly love to prosecute its residents who escape paying parking fines and other taxes because they have declared a "legal residence" (humble though it may be) in their summer camping grounds of Vermont and so have registered their cars there. Like nomads everywhere, these mobile urban residents attempt to avoid the city's exactions by keeping just beyond its legal grasp.

Nomadic pastoralists constitute the largest of the world's mobile populations and, because they have historically occupied marginal regions of mountains, steppe, and desert, they tend to straddle the frontiers between nation-states. Until modern times, these frontiers were vaguely defined and there was little purpose in trying to assume control of regions that cost more to hold and administer than they contributed in revenue. Even the greatest sedentary states never enforced claims over vast wastelands they could not exploit. Control of distant territory was therefore so loose or so indirect that the political relationship of lands like Tibet and Mongolia to China was often unclear. With the expansion of European states throughout the world, however, a new concept of state sovereignty emerged which demanded fixed boundaries between nation-states and asserted that governments within such boundaries had a monopoly on the legitimate use of force. Since the European states abhorred the idea that any place in the world might be allowed to go unclaimed and unbounded, they proceeded to create fixed boundaries in regions where none had ever existed before. Such lines were, of course, arbitrary and initially meaningless to the indigenous populations.

When governments attempted to make such lines on a map true barriers, the movement of nomads suddenly became a political problem. The Masai, for example, found themselves divided between Tanzania and Kenya and were expected to refrain from moving their cattle over a boundary that made little sense to them. What was ordinary everyday behavior like trading with neighbors or visiting kinfolk was now redefined as "smuggling" or "illegal immigration." Similarly, the Bedouin found themselves migrating between a host of new nations carved out of the Arabian Peninsula, many of which now looked upon their deserts as potential oil fields. Afghan nomads found that their traditional migration routes which crossed the border between Afghanistan and Pakistan left them vulnerable to disputes between these two countries.

Nomads, of course, have naturally viewed such restrictions upon their movements as illegitimate, since they had been moving across these territories long before any of these states were created and their boundaries drawn. The usual government response to such opposition has been to insist on the settlement of nomads, regardless of the consequences. More than any other issue, the movement of nomads has remained a source of continual friction between nomadic peoples and nation-states.

Economic Organization

Despite any political problems nomads may cause, in each of the areas we have examined, pastoralism continues to play an important productive role and contributes measurably to local and national economies. Far from being unchanging or out of touch with the world, we have seen that pastoral nomadism has made many adaptations to the modern world. Perhaps the biggest change occurring among pastoralists is the movement away from raising animals for subsistence to raising animals for exchange. Although they still may use yurts, tents, or cattle kraals, pastoralists in most parts of the world now depend less on consuming the direct products of their herds (milk, meat, wool, and so on) and more on their sale to the market for money. Many nomadic pastoralists are becoming ranchers: pastoral specialists in a cash economy.

This has occurred most intensively in North Africa, Arabia, the Iranian Plateau, and Central Asia, where nomads have long been tied into market networks. Among the Bedouins, the use of trucks has allowed the expansion of sheep and goat production and reduced the importance of camel raising. The nomads of Afghanistan and Iran are highly integrated into national and international trade networks. They specialize in selling meat animals to local markets, qarakul lambskins to international buyers, and even supply sheep intestines to meet the huge German demand for natural sausage casings. The Mongols and Tibetans have increased their production of cashmere goats significantly to meet increased world demand for this luxury product. The Kazaks in China have replaced most of their old varieties of sheep with better wool-bearing animals. Their increased emphasis on pastoralism since decollectivization has also become more complex, linking up with relatives who farm to produce fodder for winter storage and grain for themselves. The move toward ranching has been slowest in East Africa where pastoralists lacked the trading networks already long established in Eurasia. Yet even here, changes have occurred in which pastoralists are selling more of their animals in markets, a change that is in fact quite striking when we realize that less than a century ago, there were no large-scale markets in livestock.

This transformation has largely gone unrecognized among pastoralists because they outwardly appear to be so unchanging. For example, when a farmer switches from a subsistence crop to a cash crop, the transformation is immediately apparent in the fields. Cotton replaces wheat, coffee bushes appear on new plantations, or new irrigation ditches are dug across the landscape. But pastoralists can transform their economic relationships simply by changing the number of animals they market, by processing milk for sale instead of consuming it, or by raising one type of animal instead of another. Similarly, without asking, it is impossible to tell whether a family on migration has other holdings such as land, whether it is caring for additional animals owned by urban merchants or local villagers, or whether it is merely the pastoral component of a larger extended family which may also include members who drive trucks, work in oil fields, or serve in the military. Anthropologists have often perpetuated a nomadic stereotype by deliberately seeking out the most culturally conservative of the nomads for study. Rather than representing the norm, such ideal "pure nomads" are exceptional. And by focusing exclusively on animal husbandry while neglecting economic and political links to a wider world, nomadic pastoralism is made to appear far more isolated than it actually is.

"THE TRAGEDY OF THE COMMONS": DO NOMADS DEGRADE THE ENVIRONMENT?

One of the most fundamental criticisms made against practically all pastoral nomads is that their desire to increase the size of their herds inevitably leads to overgrazing and the destruction of grasslands. The case was put most starkly in a highly influential article by the ecologist Garret Hardin who argued that when privately owned animals depend on a communal pasture, their owners inevitably abuse, and eventually destroy, the public resource in pursuit of private gain.[7] Everyone's property is no one's responsibility, so if left unchecked, any such common resource will eventually become so degraded that no one can use it and everyone loses. Since it is widely believed that most nomadic pastoralists employ some form of communal pasture, many analysts have taken Hardin's analysis to heart and have predicted that sooner or later the world's pastoralists, particularly in East Africa and the neighboring Sahel, will bring about their own destruction.

Such a dire outcome would have indeed put nomads out of business centuries ago if a dynamic process of unrestricted competition were truly at work. However, pastoralists have always been aware of this danger and have had a variety of ways to restrict access to "common" pasture. Tribal boundaries usually coincided with pasture boundaries and these were defended against outsiders so that the use of a common pasture open to "everyone" was actually restricted to a limited number of people (much as some resort towns restrict beach use to residents only). Such a process is often disguised because, as we saw with the tribal il-ra in southern Iran, boundaries shift seasonally as nomads move from one pasture to another. What appears to outsiders as the spontaneous arrival and departure of nomadic groups is in fact a closely regulated system for resource use. Similarly, observers often confuse the right of free transit with the unrestricted use of pasture. Among the Kazaks and Tibetans, the right to such transit grazing is assured, but only as long as it does not exceed one or two days. In northern parts of Afghanistan and Iran, regions where pastures are so dependable that nomads can return year after year to the same place, their use is limited to a particular family or descent group. Other pastoralists wishing access must pay for the privilege. Within nomadic confederations, tribal leaders such as the Basseri khans periodically redistributed grazing rights among camping groups to bring them into line with changes in population. In arid areas such as Arabia, pasture remains free to all, but access to wells is restricted, thereby limiting its use only to those who also have access to water. In East Africa, where a man's cattle are scattered among a number of different herds to reduce risk of loss, the mixed ownership in any one herd means that an individual does not benefit by abusing the pasture at the expense of his neighbors since his own cattle in their herds will also suffer.

More often than not, the resource problems associated with overgrazing have been a function of innovations that have disrupted a previously established balance. Changes in technology and the cash value of livestock in particular can combine to produce destructive pressure on limited resources. Syria's grasslands, for example, became seriously overgrazed only after the introduction of trucks allowed people to move both more livestock and water to previously distant pastures, something not possible before. In Iran during the 1970s, urban merchants, drawn by the promise of large profits, set up a severe competition for resources when they moved large numbers of sheep into areas that had been previously reserved for the use of resident nomads. In the African Sahel, where water had been the limiting variable, the introduction of bore-hole wells with pumps permitted the number of animals to rise well above the carrying capacity of the land surrounding such wells. The restrictions that modern states have placed on movement, especially across arbitrary international boundaries, has also created problems of resource management where seasonal pastures now lie in different countries.[8]

More insidious has been the difficulty nomads have had in retaining rights to their land. Most governments assume that any land not permanently occupied is the property of the state. That pastoralists have historically used these pastures on a seasonal basis is rarely enough to establish legal property rights, previously a moot point when the nomads themselves controlled their own territories. To sedentary people, pasture land is just another form of wasteland that could stand improvement by giving it to farmers for plowing and growing crops. The success of such projects, however, often has been short-lived because in semi-arid zones, where most pastoralists reside, unirrigated agriculture depends on good rains. When these fail so do the crops. The bare land is eroded by the wind, and the new settlers must abandon it. Yet the vast rate of population growth throughout the developing world is creating so much pressure to expand agricultural production that new farming schemes are almost always preferred over continued pastoral use, even in areas that are not well suited for agriculture.

Extensive nomadic pastoralism may well represent a better long-term strategy for production because it protects the environment and makes productive use of the land. Nevertheless, it is difficult to say for certain whether some pastoral systems are more stable than others because there is a lack of long-term data for most parts of the world. Pastoralists have historically experienced many cycles of herd growth and collapse, good weather and bad, and high and low prices for their products. But few studies on pastoralism can determine whether perceived pressure on the range land is a consequence of traditional pastoral techniques, a low point of some climatic cycle of aridity, or the result of changed herding practices. Instead, the focus has been on what is observable in the short term and using that data to extrapolate current trends into the future. Thus the sight of a goat stripping the leaves from the last tree on the edge of the Sahara is enough evidence for many analysts to conclude that it is the nomads who are the villains responsible for the desert's spread. But, on the other hand, if the advance or retreat of the desert margin by hundreds of kilometers is the result of long-term periodic cycles of drought and rain, we may be blaming the victims simply because they are always found at the site of the disaster. Similarly, government planning that relies on short-term data can have negative consequences over the long term where patterns of aridity are highly variable. For example, the allocation of pasture land to Masai ranching schemes in Kenya in the 1960s was based on data derived from a series of relatively good rainfall years and proved seriously inadequate when drought hit a decade later and reduced the ranches productivity. In Tibet, we saw that faulty statistics convinced the Chinese government that herds were rapidly growing beyond the capacity of the grassland to support them, when in fact they were not growing at all. The nomads were held responsible and forced to cull the nonexistent surplus from their herds at great cost to themselves.

If, as we have argued above, nomadic pastoralism has the potential for development and can adapt successfully to the modern world, then why do we only hear about the disasters and difficulties? This is because, like expanding populations of subsistence farmers, nomads eventually produce more people than can be supported by an extensive pastoral economy. While pastoralism may continue to thrive, not all pastoralists will. This should come as no surprise. The balance between people, animals, and pasture has always depended on a process of continual

Many Kazak men and boys in the Altai Mountains of Xinjiang now dress in Chinese style clothes but still display a strong cultural preference for there own traditions such as the horse races which attracted these spectators.

sedentarization of pastoralists over time. This may occur at the family level as among the Basseri, where unsuccessful pastoralists are forced to sell their animals to pay their debts and enter the landless peasantry, and where rich pastoralists invest in land and eventually leave the nomadic life to become landlords. Or it may take place on a large scale such as when tribes coming out of Arabia and Mongolia moved into neighboring sedentary areas as conquerors and settled down. Today, young men in

Africa may seek out wage labor in the cities or mines in hopes of later building a herd back home. Some succeed while others join the urban proletariat permanently. Only in Tibet did we find a situation in which the migration flow was from village farm to nomad camp. It is therefore naive to assume that everyone born into a nomadic pastoral society will inevitably remain a pastoralist. But it is equally wrong to assume that because pastoralism cannot support an infinitely expanding population that it is also incapable of sustaining a stable core population quite well. Only a 150 years ago, more than half the American population lived on farms and now less than 3 percent do, but we do not consider this to be evidence that agriculture itself is outmoded or unsustainable. Similarly extensive pastoralism may continue to thrive even as large numbers of nomadic pastoralists sedentarize and take up other occupations.

T H E   E N D

We began this book with an image, that of nomads on the move, appearing and disappearing as if they were a mirage, a people of mystery. But as we have seen, the mystery of nomadic life lies mostly in the imagination of the outside observer. For the nomad who erects her tent at the end of each day's migration, surrounded by familiar faces and objects, listening to the bleat of lambs as she milks the ewes each evening, it's just another day. In one part of the globe after another we have seen that the world of the nomad may be different from that of his sedentary neighbor, but only because it conforms to a different set of rules. And nomads never truly disappear, they only change their campsites. It is we sedentary folk who need to widen our own horizons.

N O T E S

1. Burton Watson, trans., *Records of the Grand Historian of China*, translated from The Shih-chi of Ssu-ma Ch'ien (New York: Columbia University Press, 1961), II, 228–29.

2. Ibn Khaldun, *The Muqaddimah*, trans. Frans Rosenthal, ed. N. Dawood (Princeton: Princeton University Press, 1967), p. 118.

3. Edward Gibbon, *The Decline and Fall of the Roman Empire* (London, 1901), 1, 624.

4. E. A. Thompson, *A History of Attila and the Huns* (Oxford: Oxford University Press, 1948), p. 27.

5. Arthur Waldron, *The Great Wall of China* (Cambridge: Cambridge University Press, 1990).

6. Ibn Khaldun, *The Muqaddimah*, p. 118.

7. Garret Hardin, "The tragedy of the commons," *Science*, 162 (1968), 1243–48.

8. Dawn Chatty, *From Camel to Truck: The Bedouin in the Modern World.* New York: Vantage, 1986; John Shoup, "Nomads in Jordan and Syria," *Cultural Survival Quarterly*, 8, 1 (1984), 11–13; Jeremy Swift, "Sahelian Pastoralists: Underdevelopment, Desertification and Famine," *Annual Review of Anthropology*, 6 (1977), pp. 457–78; Lois Beck, *The Qashqa'i of Iran* (New Haven: Yale University Press, 1986), pp. 252–71.

FURTHER READINGS

Barfield, Thomas, J., ed., "Nomads: Stopped in their Tracks?" *Cultural Survival Quarterly*, 8, no. 1 (1984), 2–73.

Baxter, T.W. and Richard Hogg, eds., *Property, Poverty, and People: Changing Rights in Property and Problems of Pastoral Development.* Manchester: Department of Anthropology, University of Manchester, 1990.

Galaty, John G., and others, eds., *The Future of Pastoral Peoples.* Ottawa: International Development Research Center, 1981.

Galaty, John, and Philip Salzman, eds., *Change and Development in Nomadic and Pastoral Societies.* Leiden: Brill, 1981.

McCay, Bonnie, and James Acheson, eds., *The Culture and Ecology of Communal Resources.* Tucson: University of Arizona Press, 1987.

Salzman, Philip , ed., *When Nomads Settle: Processes of Sedentarization and Response.* New York: Praeger, 1980.

*B*IBLIOGRAPHY

Aberle, David, *The Kinship System of the Kalmuk Mongols*. Albuquerque: University of New Mexico Press, 1953.

Abu-Lughod, Lila, *Veiled Sentiments: Honor and Poetry in a Bedouin Society*. Berkeley: University of California Press, 1986.

Albright, W.F., *The Archaeology and the Religion of Israel*. Baltimore: Johns Hopkins University Press, 1942.

Andrews, Peter A., "The White House of Khurasan: The Felt Tents of the Iranian Yomut and Goklen," *The Journal of the British Institute of Iranian Studies*, 11 (1973), 93–110.

Anthony, David, and Dorcas Brown, "The Origins of Horseback Riding," *Antiquity*, 65 (1991), 22–38.

Asad, Talal, "Political Inequality in the Kababish Tribe," in *Studies in Sudan Ethnography*, eds. Ian Cunnison and Wendy James. New York: Humanities Press, 1972.

Bacon, Elizabeth, "Types of Pastoral Nomadism in Central and Southwest Asia," *Southwestern Journal of Anthropology*, 10 (1954), 44–68.

Bacon, Elizabeth, *Central Asians under Russian Rule*. Ithica: Cornell University Press, 1980.

Barfield, Thomas, "The Hsiung-nu Imperial Confederacy: Organization and Foreign Policy," *Journal of Asian Studies*, 41 (1981), 45–61.

Barfield, Thomas, *The Central Asian Arabs of Afghanistan*. Austin: University of Texas Press, 1981.

Barfield, Thomas, *The Perilous Frontier: Nomadic Empires and China*. Cambridge, MA and Oxford: Blackwell, 1989.

Barth, Fredrik, "The Land Use Pattern of Migratory Tribes of South Persia," *Norsk Geografish Tidsskrift*, 17 (1959), 1–11.

Barth, Fredrik, *Nomads of South Persia*. Boston: Little, Brown, 1961.

Barthold, V.V., *Turkestan down to the Mongol Invasion*. London: Gibb Memorial Series, 1968.

Bates, Daniel, *Nomads and Farmers: A Study of the Yoruk of Southeastern Turkey*. Ann Arbor: Anthropological Papers of the Museum of Anthropology, 52, University of Michigan Press, 1973.

Bawden, Charles, *The Modern History of Mongolia*. New York: Praeger, 1968.

Baxter, P.T.W., and Uri Almagor, eds., "Introduction," in *Age, Generation and Time: Some features of East African Age Organizations*, pp. 1–35. New York: St. Martins Press, 1978.

Beck, Lois, *The Qashqa'i of Iran*. New Haven: Yale University Press, 1986.

Black, Jacob, "Tyranny as a Strategy for Survival in an 'Egalitarian' Society: Luri Facts versus Anthropological Mystique," *Man*, 7 (1972), 614–634.

Black-Michaud, Jacob, *Sheep and Land: The Economics of Power in a Tribal Society*. Cambridge: Cambridge University Press, 1986.

Bourgeot, Andre, "Pasture in the Malian Gourma: Habitation by Humans and Animals," in *The Future of Pastoral Peoples*, eds. John Galaty and others. Ottawa: International Development Research Centre.

Boyle, J.A., "Dynastic and Political History of the Il-Khans," in *The Cambridge History of Iran, vol. 5: The Saljuq and Mongol Period*, ed. John Boyle. Cambridge: Cambridge University Press, 1968.

Boyle, John A., trans., *The History of the World Conqueror of Ata Malik Juvaini*. Manchester: Manchester University Press, 1958.

Bulliet, Richard, *The Camel and the Wheel*. Cambridge: Harvard University Press, 1977.

Burnham, Philip, "Spacial Mobility and Political Centralization in Pastoral Societies," in *Pastoral Production and Society*, ed. L'Équipe écologie et anthropologie des sociétés pastorales. Cambridge: Cambridge University Press, 1979.

Chang, K.C., *Archaeology of Ancient China*. New Haven: Yale University Press, 1977.

Chatty, Dawn, *From Camel to Truck: The Bedouin in the Modern World*. New York: Vantage, 1986.

Chayanov, A.V., *The Theory of Peasant Economy*. Madison: University of Wisconsin Press, 1986.

Cleaves, Francis, trans., *The Secret History of the Mongols*. Cambridge: Harvard University Press, 1982.

Cole, Donald, *Nomads of the Nomads, The Al Murrah Bedouin of the Empty Quarter*. Arlington Heights, IL: AHM Publishing Corporation, 1975.

Coon, Carlton, *Caravan, The Story of the Middle East*. New York: Holt, Rinehart and Winston, 1964.

Cooper, Marion C., *Grass*. New York: Putnam, 1925.

Cronin, Vincent, *The Last Migration*. New York: Dutton, 1957.

Dahl, Gudrun, and A. Hjort, *Having Herds: Pastoral Herd Growth and Household Economy*. Stockholm: University of Stockholm, Department of Social Anthropology, 1976.

de Rachewiltz, Igor. "Yeh-lü Ch'ü-ts-ai (1189–1243): Buddhist Idealist and Confucian Statesman," in *Confucian Personalities,* eds. Arthur Wright and Denis Twitchett. Stanford: Stanford University Press, 1962.

Deshler, W.W., "Native Cattle Keeping in Eastern Africa," in *Man, Culture and Animals,* eds. Anthony Leeds, and A.P. Vayda. Washington, D.C.: American Association for the Advancement of Science, 1965.

Downs, James F., "Livestock, Production and Social Mobility in High Altitude Tibet," *American Anthropologist,* 66 (1964), 1115–1119.

Downs, James, "The Origin and Spread of Riding in the Near East and Central Asia," *American Anthropologist,* 63 (1961), 1193–1203.

Dyson-Hudson, Rada and Terrence McCabe, *South Turkana Nomadism: Coping with an Unpredictably Varying Environment.* New Haven: HRAF Press, 1985.

Ekvall, Robert B., "Peace and War among the Tibetan Nomads," *American Anthropologist,* 66 (1964), 1119–48.

Ekvall, Robert B., *Fields on the Hoof.* New York: Holt, Rinehart and Winston, 1968.

Evans-Pritchard, E.E., *The Nuer, A Description of the Modes of Livelihood of a Nilotic People.* Oxford: Oxford University Press, 1940.

Evans-Pritchard, E.E., *The Senusi of Cyrenaica.* Oxford: Oxford University Press, 1949.

Feilberg, C.G., *La Tente Noir.* Copenhagen: Gyldendal, 1944.

Ferguson, James, "The Bovine Mystique: Power, Property and Livestock in Rural Lesotho," *Man,* 20 (1985), 647–74.

Fletcher, Joseph, "Turco-Mongolian Monarchic Tradition in the Ottoman Empire" in *Eucharisterion: Essays Presented to Omeljan Pritsak,* eds. Ihor Sevcenko, and Frank Sysyn, *Harvard Ukranian Studies,* 3–4 (1979–80), I, 236–51.

Free, Joseph, "Abraham's Camels," *Journal of Near Eastern Studies,* 3 (1944), 187–93.

Garthwaite, Gene, *Khans and Shahs: A Documentary Analysis of the Bakhtiari in Iran.* Cambridge: Cambridge University Press, 1983.

Gauthier-Pilters, Hilde, *The Camel: Its Evolution, Ecology, Behavior, and Relationship to Man.* Chicago: University of Chicago Press, 1981.

Gibbon, Edward, *The Decline and Fall of the Roman Empire,* (3 vols.), New York: Modern Library, n.d.

Gluckman, Max, "Marriage Payments and Social Structure among the Lozi and Zulu," in *Kinship,* ed. Jack Goody. Baltimore: Penguin, 1971.

Goldschmidt, Walter, *Kambuya's Cattle: The Legacy of an African Herdsman.* Berkeley: University of California Press, 1969.

Goldstein, Melvyn, and Cynthia Beall, "The Impact of China's Reform Policy on the Nomads of Western Tibet," *Asian Survey,* 29 (1989), 619–41.

Goldstein, Melvyn, and Cynthia Beall, *Nomads of Western Tibet: The Survival of a Way of Life.* Berkeley: University of California Press, 1989.

Goody, Jack, *Production and Reproduction.* Cambridge: Cambridge University Press, 1976.

Gulliver, Phillip H., "Age Differentiation," *Encyclopedia of Social Science,* 1 (1968), 157–62.

Gulliver, Phillip H., "The Turkana Age Organization," *American Anthropologist,* 60 (1958), 900–922.

Gulliver, Phillip. H., *The Family Herds: A Study of Two Pastoral Tribes in East Africa, the Jie and the Turkana.* London: Routledge and Kegan Paul, 1955.

Hardin, Garret, "The Tragedy of the Commons," *Science,* 162 (1968), 1243–48.

Herodotus, *The History*, trans. David Grene. Chicago: University of Chicago Press, 1987.

Herskovits, M.J., "The Cattle Complex in East Africa," *American Anthropologist*, 28 (1926), 230–72, 361–88, 494–528.

Herskovits, M.J., *Economic Anthropology*. New York: Knopf, 1952.

Holder, Preston, *The Hoe and the Horse on the Plains*. Lincoln, NB: University of Nebraska Press, 1970.

Humphrey, Caroline, *Karl Marx Collective*. New York: Cambridge University Press, 1983.

Ibn Khaldun, *The Muqaddimah*, trans. Frans Rosenthal, ed. N. Dawood. Princeton: Princeton University Press, 1967.

Irons, William G., "Political Stratification among Pastoral Nomads," in *Pastoral Production and Society*, ed. L'Équipe écologie et anthropologie des sociétés pastorales. Cambridge: Cambridge University Press, 1979.

Irons, William G., *The Yomut Turkmen: A Study of Social Organization among Central Asian Turkic-speaking Population*. Ann Arbor: Anthropological Papers of the Museum of Anthropology, 58, University of Michigan Press, 1975.

Irons, William G., "Nomadism as Political Adaptation: The Case of the Yomut Turkmen," *American Ethnologist*, 1 (1974), 635–658.

Issawi, Charles, *The Economic History of Iran: 1800–1914*. Chicago: University of Chicago Press, 1971.

Jacobs, Alan, "Maasai Pastoralism in Historical Perspective," in *Pastoralism in Tropical Africa*, ed. Theodore Monod. Oxford: Oxford University Press, 1975.

Jettmar, Karl, *The Art of the Steppes*. New York: Crown, 1964.

Kelly, Raymond, *The Nuer Conquest: The Structure and Development of an Expansionist System*. Ann Arbor: University of Michigan Press, 1985.

Khazanov, Anatoly M., *Nomads and the Outside World*. Cambridge: Cambridge University Press, 1984.

Krader, Lawrence, "The Ecology of Central Asian Pastoralism," *Southwestern Journal of Anthropology*, 11 (1955), 301–26.

Krader, Lawrence, *Social Organization of the Mongol-Turkic Pastoral Nomads*. The Hague: Mouton, 1963.

Lancaster, William, *The Rwala Bedouin Today*. Cambridge: Cambridge University Press, 1981.

Lattimore, Owen, *Inner Asian Frontiers of China*. New York: American Geographical Society, 1940.

Le Strange, Guy, *The Lands of the Eastern Caliphate*. London. Frank Cass & Co., 1905.

Levine, Nancy C., *The Dynamics of Polyandry: Kinship, Domesticity, and Population on the Tibetan Border*. Chicago: University of Chicago Press, 1988.

Lienhardt, Godfrey, "The Western Dinka," in *Tribes Without Rulers, Studies in African Segmentary Systems*, eds. John Middleton, and D. Tait. London: Routledge and Kegan Paul, 1958.

Lindholm, Charles, "Kinship Structure and Political Authority: The Middle East and Central Asia," *Journal of Comparative History and Society*, 28 (1986), 334–55.

Loewe, M.A.N., "The Campaigns of Han Wu-ti," in *Chinese Ways in Warfare*, eds. Frank Kierman, and John Fairbank. Cambridge: Harvard University Press, 1974.

Meeker, Michael, *Literature and Violence in North Arabia*. Cambridge: Cambridge University Press, 1979.

Meeker, Michael, *The Pastoral Son and the Spirit of Patriarchy: Religion, Society and Person among East African Stock Keepers*. Madison: University of Wisconsin Press, 1989.

Michael, Franz, *Rule by Incarnation: Tibetan Buddhism and Its Role in Society*. Boulder, CO: Westview Press, 1982.

Mikesell, Marvin K., "Notes on the Dispersal of the Dromedary," *Southwestern Journal of Anthropology*, 11 (1955), 231–45.

Musil, Alois, *The Manners and Customs of the Rwala Bedouins*. New York: American Geographical Society, 1928.

Napier, George C., "Memorandum on the Condition and External Relations of the Turkomen Tribes of Merv," in *Collection of Journals and Reports from G.C. Napier on Special Duty in Persia 1874*. London: Her Majesty's Stationery Office, 1876.

Naumova, Olga B., "Evolution of Nomadic Culture under Modern Conditions: Tradition and Innovation in Kazakh Culture," in *Rulers from the Steppe: State Formation on the Eurasian Periphery*, eds. Gary Seaman, and Daniel Marks. Los Angeles: Ethnographics, 1991.

Oberling, Pierre, *The Qashqa'i of Fars*. The Hague: Mouton, 1974.

Olcott, Martha Brill, *The Kazakhs*. Stanford: Hoover Institution Press, 1987.

Oppenheim, Max Freiherr von, *Die Beduinen, Volume 1*. Leipzig: Otto Harrassowitz, 1939.

Perry, John, "Forced Migration in Iran during the 17th and 18th Centuries," *Iranian Studies*, 8 (1975), 199–215.

Peters, Emrys, "Some Structural Aspects of Feud among the Camel Raising Bedouin of Cyrenaica," *Africa*, 32 (1967), 261–82.

Petrushevsky, I.P., "The Socio-economic Condition of Iran under the Il-khans," in *The Cambridge History of Iran, vol. 5: The Seljuq and Mongol Period*, ed. J.A. Boyle. Cambridge: Cambridge University Press, 1968.

Picardi, A.C., and W.W. Seifert, "A Tragedy of the Commons in the Sahel," *Technology Review*, 42 (May 1976).

Porter, Philip W., "Environmental Potentials and Economic Opportunities—A Background for Cultural Adaptation," *American Anthropologist*, 67 (1965), 409–20.

Radcliffe-Brown, A.R., "The Mother's Brother in South Africa," in *Structure and Function in Primitive Society*. New York: Free Press, 1965.

Rosenfeld, Henry, "The Social Composition of the Military in the Process of State Formation in the Arabian Desert," *Journal of the Royal Anthropological Institute*, 95 (1965), 75–86, 174–94.

Rudenko, Sergei, *Frozen Tombs of Siberia: The Pazyryk Burials of Iron Age Horsemen*. London: Dent & Sons, 1970.

Sahlins, Marshall, "The Segmentary Lineage: An Organization for Predatory Expansion," *American Anthropologist*, 63 (1960), 332–45.

Sahlins, Marshall, *Tribesmen*. Englewood Cliffs, NJ: Prentice-Hall, Inc., 1968.

Sandorj, M., *Manchu Chinese Colonial Rule in Northern Mongolia*. New York: St. Martins Press, 1980.

Schneider, Harold, "The Subsistence Role of Cattle among the Pokot and in East Africa," *American Anthropologist*, 59 (1957), 278–300.

Schneider, Harold, *Livestock and Equality in East Africa: The Economic Basis for Social Structure*. Bloomington: Indiana University Press, 1979.

Shaughnessy, Edward, "Historical Perspectives on the Introduction of the Chariot in China," *Harvard Journal of Asiatic Studies*, 48 (1988), 189–238.

Shoup, John, "Nomads in Jordan and Syria," *Cultural Survival Quarterly*, 8, no. 1, (1984), 11–13.

Spuler, Bertold, ed., *History of the Mongols: Based on Eastern and Western Accounts of the Thirteenth and Fourteenth Centuries*. Berkeley: University of California Press, 1972.

Stauffer, Thomas R., "The Economics of Nomadism in Iran," *Middle East Journal*, 19 (1965), 284–302.

Stenning, Derrick, "Household Viability among the Pastoral Fulani," in *The Development Cycle in Domestic Groups*, ed. Jack Goody. Cambridge: Cambridge University Press, 1965.

Sweet, Louise, "Camel Raiding of North Arabian Bedouin: A Mechanism of Ecological Adaptation," *American Anthropologist*, 67 (1965), 1132–50.

Swift, Jeremy, "Sahelian Pastoralists: Underdevelopment, Desertification and Famine," *Annual Review of Anthropology*, 6 (1977), 457–78.

Tapper, Richard, *Pasture and Politics: Economics, Conflict and Ritual among the Shahsevan Nomads of Northwestern Iran*. New York: Academic Press, 1979.

Thompson, E.A., *A History of Attila and the Huns*. Oxford: Oxford University Press, 1948.

Thompson, Leonard, "Conflict and Cooperation: The Zulu Kingdom and Natal" in *The Oxford History of South Africa*, eds. Monica Wilson and Leonard Thompson. Oxford: Oxford University Press, 1969.

Waldron, Arthur, *The Great Wall of China*. Cambridge: Cambridge University Press, 1990.

Watson, Burton, trans., *Records of the Grand Historian of China*, (2 vols.) translated from *The Shih-chi of Ssu-ma Ch'ien*. New York: Columbia University Press, 1961.

Weir, Shelagh, *The Bedouin, Aspects of the Material Culture of the Bedouin of Jordan*. London: World of Islam Festival Publishing Co. Ltd., 1976.

Wilson, Monica, "The Nguni People" in *The Oxford History of South Africa*, eds. Monica Wilson and Leonard Thompson. Oxford: Oxford University Press, 1969.

Woods, John, *The Aqquyunlu: Clan, Tribe, Confederation*. Minneapolis: Bibliotheca Islamica, 1976.

Yü, Ying-shih, *Trade and Expansion in Han China: A Study in the Structure of Sino-Barbarian Economic Relations*. Berkeley: University of California Press, 1967.

INDEX